Electing America's Governors: The Politics of Executive Elections

David L. Leal

palgrave
macmillan

First published in 2006 by
PALGRAVE MACMILLAN™
175 Fifth Avenue, New York, N.Y. 10010 and
Houndmills, Basingstoke, Hampshire, England RG21 6XS.
Companies and representatives throughout the world.

PALGRAVE MACMILLAN is the global academic imprint of the Palgrave Macmillan division of St. Martin's Press, LLC and of Palgrave Macmillan Ltd. Macmillan® is a registered trademark in the United States, United Kingdom and other countries. Palgrave is a registered trademark in the European Union and other countries.

ISBN-13: 978-1-4039-7528-7
ISBN-10: 1-4039-7528-0

Library of Congress Cataloging-in-Publication Data

Leal, David L.
    Electing America's governors: the politics of executive elections/David L. Leal.
    p. cm.
    Includes bibliographic references (p.).
    ISBN 1-4039-7528-0
    1. Governors—United States—Election. I. Title.

JK2447.L43 2006
324.973—dc22   2006041578

A catalogue record for this book is available from the British Library.

Design by Macmillan India Ltd.

First edition: September 2006

10 9 8 7 6 5 4 3 2 1

Printed in the United States of America.

Table of Contents

List of Figures

List of Tables

Preface

I am happy to publish this book at a time when the study of state politics is coming into its own. Not very long ago, it seemed that few cared about the states. While some outside the field occasionally repeated the well-known phrase that states were "laboratories of democracy," they rarely said it as if they meant it. My interest in state politics was kindled by the work of a small number of foresighted scholars who carried the flag and waited for the political science discipline to catch up with them. Since that time, we have seen the beginning of a well-respected journal (*State Politics & Policy Quarterly*), the creation of an annual state politics conference, and a growing state politics organized section in the American Political Science Association (APSA). "Real world" political observers also seem more interested in state politics, state political figures, and state-national relations. I hope that these positive trends continue, as scholars and practitioners alike have much to learn from the study of the states and our federal system.

I would first like to acknowledge the people who assisted me with this project by discussing ideas, reading drafts, providing comments on chapters and conference papers, sharing data, and generally encouraging my study of state politics. They include Morris Fiorina, Gary King, Steve Ansolabehere, and Thad Beyle, as well as Richard Winters, Jeff Cohen, Jim King, Tom Carsey, Larry Sabato, and Ken Meier. I also acknowledge the more general but no less valuable support and encouragement of the late H. Douglas Price, Michael Shinagel, Jim Campbell, Frank Zagare, Charles Lamb, Frederick Hess, Brad Mann, Maurits van der Veen, Sean Johnson, and David Pervin. I would also like to acknowledge the support of the National Science Foundation, the Mellon Foundation, Harvard University, the State University of New York at Buffalo, and the University of Texas at Austin for helping to make this project possible.

This book is dedicated to my mother, Esther Leal, for all she has done for me over the years. My wife, Kelley, deserves innumerable thanks for all her support. My late father and grandfather, Louis and

Pedro, were sources of humor, support, inspiration, and encouragement for many years. My grandmother, Marian, a former high school
English teacher, provided a very practical assistance by editing much of
the manuscript.

Because of space considerations, some material could not be
included in this book. This includes the first-stage regressions for the
two-stage least-squares (2SLS) regression models in Chapters 2 and
3, the descriptive statistics for the dependent and independent variables used in the empirical chapters, and the discussion of the sources
and codings of the variables (although the key variables are already
discussed in the chapters). This information can be obtained from the
author, who can be contacted at dleal@post.harvard.edu.

One day in 1972, when I was four years old, I announced my support for Richard Nixon in that year's presidential contest. When my
parents asked why, I said it was because he was one of Santa's rein-
deer. I hope that my understanding of the political system has
improved over time, but it is up to the reader to decide.

1

Introduction: Why Study How Governors Are Elected?

For the last two decades, political scientists have exhaustively studied congressional elections but have paid much less attention to how governors are elected.[1] This leads to two related questions: What explains this overwhelming attention to House and Senate elections, and Why should we care how governors are elected?

A starting point for answering these questions is that the relative importance of state and federal offices has not remained constant over the twentieth century. Since the Great Depression, federal offices have been largely considered more important than state governorships. As Sabato (1983, xiii) pointed out, for decades "most of the significant developments and innovations in government originated in Washington, D.C." State governments, in contrast, have been perceived by many as backward, lethargic, or in need of federal oversight. Kaplan and O'Brien (1991, vii) noted that in the 1960s and 1970s,

> doubts that the states could be counted on to make social policy seemed confirmed by reality. Governors and their aides were rarely asked to attend federal policy conferences in Washington. Very few states seemed to care about the tremendous growth in federal aid programs directed at poverty and social-welfare issues. Federal/city relationships supplanted federal/state linkages, constituting, in effect, a de facto constitutional amendment.

However, this national distribution of power changed as states, and therefore their governors, regained power vis-à-vis the federal government.[2] Hanson (1998, 20) wrote that the states "now occupy a central position in domestic policymaking under the New Federalism."[3] As Herzik (1991, 25) put it, "the quality of life enjoyed, and indeed expected, by most Americans is in large part a function of state government policy." State governments have not only grown into active participants in the policy game, but they sometimes even drive national policy debates.

A second important change is that governors have gained a great deal of authority within their states over the last few decades (Beyle 1990). As Ransome (1982, 3) pointed out, "The citizens of a state have an important stake in the governorship because the governor's increased power and importance strengthen his ability to take action that can affect their lives." As the states assume greater responsibility for domestic policymaking, governors also find their influence on the outcomes increasing.

These changing circumstances suggest the importance of learning how individuals have attained gubernatorial office. While elections to a trivial office are of little concern, elections to powerful and consequential offices deserve sustained and comprehensive attention. The nature of academic specialization means that many electoral scholars may not be aware of these important changes and may therefore see little reason to refocus their scholarly attention on the state level.

Such increases in state and gubernatorial influence might be reason enough to study how men and women find their way into the fifty executive offices. Gubernatorial elections, moreover, also provide a useful way to better understand fundamental electoral topics that have been studied almost exclusively in the congressional context. Questions such as how candidate expenditures affect election outcomes, whether issues play a role in voting decisions, what determines why some kinds of candidates run for office while others do not, what drives voter turnout—and many others—have only occasionally been studied in the context of gubernatorial elections.

In addition, most election studies focus on offices that have different constituencies—particularly the House, the Senate, and the presidency. Governors share the same voters as do senators, so an unanswered question is whether contests for these two statewide offices have similar electoral dynamics. If elections for governor and senator are found to be very similar, then gubernatorial elections might require less scholarly attention. One of the goals of this book is therefore to compare elections for these two powerful offices. The chapters will compare their findings with those in the extant Senate elections literature, and Chapters 6, 7, and 8 will directly compare data on the nature of political competition in both contests. As will be shown, these elections are very different in all aspects but one.

The above points will be explored at greater length below, followed by a preview of the chapters and a description of the three data sets used in the book. In addition, the theme of gubernatorial elections as executive elections will be introduced. Several of the important differences between contests for governor and senator may not be random, but may have their roots in the executive nature of the former. Parallels between presidential and gubernatorial contests will therefore be explored, as these offices inhabit similar institutional settings and may share noteworthy electoral features.

Growing Gubernatorial Power

As noted earlier, there is little debate that the office of governor has grown in importance over the last few decades. Sabato (1983, 2) found that

> governors as a class have outgrown the term "good-time Charlie." Once the darling of society pages, governors today are more concerned about the substantive work of the office than about its ceremonial aspects. Once parochial officers whose concerns rarely extended beyond the boundaries of their home states and whose responsibilities were slight, governors have gained major new powers that have increased their influence in national as well as state councils. Once maligned foes of the national and local governments, governors have become skilled negotiators and, importantly, often crucial coordinators at both of those levels. Once ill prepared to govern and less prepared to lead, governors have welcomed into their ranks a new breed of vigorous, incisive, and thoroughly trained leaders.

Beyle (1990) also found that the power of the governor has increased over the last several decades across almost all measures, including veto power, appointment power, staff,[4] and budget authority.[5] Herzik and Brown (1991) agreed that governors now have the formal powers[6] and staff that allow them to be more effective actors in the policymaking process.[7]

By the 1980s, the political institutions surrounding the governor had also been modernized, greatly aiding gubernatorial ability to promote change.[8] The governor is also the one actor within a state who is able to set goals for, impose coherence upon, and lead the state bureaucracy (Beyle and Muchmore 1983). Ransome (1982, 3) noticed such changes, writing that

> during the last thirty years the American governor has emerged as a policy leader of no mean proportion. He also is emerging gradually as

a leader in terms of more recently gained powers in the field of state management. His office has become the primary center of public attention at the state level, and his actions and speeches have considerable influence in molding public opinion. This tendency toward a strong governor means that his office has increased in importance.

Many other scholars have echoed these sentiments. Cox (1991, 55) agreed that understanding "the shift from a custodial, administrative style to a proactive style is key to understanding the modern role of the governor." Svoboda (1995, 135) concluded that "in most states, the governor is now the most powerful political personality."[9] Herzik and Brown (1991, ix) found that "governors are the most salient political actors in state government . . . over the past three decades governors have assumed an ever greater role in the state policy process."

One symbolic illustration of growing gubernatorial power is how statewide officeholders are listed in the biennial *Almanac of American Politics,* which George Will has described as the "Bible of American Politics." For years, the *Almanac's* individual state descriptions first discussed the two senators and then the governor. Starting with the 1986 edition, however, the order reversed: the governors were placed first and the senators were second. No explanation was given, but it was an appropriate recognition of contemporary gubernatorial power and responsibility.

The Growing State Role in Public Policy

As mentioned above, the movement toward devolving power and obligations from the federal government to the states increased the role of the governor in a wide range of policy areas. Governors have not always been consulted about these changes. Beyle (1992, 8–9) found that "what John Shannon suggested as an important legacy of the Reagan revolution—'fend-for-yourself-federalism'—has come to pass with a vengeance . . . [covering] virtually all facets of federal activity because governmental units at each level—national, state, and local—must find ways to go it alone in facing their problems."

In fact, the federal government sometimes did more than leave the states alone; it sometimes transferred "sizable program commitments to the state and local governments without offering enough financial support to assist them in carrying out their new responsibilities" (Beyle 1990, 1).

While these cuts and impositions were taking place, the New Federalism did empower the states in some ways. Kaplan and O'Brien

(1991, 5) observed that the Reagan administration's consolidation of grant programs into block grants had several important implications for the states. First, consolidation reduced the total amount of money given to the states. Second, "there was a significant reduction in federal regulations accompanying the flow of funds."[10] Third, "a certain percentage of the funds distributed under several of the block grants could be redirected to other purposes at the option of the states. This increased state discretion regarding the types of programs to be supported and how to apportion the cuts" (5). While many of the states may have preferred the previous arrangements, they did receive at least some regulatory and fiscal latitude under the new system.

More generally, in an era of limited resources at the federal level and lingering public concern that the federal government is "part of the problem," new programs or policy innovations are increasingly likely to come from state capitals instead of Washington, D.C. (Hanson 1998). As Beyle noted, "The states are getting to be where a lot of the action is."[11]

For a variety of reasons, governors have not been shy about exercising their powers. Sabato (1983, 10) found that while governors in the 1950s rarely attempted ambitious projects,

> by the early 1980s the agenda conceived by the governors was a crowded one. Even in times of economic difficulty, an exceedingly wide range of social, health, and education programs, with devotion to urban needs in particular, was evident. Innovations in all major policy areas now abound in the states, and the federal government has found itself outstripped in several fields.

Rosenthal (1992, viii) agreed that "the states are where it's at today, and where it will be tomorrow. And governors are the principal actors on the scene."

Osborne (1990) examined how some governors were forced to take proactive policy roles in the 1980s because of economic transformations. When unemployment increased, governors "could not afford to wait for the next recovery, or to evoke the nostrums of free-market theory" (2).[12] Kaplan and O'Brien (1991, vii) agreed that state action at this time was "precipitated by the economic and fiscal problems facing many local governments in the early part of the decade [1980s]." Given these challenges, creativity and leadership on the part of state chief executives became more important than ever.

States have been involved in a variety of policy areas. Osborne (1990) discussed a number of state economic enhancement programs, noting that education was a priority of many state governments during the 1980s. Kaplan and O'Brien (1991, 120) similarly found that "most of the governors [we interviewed] were education governors . . . It was the favored issue focus of the majority of governors." But they also discovered state involvement in other issue areas, some of which were previously thought to reside largely in the domain of the national government: "States have been pushed and, in some cases, have pushed themselves to the forefront of health . . . and welfare policy making" (vii). While state policy activism depends on budgetary considerations, as only the national government can operate consistently in the red, states have little reluctance to spend when revenues are available.[13]

The impact of contemporary governors is felt beyond state lines. They play an increasing role in policymaking across the nation and often oversee programs that become important elements in federal-level debates. Governors and state governments are involved in some of the most important policy issues of the day. From welfare to education to health care, governors are not only spending money given by Washington on programs mandated by Washington, but are also conducting experiments that subsequently drive the national agenda. The old saying that states are "laboratories of democracy," while almost a cliché, is more fitting today than at any other time in recent history.[14]

One prominent example is welfare reform. The reform bill passed by Congress and signed by President Clinton in 1996 assigned welfare money to the states in block grants and gave them substantial leeway to modify the program. This was not just a federal initiative; it was partly the consequence of states seizing the initiative by applying for and receiving waivers from federal law to conduct their own experiments. These programs were well known to Congress as it debated and then passed its own major revision of the entitlement.

Education reform is another area where state action preceded federal change. In 1991 Minnesota became the first state to experiment with charter schools, and one of its senators (Republican David Durenberger) also introduced charter legislation in Congress. The first federal charter support law was finally passed in 1994, at which time a dozen states had already moved forward with their own plans.[15] The federal program soon grew from $6 million to $100 million, but without the state efforts it might not have been considered by Congress until much later.[16] In addition, many of the components of the "No Child Left Behind" legislation were first developed at local and state levels in Texas—reforms that Governor Bush helped take national when he became president.

Governors have also been increasingly active players in health care debates within their own states and on the national stage. Schneider (1991, 1989) showed that while governors had little influence on Medicaid between 1975 and 1981, they were able to affect expenditures between 1982 and 1985. Nationally, the health care debate in the first Clinton term was partially structured by the Hawaii and Oregon plans. The state of Hawaii used an employer mandate and achieved nearly universal coverage, while Oregon adopted a form of health care rationing. All sides of the national debate carefully analyzed both plans.

The *New York Times* claimed that this flurry of innovation was caused in part because governors with "presidential ambitions (mostly Republicans) are eager to claim credit for flashy initiatives with national ramifications."[17] This was made possible, it continued, because "state governments are often not as partisan" as the federal government.[18] If this is true, it suggests that the state role in policymaking will continue to increase.

There is one additional way governors have been influential outside of their own states. Dantico and Mushkatel (1991, 173) showed how governors are capable of cooperating to solve common problems, which they referred to as "multistate policymaking" (see also Gross 1989 and Grady 1989).

The contemporary judiciary is also involved in the federalism issue. The Rehnquist Court saw the first sustained questioning, since the New Deal, of the use of the commerce clause to justify congressional legislation. While the substantive results of this "federalism revolution" are modest to date (Tushnet 2005), a future court that builds on this logic could significantly limit the reach of national government and thereby further increase the power of the states. As Tushnet (2005, 278) noted, "The federalism revolution would stay within narrow bounds as long as the Court's conservatives were divided. Thomas [and his concurrent opinion in the *Lopez* case] showed where new justices might take the Rehnquist Court's decisions."

Understanding Elections

To study an office without understanding the dynamics that bring people into that office is an incomplete examination. Congressional scholars first realized this several decades ago, as a burgeoning research agenda on elections demonstrates. Now governors are attracting more scholarly attention, but the electoral foundations of the office remain relatively unknown.

Because most electoral studies involve either the House or the Senate, much of what we know in this field holds true largely in these two contexts. While the congressional elections literature is certainly important, it is limited, as it compares the electoral dynamics of one legislative office with those of another legislative office. This book will comprehensively compare gubernatorial elections with legislative elections for the first time. This comparison will allow us to draw some conclusions about which dynamics are common to all elections and which are unique to those for particular offices.

Consider the issue of campaign expenditures. For two decades, scholars have debated whether incumbent expenditures affect the electoral bottom line, and if so, how they compare with challenger expenditures. Research in this field has not often explored the effects of campaign expenditures across American political institutions. By comparing the results of Chapters 2 and 3 with congressional campaign finance studies, this book will contribute to the development of a general understanding of how money is associated with election outcomes. It might also motivate other scholars in this debate to test their theories in both the gubernatorial context as well as the congressional context.

As mentioned earlier, this book will consider a wide variety of other electoral questions. In addition to studying campaign expenditures, Chapters 2 and 3 explore the effect of candidate political experience and changes in economic and social conditions on election outcomes. Chapter 4 studies the determinants of voter turnout, and Chapters 5 and 6 examine why some politically experienced candidates run for governor while others do not. Chapters 7 and 8 discuss campaign intensity and competitiveness and the growing role of third-party and independent candidacies. All these efforts, as well as the methods and data that are used, will be discussed in more detail below in the chapter previews.

Understanding Executive Elections

American politics is characterized by an overwhelming number of elections for legislative and executive offices. Scholars have spent only limited time trying to understand how these contests compare. One important reason for this is that the most common executive election studied is the most powerful one, the presidency, and this field suffers from the much noted "low n" problem. In the time period of this study, for example, there were only five contests, and much of the commentary inevitably focuses on the unique determinants of each.

There is, therefore, a need to examine contests for another executive office in order to better understand the full range of campaign dynamics. Perhaps presidential and gubernatorial elections share features that may not resemble those found in elections to legislative bodies. On the other hand, perhaps executive and legislative elections are very similar. At this point, however, the literature does not contain enough evidence from which we can draw any firm conclusions.

This book not only compares gubernatorial elections with Senate contests but also discusses whether the differences between them are based on their contrasting institutional settings. It examines the literature on presidential elections for dynamics and hypotheses that might apply to governors and suggests that several of the key differences between gubernatorial and Senate elections reflect the nature of the respective offices. This book can only raise and begin to explore the possibility of an executive perspective on elections, not completely develop one, but in doing so it helps to advance a comparative perspective that has received only limited attention.

Outline of the Chapters

The chapters in this book are based in large part on a campaign finance data set encompassing contests from 1980 to 1996, as well as on two other data sets. As mentioned earlier, the book not only examines multiple electoral topics that have been largely confined to the congressional elections literature, but it also compares gubernatorial elections with Senate elections in two important ways.

Chapters 2 to 5 compare their findings with research previously conducted on the same topic in Senate elections. Chapter 2 addresses the aforementioned long-standing debate in the campaign finance literature on the effect of incumbent and challenger expenditures on election outcomes. Chapters 3–5 cover how national and state social and economic changes affect the vote, the determinants of voter turnout, and the emergence of quality challengers to incumbents. The second way gubernatorial and Senate elections are compared is found in Chapters 6–8, which directly collect and compare gubernatorial and Senate data on political competition, third-party and independent campaigns, and political ambition for statewide office.

One picture that emerges is that gubernatorial elections differ in important ways from Senate elections. Although both offices share the same constituency and often have concurrent elections, it would be a mistake to assume that the electoral dynamics are therefore similar. This book will present evidence that both politicians and voters see gubernatorial and Senate offices differently.

Chapter 2 addresses the long-running debate on whether incumbent spending is associated with election outcomes and, if so, how it compares with challenger spending. Early research on congressional elections suggested that there was no relationship between the money spent by incumbents and the votes they received on election day. The explanation for this counterintuitive result was that incumbents have so many advantages, such as name recognition and official resources, that campaign expenditures do not provide any extra benefit. This perspective is mostly associated with the research of Jacobson on House elections,[19] although others have drawn different conclusions with different models.[20] Research on Senate elections has generally argued that incumbent spending is statistically significant but substantively only one-third as important as challenger spending,[21] although Stewart (1989) found both to be of roughly equal importance.

Recent research has rethought the role of candidate quality in election models in order to avoid the "simultaneity problem."[22] The result is a two-stage least-squares (2SLS) model that more effectively isolates the impact of candidate spending, and this approach is used in Chapters 2 and 3. The data show that incumbent spending is just as useful as challenger spending and that it has substantive effects that are neither too small to be of interest nor too large to be believed. This proves to be the only important exception to the rule that gubernatorial and Senate elections differ substantially.

Chapter 3 investigates how changes in economic and social conditions might influence the decisions of voters at the polls. This chapter is unique among "retrospective[23] voting" research because it examines noneconomic variables, such as the state crime rate and SAT scores. It finds that voters punish incumbents when the state crime rate increases. One explanation for this effect is found in research on how the news media cover state politics. Tidmarch, Hyman, and Sorkin (1984) found that issues commonly thought to be more susceptible to state control, such as crime and education, were more likely to be covered in gubernatorial elections. It is therefore not surprising that voters hold governors responsible for one of these state factors.

Open seat candidates are affected by national political and economic conditions, but not by state-level factors. Specifically, if an open seat candidate is of the same party as the president, he or she receives fewer votes. In addition, if the candidate is from the same party as the president and the national unemployment rate increases, the candidate receives fewer votes In other words, open seat elections take on some of the characteristics of a national referendum on the president.

Chapter 4 explores voter turnout. Apart from testing the variables usually seen in this literature, it asks whether the economic and social change measures from Chapter 3 play any role. It finds that the state tax rate variable is significant, indicating that rising taxes are positively associated with turnout in incumbent elections. In open seat elections, we see how bad news can spur turnout, as a higher state unemployment rate is associated with higher turnout. There is also a national factor at work in open seat elections; as national per capita income increases, so does turnout. Perhaps the lack of an incumbent allows voters to be influenced by factors outside the state.

This chapter also shows that campaign expenditures affect turnout in incumbent and open seat elections differently. In incumbent elections, the ratio of the money spent by the biggest spender to the money spent by the lowest spender (which is used again in Chapter 7 to measure campaign intensity) is negatively associated with turnout. In open seat elections, it is the total amount of money spent by the two candidates that increases turnout, not the ratio. In open seat elections, it is therefore not the closeness of the contest that matters but the amount of political "noise" an election generates. This is what one should expect; open seat elections usually receive more attention than do incumbent contests, so total expenditures lead to higher turnout because these elections are already in the public eye. In incumbent contests, what matters is whether or not the challenger is able to contest the election vigorously. Voters have less reason to turn out for a race that is only weakly contested. Once again, this shows how the dynamics of gubernatorial elections are more complex than some previous research has suggested.

Chapter 5 revisits the question of candidate quality by examining which political and economic factors are associated with the emergence of quality challengers to incumbents. Previous scholarship has investigated this question in gubernatorial,[24] Senate,[25] and House[26] elections and has also explored the ability of higher-quality Senate challengers to spend more money on their campaigns.[27] The problem with many of these models, as Lublin (1994, 229–230) noted, is that they make "assumptions about the relative value of prior posts in running for the House or Senate that have little empirical justification." The value of these prior posts in furthering electoral goals is tested in Chapters 2 and 3, and this information is used to determine which specification of the challenger quality measure is best. A comprehensive model explaining the emergence of such candidates is then tested in the gubernatorial context. Once again, the results show that it would be a mistake to assume that gubernatorial and Senate election dynamics are the same. First, different factors appear to affect the decision of higher quality candidates to challenge an incumbent than previous research suggests. The results differ not just from previous Senate and House research, but also from the one previous gubernatorial study. Second, the aggregate challenger quality variable is not associated with challenger expenditures in gubernatorial elections, whereas Squire (1989) found that it was in Senate elections. This reinforces the findings from Chapters 2 and 3 on the unimportance of a candidate's prior political experience in gubernatorial elections.

Chapter 6 begins the direct comparison of gubernatorial and Senate election data by examining which political and personal factors structure the decision of House members to run for governor or for the Senate. The results validate the strategy of separately analyzing the decision to run for these two offices, as there are differences in which factors affect the decision to run for each. Most importantly, the Senate model closely mirrors the aggregate model typically used in the literature,[28] while the gubernatorial model does not. There are far fewer significant variables in the gubernatorial model than in the Senate model, suggesting that ambition in the former is not well structured. As the chapter discusses, this not only points out another difference in the electoral dynamics for these two offices, but it may help explain why House members are not as effective candidates for governor as they are for senator.

Chapter 7 compares several important elements of electoral competition in gubernatorial and Senate elections. While there has been some research comparing House and Senate elections,[29] there have been few comparisons of elections to the two major statewide offices.[30] This chapter begins with the finding that governors are about twice as likely to be defeated as are senators. One explanation for this might be that governors face a greater level of competition than senators. Westlye (1991) showed that not all Senate elections are the competitive races of lore. He found that while some are "hard fought," others are "low key" and better resemble lopsided House campaigns. Chapter 7 finds that gubernatorial elections are significantly more likely to be hard-fought than are Senate elections, both for incumbent and open seat contests.

Gubernatorial campaign expenditures are also compared with expenditures in Senate elections, using the gubernatorial data set and U.S. Federal Election Commission (FEC) data. Total amounts of money spent as well as spending ratios are discussed. The data show that governors outspend senators and that gubernatorial challengers outspend Senate challengers. When expenditures are calculated per capita, however, the Senate candidates outspend gubernatorial candidates across the board.[31] Nevertheless, the ratio of incumbent to challenger spending, whether overall or per capita, shows that senators are better able to outspend their challengers than are governors. This finding helps us better understand the greater gubernatorial electoral insecurity vis-à-vis senators.

In addition, the personal and political backgrounds of successful and unsuccessful gubernatorial and Senate candidates are compared, and the results are contrasted with findings from earlier time periods in Schlesinger (1966) and Sabato (1983). Some of the trends noticed by Sabato from 1900 to 1980 are shown to continue into the present. Schlesinger's (1966) theory of manifest office is also tested for gubernatorial and Senate elections and is found to hold true for elections in the 1980s and 1990s. The data further suggest that no particular prior office better enables a candidate to either win an election or engage in a hard-fought campaign. This reinforces the previously noted lack of significance of the candidate political experience variables in the election models.

Finally, data on partisan trends in incumbent and open seat elections are analyzed over time. Comparisons of partisan outcomes and electoral intensity are also examined for simultaneous gubernatorial and Senate elections. Westlye (1991) noted that many hard-fought races are often followed two years later by a low-key contest. This chapter asks whether concurrent gubernatorial and Senate campaigns have similar levels of electoral competition and similar partisan outcomes. Although there are only a limited number of observations, the data suggest a tentative answer of yes to both questions.

Chapter 8 explores one of the most unique features of gubernatorial elections: candidates who run without major party affiliations occasionally win. From 1980 to 1996, third-party and independent candidates captured the governor's mansion in Alaska, Connecticut, and Maine and received a significant percentage of the vote (10 percent or more) in fifteen other elections. This stands in marked contrast to Senate elections, where no candidate outside the two-party context won a seat, and only five candidates received 10 percent or more of the vote (despite almost one-third more Senate elections than gubernatorial elections).

This last chapter discusses these campaigns and the candidates behind them. How do they compare with major party general election candidates in terms of previous electoral experience and money raised? Is support for their candidacies increasing, decreasing, or holding steady? Are there any common themes to their efforts? What led these candidates into the independent category, and what were their previous relationships with the Democrats and Republicans? The chapter concludes by discussing why voters are more willing to elect independents to this office than to any other and what this might mean for the future of gubernatorial elections.

Chapter 9, the conclusion, summarizes the dynamics of gubernatorial campaigns and discusses how they differ from those in Senate elections. It also brings together the findings on how presidential and gubernatorial elections share important electoral features.

The Data and Models

One innovative aspect of this project is the use of a data set of candidate campaign expenditures in gubernatorial elections from 1980 to 1996. This data set is used in six of the eight chapters; it is especially important to the chapters on campaign finance (Chapter 2), retrospective voting (Chapter 3), voter turnout (Chapter 4), and electoral competition in gubernatorial and Senate elections (Chapter 7). Although such expenditure data are commonly used in the study of House and Senate elections, they have not been comprehensively examined in the gubernatorial context.

The total number of gubernatorial elections for which campaign finance data exist is 185. The data were divided into two different data sets. The first includes 112 general elections featuring an incumbent, and the second includes 73 open seat elections featuring 146 general election candidates.. This is not a sample; rather, it represents all the data available for the elections the chapters examined.[32]

The campaign finance data were obtained in three ways. Approximately one-half were obtained through telephone calls to state election commissions and secretary of state offices during the summer of 1996 and spring of 1997. Additional observations were obtained by the inspection of archival records in Alabama, California, Massachusetts, and Mississippi. The remaining data were obtained courtesy of Professor Thad Beyle at the University of North Carolina at Chapel Hill. Over the years, he has diligently requested candidate expenditure data from state agencies, and about half of the observations in the data set came from him.

When I began this data-collection effort, I found that within each state, information was initially collected by the secretary of state or a state elections board and then typically sent to the state archives after a period of time. The treatment of the data by each state varies widely, however. Some states published extensive reports at the end of each election cycle; they listed how much money was raised and spent by the candidates, detailed individual contributions and items of expenditure, and included factors such as beginning and ending cash on hand. Other states required candidates to report a minimal amount of information, made no attempt to analyze or publish it, and required researchers to personally travel to state archives to inspect the records.

The effort required in the 1980s and 1990s to assemble such gubernatorial election data stands in contrast to the relative ease of data collection experienced by scholars of congressional elections. For these contests, the FEC collects and makes publicly available financial expenditure and contribution data for all federal candidates. The relative difficulty in collecting state election data is another reason why election researchers have focused so exclusively on federal campaigns.

A second data set was also collected for the first chapter on political ambition, Chapter 6. As discussed above, this chapter models the factors structuring the decision by a House member to run for higher office (governor or senator) or to stand for reelection. The data set examines election decisions from 1984 to 1996 and consists of 1,615 separate decisions.

The methodological approaches in this book run the gamut of available methods. The most complex statistical models are found in Chapters 2 and 3, which use 2SLS analysis. Chapters 4 and 6 use ordinary least-squares (OLS) analysis, while Chapter 6 uses logistic regression. Chapter 7 examines data in a more aggregate manner, while Chapter 8 is based on case studies.

The division of the first data set into two separate parts in Chapters 3 and 4 is an important innovation. Although substantial differences between incumbent and open seat elections have been demonstrated in the campaign finance literature over the last two decades, the retrospective voting and turnout literatures have not distinguished between the two. Instead of including both elections in the same data set, and therefore in the same regressions, Chapters 3 and 4 separately analyze incumbent and open seat elections. The results demonstrate the usefulness of this approach, as important differences are shown to exist between the two.

Chapter 6 also uses disaggregation. Most previous political ambition studies use a dependent variable coded 1 for the decision to run for either governor or Senate and 0 for the decision to seek reelection. This specification is problematic because the founder of the ambition literature (Schlesinger 1966) quite clearly noted that the paths to each office were distinct. This chapter therefore examines three dependent variables: (1) the decision to run for governor or for reelection; (2) the decision to run for the Senate or for reelection; and (3) for comparative purposes, the usual aggregate measure. As mentioned above, the results demonstrate that very different forces structure gubernatorial and Senate ambition.

An additional innovation of the book is the cross-fertilization of several different electoral literatures. While the campaign finance, retrospective voting, and turnout literatures have coexisted in the same journals for two decades, they have learned only a limited amount from each other. This is especially surprising in the case of the first two, as they both test models explaining the same dependent variable.

Chapter 3 therefore combines a number of the political variables usually found in the campaign finance literature with the state and national economic change measures usually found in "retrospective research." Only one previous retrospective voting study has tested candidate expenditure variables (Chressanthis and Shaffer's Senate study [1993]), and no research has controlled for candidate quality variables in any retrospective model. In addition, two measures of state-level noneconomic change (crime and education) are tested for the first time in a retrospective model, an innovation that proved fruitful.

The chapter on voter turnout, Chapter 4, also includes variables tested in Chapters 2 and 3. Because economic and noneconomic change variables and other political measures affect how voters make decisions, the question naturally arises as to whether these factors also influence the decision to vote. No previous research had tested these possibilities, and the chapter suggests that two such variables affect turnout.

Chapters 7 and 8 use a more qualitative, or at least a nonregression, approach. Chapter 7 compares key measures of electoral competition in elections for gubernatorial and Senate office. These include campaign intensity, campaign expenditures, and candidate quality. Chapter 8 discusses the candidates who ran for office without a

Democratic or Republican label, including both third-party candidates and independents. It examines patterns and commonalities in their campaigns and discusses what this suggests for the political future of the states.

Chapter 2 will now begin the study of gubernatorial elections by asking one of the most important questions in politics and political science—how do campaign expenditures affect election outcomes?

2

Election Outcomes: Campaign Expenditures
and Candidate Quality

This chapter investigates the relationship between campaign expenditures and voting in gubernatorial elections from 1980 to 1996. To date, the overwhelming majority of studies on campaign finance have analyzed congressional elections. This research was in large part stimulated by the Federal Election Campaign Acts (FECA) of the early 1970s. Although Congress had passed financial disclosure laws as early as 1910 and 1911, they were not effective until strengthened by the 1971 FECA. The FECA amendments of 1974 created the Federal Election Commission (FEC), which became the central collection point for publicly available campaign finance disclosure reports. Scholars could thereafter obtain expenditure data for all House and Senate elections from this single source. As discussed in the introduction, no equivalent to the FEC exists for gubernatorial elections. This has made research on state-level campaign finance issues more difficult.

Most research within the congressional elections field focuses on elections to the House of Representatives. The primary reason is that there are more House elections than Senate elections and thus more of the observations necessary for regression analysis. As the House of Representatives has almost four and one-half times the number of members than the Senate, as well as two-year rather than six-year terms, House elections provide enough data points to test most hypotheses or specifications. Although some important research has been conducted on Senate elections, as will be discussed below, it is limited by both the number of articles written and the number of scholars who have written them.

Despite the lack of academic attention that has been paid to this subject, there are two primary reasons scholars might care about the role of money in gubernatorial elections. First, as discussed in the introduction, governors have become much more powerful vis-à-vis the federal government and other state politicians in recent decades. As expenditures are thought to play a key role in how candidates win office, our understanding of what brings men and women into this increasingly important office is incomplete without an understanding of this subject. Second, the study of expenditures provides evidence toward a general theory of how money affects political outcomes. There is very little research comparing the role of campaign expenditures across political institutions; at this point, the only comprehensive comparisons are between House and Senate elections. This means that political scientists do not know whether money plays a consistent role in elections across various levels of government. By focusing on gubernatorial elections, this chapter therefore fills a research gap that has existed for decades.

In general, there should be no question that money is important in gubernatorial campaigns. Sabato (1983) has shown how the same expensive electioneering techniques used in congressional elections, such as opinion polls, direct mail, and television advertising, and the growth of personal campaign organizations, are now common in gubernatorial elections.[1]

Ransome (1982, 172) noted that not only had the cost of gubernatorial campaigning "skyrocketed" by the early 1980s, but the sophistication of campaign techniques had increased as well:

> A successful candidate had to hire a political consultant or a public relations firm specializing in the management of political campaigns. The candidate also had to make extensive use of television, which has come to be decisive in the gubernatorial popularity contest. When the cost of a political consultant and the sums spent for television are added to the cost of traditional campaign techniques, they make almost any gubernatorial campaign prohibitively expensive.

Expenditures are more important today than in recent history because of the declining roles of political parties. A candidate today can expect no financial assistance in the primary and relatively little direct assistance in the general election; the end of patronage also eliminated the armies of volunteer workers at the command of local party leaders. Instead, expenditures buy what Sabato (1980) called "party substitutes"—including public opinion polls, television advertising, and political consultants—to maximize campaign effectiveness. Beyle (1986, 20) noted that "money isn't everything in gubernatorial politics, but it can buy most anything else that is."[2] In addition, a relatively small amount of quantitative research suggests that money may, in some limited ways, play a role in gubernatorial elections (Patterson 1982; Morehouse 1990). This research will be discussed in the following section.

Using the data set described in the introduction, this chapter will examine the effect of campaign expenditures by incumbents, challengers, and open seat candidates on election outcomes. Doing so requires some thinking about other issues in campaign finance research, especially the role of the political experience of challengers and the use of instrumental variables.

Discussion

A. Expenditures in House Elections

The scholarly campaign finance debate largely began with Jacobson in 1978 and continued through various articles and books by Jacobson[3] and his critics. Jacobson's key finding was that "spending by *challengers* has a substantial impact on election outcomes, whereas spending by *incumbents* has relatively little effect."[4] The others who had previously examined the newly collected FEC data in the mid-1970s generally assumed that incumbent and challenger money had the same effect.[5] Jacobson (1978, 469) explained his results by arguing that "campaign expenditures buy nonincumbents the necessary voter recognition already enjoyed by incumbents prior to the campaign."

Jacobson also found that although incumbents were able to adjust their level of spending to match the seriousness of the challenge, this did not provide much help at the polls. In fact, the simple correlation between incumbent spending and challenger votes was positive, which suggested that the more incumbents spent, the worse they did. Jacobson (1985, 13) explained: "This does not mean that incumbents lose votes by spending money, but rather that they spend more the more strongly they are challenged, and the stronger the challenge, the worse for the incumbent."

Green and Krasno (1988) have been the primary critics of Jacobson's approach.[6] They brought up three main problems. The first was that Jacobson's model did not adequately control for challenger political quality (CPQ). The effect of challenger spending was therefore overestimated, and the effect of incumbent spending underestimated. Second, they argued that Jacobson did not adequately take into account the reciprocal causation effect. They modified Jacobson's two-stage least-squares (2SLS) approach by suggesting that challenger spending can be assumed to be exogenous, and they included CPQ in the second-stage regression. Third, they found that Jacobson's linear assumption could be fruitfully replaced with a model using interaction effects and logged variables.

Jacobson (1985, 39) strongly suspected that "no simultaneous equation model of this type can be suitably identified. Any measurable variable known to affect the vote should also affect campaign contributions; and it is difficult to think of any measurable variable that would systematically influence contributions (and thus expenditures) without independently affecting the actual vote."[7]

Ansolabehere and Snyder (1995, 3) argued that a key problem with previous research was that it did not adequately take into account the way candidate quality affected election outcomes. They argued that Green and Krasno (1988) were wrong to construct a single measure of challenger quality: "Politicians draw on many assets—experience, contacts, personal wealth, a winning smile—all of which affect money and votes, but in different ways" (4). They saw two dimensions to candidate quality—the ability to raise money and the ability to attract votes—and they used as instrumental variables the measures that affected only the marginal cost of raising money but had no direct impact on the vote.

Using this approach, Ansolabehere and Snyder (1995) found that challenger and incumbent expenditures were approximately in the same range. While they therefore ended up on the same side of the debate as Green and Krasno (1988), they argued that the latter were right for the wrong reasons. And while they acknowledged their debt to Jacobson for his original insight into candidate quality, they found his conclusions incorrect.

B. Expenditures in Senate Elections

In a 1988 article, Abramowitz studied all Senate races from 1974 to 1986 that featured an incumbent.[8] He used ordinary least-squares (OLS) and sixteen independent variables to examine incumbent vote totals. The size of the coefficient for challenger spending was three times that of the coefficient for incumbent spending. In fact, challenger expenditure was the single most important factor affecting the incumbent's reelection campaign, with challenger political experience next in importance.

Grier (1989) studied Senate elections from 1978 to 1984 featuring incumbents, finding that incumbent spending had a significant and positive outcome on an incumbent's vote. The coefficients in the OLS regressions suggested that challenger dollars were about three times more effective than incumbent dollars in affecting incumbent vote.

Jacobson (1985) also investigated Senate elections, but his model was more circumscribed than his House elections model and included the two independent variables of challenger and incumbent spending along with a party measure.[9] The challenger variable was significant in both of the election years he studied, while the incumbent measure was significant only in one.

Stewart (1989) took into account some of the points made by Green and Krasno (1988), such as the endogeneity of the spending variable and the need for instruments, although he did not use their challenger quality variable. His 2SLS models were somewhat unusual because they examined separate models for incumbent and challenger vote returns. He explained that this was because partisanship, spending, and political coattails might not affect incumbent and challenger votes symmetrically. On the crucial question of incumbent versus challenger spending, Stewart (1989) found comparable effects on average. One difference was that incumbents were favored by the expenditure dynamics in large states, whereas challengers were advantaged in smaller states.

Gerber (1998) followed along the lines of Ansolabehere and Snyder (1995), estimating the vote for Senate incumbents using three instrumental variables. He discovered that the effects of incumbent and challenger spending canceled each other out, whereas the simple but misleading OLS model showed that challenger spending had a far greater effect on votes than did incumbent spending. This chapter tests whether the instrumental variable approach will find similar effects in gubernatorial elections and thereby contribute to the quest for a general understanding of how money functions in elections.

C. Expenditures in Gubernatorial Elections

Patterson (1982) conducted one of the few previous quantitative studies of gubernatorial elections. Using a dataset of thirty-four 1978 gubernatorial elections, he found none of the variables in the Jacobson model to be significant. This regression was mentioned only briefly, and his main model organized the data not according to challengers and incumbents, but according to party. Expenditures by the Democratic and Republican candidates, Democratic Party strength (the average proportion of the party vote for governor in each state for elections from 1958 to 1976), and incumbent tenure were all significant and in the expected direction. He concluded that "gubernatorial elections are not the same as congressional elections" (468).

One feature to note is that Patterson included both incumbent and open seat elections in the same regressions. The variable for tenure was supposed to take this into account, although it was not a dummy variable. Open seat elections were coded as zero, and incumbents were coded for the number of years served, but this did not seem to take into account the substantial differences between these two types of elections. Patterson's study was an important initial effort to extend congressional elections research to the gubernatorial field, but the subsequent campaign finance literature has largely examined incumbent and open seat elections separately.

Squire (1992) investigated the influence of money on gubernatorial election returns in a single electoral cycle (1987–1988). He separately analyzed incumbent and open seat elections, but because there were only ten observations in each four-variable OLS model, he noted that "the results should be viewed with great caution" (139). The variables included candidate quality, candidate party strength, expenditures, and opponent's expenditures. The results showed that money was positively associated with vote share for incumbent elections but not for open seat elections. No other variables were statistically significant.

The varying results from these two exploratory efforts reinforce the general point that it is risky in campaign finance studies to examine data from one year alone. It is surprising that scholars have not followed up on these findings with data from other years.

With the exception of Morehouse (1990), there is little other work involving gubernatorial campaign finance issues. Morehouse quantitatively investigated the relative effect of party organization and campaign expenditures on gubernatorial primary election outcomes in 1982. She found that where parties endorse candidates through conventions, money is not a crucial explanation for candidate success. On the other hand, where parties do not endorse, money is the primary explanatory factor.[10]

The Models

A. Overview

This chapter adopts the Gerber (1998) and Ansolabehere and Snyder (1995) approaches discussed above. The following subsections will discuss the data, as well as the independent and instrumental variables. The specifications of the incumbent and open seat election models are then shown.

B. Data

This chapter uses the campaign finance dataset discussed in the introduction. It is divided into two datasets: the first contains 112 general elections featuring an incumbent, and the second contains 146 general election candidates for open seats. Together, they cover all elections from 1980 to 1996 in all fifty states for which data are available.

As a group, the general election challengers to incumbents have had a high level of previous political experience. Five percent held federal office, 28 percent had statewide experience, 30 percent were from the state legislatures, 10 percent were former governors, and 10 percent held city or local office. This means that over 80 percent of challengers held some type of elected political office. Because an additional 16 percent had worked in politics or held an appointed political position, almost all of the challengers were concurrently or previously involved in politics in a significant way.

Aside from the former governors, not many of the challengers had previously run for statewide office. Seven percent had tried for the office of governor or senator in the previous election cycle, while about 3 percent had made a similar effort in a previous election. It appears that after running an unsuccessful statewide campaign, candidates either leave politics or run for a lower office. Whether this is because they have somehow lost credibility among state political elites or the public or have voluntarily lowered their sights is not discernible from this dataset.

The median age of challengers and incumbents was virtually the same, with incumbents being one year older than challengers (fifty years). Challengers appeared to be wealthier than incumbents, however. Sixteen percent of challengers were so coded, compared with only about 9 percent of incumbents. About 3 percent of incumbents were facing a scandal. As might be expected, incumbents did better in their primaries than did challengers. Incumbents won with an average vote of about 85 percent, while challengers took 66 percent.

C. Independent Variables

The incumbent analysis includes variables for incumbent spending and challenger spending. The general theory that incumbent and candidate spending may have different effects is long-standing in the elections literature and is based on the greater visibility of the incumbent. Jacobson (1990, 334–335) wrote:

> Incumbents, exploiting the extensive communication resources
> available to every member of Congress, saturate their districts with

information about themselves, their virtues and services, before the formal campaign begins . . . Challengers, in contrast, typically begin the campaign in obscurity. Because voters are demonstrably reluctant to vote for candidates they know nothing about, challengers have a great deal to gain by making themselves better (and, of course, more favorably) known to the electorate.

There should be no doubt that governors are highly visible among the citizens of their states. In fact, after the president and vice president, the governor is the most well-known political figure in a state.[11] The two expenditure variables were deflated with the consumer price index. This deflated figure was then divided by the population of the state (in thousands), as found in various editions of the *Statistical Almanac of the United States*. Such a transformation is common to almost all previous campaign finance studies. An alternative approach is to include the deflated and logged expenditure measures in the second-stage regression and use state population as an instrumental variable. If this is done, the population variable is statistically significant in each first-stage regression, but the significance of the second-stage variables does not change in any important way. While this was the Gerber (1998) approach, it does not make any substantive difference how the state population data are used in this chapter.

Four variables take into account the experience of the candidates in their party primaries. The first two measure the primary vote received by each candidate, with those who did not face a primary coded at 100 percent. The next two measure the number of candidates in each party primary. While there is evidence that divisive primaries reduce general election support for the primary winner in presidential elections,[12] the evidence is mixed for Senate elections.[13]

One theoretical explanation for this potential dynamic is that some voters grow psychologically attached to the losing candidate they supported in the primary and therefore find it difficult to vote for someone else in the general election.[14] It has also been suggested that party activists who supported the losers become especially alienated from the winner.[15] There may also be some endogeneity, especially for incumbents, whereby weaker candidates attract stronger primary competition while stronger candidate scare away quality opponents.

Conversely, Ware (1979) argued that there are reasons to expect divisive primaries to help the eventual winner. Since the media typically ignore primaries, they may give greater attention to a close contest and, therefore, to the winner. An early race may also cause the winner to begin activities such as fundraising and advertising early in the electoral calendar. This could lead to higher name recognition and may give the campaign team an additional opportunity to hone their electoral skills.

The political experience of the challengers and open seat candidates must also be taken into account. Five dummy variables are therefore used to measure current or last electoral office: former governor, other statewide office, state legislative office, federal office, and city or county office. The federal measure includes both House members and Senators because only a few of the latter ran for governor. Whether this variable or separate variables for the two offices are used makes no difference to the regression results. The aggregate measure is used in the model to reduce the number of independent variables.

The fame or name recognition of the challengers might also be related to their capacity to win a greater percentage of votes. Candidates who start with wide public recognition are thought to pose a stronger threat to incumbents than are those who begin unknown, as voters are more willing to vote for a name they know. The campaign also needs to spend less time familiarizing the public with the candidate; it can therefore begin boosting the positives of the candidate or the negatives of the opponent much sooner. Candidates who are related to former or current politicians will hope that the association with such familiar and previously successful political personalities will benefit their campaigns.

Although the most common form of fame and name recognition is through family relations to a former elected official, it sometimes comes through other avenues. Eddie Basha, for example, was already well known in Arizona when he challenged Fife Symington in 1994. His name and face appeared across the state in advertisements for his supermarkets, so he was included in this variable. George W. Bush was the son of a former president of the United States when he ran for governor of Texas in the same year, so he was similarly coded.

Some candidates gain unwanted recognition through scandals, so a variable for this was also included. This measure may take into account only small- or medium-sized scandals, as the most serious scandals may convince a potential candidate not to run.

The baseline state-level party support for the challenger was specified as the average two-party percentage vote for the presidential candidates of the challenger's party over the last four presidential elections. The expectation is that the higher this level, the greater will be the support for the challenger. It might be argued that presidential voting is a misleading measure of state party support, especially in the south. One alternative specification of this factor is the Erikson, Wright, and

McIver (1993) measure of state partisan identification, which will also be tested in these models.

A dummy variable measures whether the incumbent governor is from the same party as the president. If this is negatively correlated with the vote, it would suggest a dynamic similar to Erikson's (1988) "presidential penalty thesis," whereby voters choose to punish the president by voting against House candidates of his party during midterm elections. A divided government dynamic is also possible, whereby the public wants executives from different parties. Fiorina (1992) showed that voters often choose presidents and congresses, as well as governors and legislatures, from different parties. Whether the voters might choose divided government between the state and federal levels is unclear and has not been previously examined.

It might be argued that the formal powers of a governor, which vary from state to state, could affect the odds of reelection.[16] Some governors are generally considered "strong" and others "weak." Holbrook (1993, 268) investigated this possibility and concluded that there is "no relationship between gubernatorial power and gubernatorial elections."

D. Instrumental Variables

The model uses five instrumental variables in the first stage of the 2SLS regression. These variables are expected to affect money raised but not to directly affect election day votes. Some challengers may not have previous electoral experience, but they may have held appointed positions or worked as political aides or campaign consultants. Ansolabehere and Snyder (1995, 22) noted that these candidates "have all of the political connections and acumen of elected officials but lack the exposure brought by running for and winning office . . . they often do know who to ask and how to ask for campaign contributions." In a similar vein, Westlye (1991, 28) noted that some candidates "had served as party officials at the county or state level . . . these challengers were not unfamiliar with political organization and elections but were essentially invisible to the electorate at the start of their own campaigns."

The personal wealth of the candidate is another important factor in fundraising but is unlikely to affect the vote directly. While some candidates may charge a wealthy opponent with trying to "buy" the election, anecdotal evidence suggests that voters rarely heed this warning. The wealth of both incumbents and challengers is noted.

Ansolabehere and Snyder (1995, 25) also argued that "all other things being equal, older candidates may not have the energy to go to

as many fundraisers as their younger and more eager counterparts."
The ages of both incumbent and challenger are therefore included.

E. Incumbent Election Model

Some scholars have analyzed election years separately. Jacobson
(1985, 16) tested an identical model in each election featuring an
incumbent from 1972 to 1982 and found that "the marginal impact
on the vote of a challenger's dollar has evidently diminished over the
years."[17] Green and Krasno (1988), however, suggested that when
Jacobson's data are analyzed by year, the results are unstable for
both OLS and 2SLS regressions. Yearly analysis is not possible with
gubernatorial data, as the number of races featuring an incumbent
does not provide a sufficient dataset for regression analysis in any
given election.

The second-stage model, based on the Ansolabehere and Snyder
(1995) and Gerber (1998) approaches, is therefore:

$$
\begin{aligned}
\text{Incumbent Vote} = \alpha\ & + \beta_1 \ln(\text{Incumbent Expenditures}) \\
& + \beta_2 \ln(\text{Challenger Expenditures}) \\
& + \beta_3 (\text{Incumbent Primary Margin}) \\
& + \beta_4 (\text{Challenger Primary Margin}) \\
& + \beta_5 (\text{Number of Candidates in} \\
& \qquad \text{Incumbent Primary}) \\
& + \beta_6 (\text{Number of Candidates in} \\
& \qquad \text{Challenger Primary}) \\
& + \beta_7 (\text{Incumbent Scandal}) \\
& + \beta_8 (\text{Incumbent Same Party as} \\
& \qquad \text{President}) \\
& + \beta_9 (\text{State Party Support}) \\
& + \beta_{10} (\text{Challenger Former Governor}) \\
& + \beta_{11} (\text{Challenger Federal Office} \\
& \qquad \text{Experience}) \\
& + \beta_{12} (\text{Challenger Statewide Office} \\
& \qquad \text{Experience}) \\
& + \beta_{13} (\text{Challenger State Legislative} \\
& \qquad \text{Experience}) \\
& + \beta_{14} (\text{Challenger City or County Office} \\
& \qquad \text{Experience}) \\
& + \beta_{15} (\text{Challenger Fame/Name} \\
& \qquad \text{Recognition}) + \varepsilon,
\end{aligned}
$$

where α is the intercept.

The five instrumental variables added to the first-stage model are incumbent age, challenger age, incumbent wealth, challenger wealth, and challenger experience as a political staffer or consultant.

These results will also be compared with those generated from other models of statewide elections found in the campaign finance literature. The first model replicated is the simple Jacobson (1978) model of Senate elections. As discussed above, his model used OLS:

$$\text{Vote} = \alpha + \beta_1 \ln(\text{Incumbent Expenditures})$$
$$+ \beta_2 \ln(\text{Challenger Expenditures})$$
$$+ \beta_3(\text{Challenger Party}) + \varepsilon.$$

Also tested is Patterson's (1982) adjusted replication of the Jacobson OLS model:

$$\text{Vote} = \alpha + \beta_1 \ln(\text{Incumbent Expenditures})$$
$$+ \beta_2(\ln \text{Challenger Expenditures})$$
$$+ \beta_3(\text{Challenger Party}) + \beta_4(\text{Challenger Party Strength})$$
$$+ \beta_5 \ln(\text{State Population}) + \varepsilon.$$

A more elaborate OLS model, similar to the one used by Abramowitz (1988) and Abramowitz and Segal (1992), is then tested. Not all of their variables are included, as some are not possible to recreate in the gubernatorial context. This model adopts their framework but is not a complete replication:

$$\text{Vote} = \alpha + \beta_1(\text{State Partisanship}) + \beta_2 \ln(\text{State Size})$$
$$+ \beta_3 \ln(\text{Incumbent Expenditures})$$
$$+ \beta_4 \ln(\text{Challenger Expenditures})$$
$$+ \beta_5(\text{Challenger Experience})$$
$$+ \beta_6(\text{Celebrity Challenger}) + \beta_7(\text{Scandal})$$
$$+ \beta_8(\text{Number of Incumbent Primary Challengers})$$
$$+ \beta_9(\text{Primary Margin}) + \varepsilon.$$

F. Open Seat Election Model

The open seat elections dataset consists of 146 candidates contesting seventy-three elections. For the open seat analysis, the dependent variable is the same as in the incumbent model, and the campaign finance variable is the amount of money spent by each candidate divided by the total amount spent by both candidates in the election.

The other independent variables include the following: the candidate's primary percentage; the number of candidates in the primary; how the presidential candidate of the candidate's party fared in the last four presidential elections; whether the candidate was a former governor; dummies for whether the candidate had experience in federal, statewide, state legislative, or city/county elected office; whether the candidate held a good occupation (lawyer, doctor, businessperson, etc.) if he or she had no previous political experience; and whether the candidate was famous or had unusual name recognition.

Whether the candidate was from the same party as the outgoing governor was controlled for because the reputation of the latter may help or hurt a candidate. As with the incumbent model, whether the candidate was from the same party as the president was also taken into consideration. The presence of a scandal was controlled for in the incumbent model, but not in open seat elections because only one such candidate faced this problem.

Because the unit of observation in an open seat election is each candidate, it is important to take into account the characteristics of the opponent each candidate faces (aside from the comparative campaign expenditure measure). To do so, seven dummy variables control for federal, statewide, state legislative, and city or county political experience, along with occupational status, fame, and whether the candidate is a former governor. As with the incumbent model, it makes no difference whether the aggregate federal variable or the separate House and Senate member variables are used.

The instrumental variables are specified slightly differently than in the incumbent model. Six measures are used, including the wealth, age, and political aide/consultant status of both the candidate and his or her opposition. Just as it was important for each observation to take into account the political background of the opposition, so should the first-stage model include instruments relevant to the opposition.

The second-stage model, also based on Ansolabehere and Snyder (1995) and Gerber (1998), is therefore:

$$
\begin{aligned}
\text{Candidate Vote} = \alpha \; + \; & \beta_1(\text{Spending Percent}) + \beta_2(\text{Primary Margin}) \\
+ \; & \beta_3(\text{Number of Candidates in Primary}) \\
+ \; & \beta_4(\text{State Party Support}) \\
+ \; & \beta_5(\text{Same Party as Outgoing Governor}) \\
+ \; & \beta_6(\text{Same Party as President}) \\
+ \; & \beta_7(\text{Former Governor}) \\
+ \; & \beta_8(\text{Federal office Experience})
\end{aligned}
$$

$$+ \beta_9(\text{Statewide Office Experience})$$
$$+ \beta_{10}(\text{State Legislative Experience})$$
$$+ \beta_{11}(\text{City or County Office Experience})$$
$$+ \beta_{12}(\text{Good Occupation})$$
$$+ \beta_{13}(\text{Fame/Name Recognition})$$
$$+ \beta_{14}(\text{Opponent Former Governor})$$
$$+ \beta_{15}(\text{Opponent Federal Office Experience})$$
$$+ \beta_{16}(\text{Opponent Statewide Office Experience})$$
$$+ \beta_{17}(\text{Opponent State Legislative Experience})$$
$$+ \beta_{18}(\text{Opponent City or County Office Experience})$$
$$+ \beta_{19}(\text{Opponent Good Occupation})$$
$$+ \beta_{20}(\text{Opponent Fame/Name Recognition}) + \varepsilon.$$

Results

Table 2.1 shows the results of the second stage of the fully specified 2SLS incumbent and open seat election models.

A. Incumbent Elections

The most important finding in incumbent elections is that both challenger and incumbent spending are statistically significant. The challenger spending variable is well within the conventional range of statistical significance ($p < .01$). The incumbent measure is also significant ($p < .10$), which is in line with the most recent research on Senate and House elections. As mentioned earlier, there has been much debate about whether incumbent expenditures have an independent influence on election outcomes, given the high name recognition and substantial political resources incumbents bring to their reelection campaigns. This chapter argues that incumbent spending is far from a waste of effort.

The simple correlation of incumbent spending with incumbent two-party vote percentage is −0.17. This negative relationship was noted in previous campaign finance research, and superficially it appears to show that the more incumbents spend, the worse they do. As in the case of congressional elections, this correlation shows the endogeneity implicit in incumbent spending. However, the correlation did not

Table 2.1 Second stage of 2SLS analysis of incumbent and open seat gubernatorial elections

Variables	Incumbent	Variables	Open Seat
Constant	0.597*** (0.148)	Constant	0.206*** (0.072)
ln(Incumbent Spending) (divided by state population)	0.148* (0.087)	Percent of Mone Raised by Candidate	0.449*** (0.146)
ln(Challenger Spending) (divided by state population)	−0.117*** (0.034)	Primary Vote Percent	0.063* (0.034)
Incumbent Primary Vote Percent	0.245** (0.112)	Number of Primary Candidates	0.001 (0.003)
Challenger Primary Vote Percent	−0.088 (0.069)	State Partisan Support	−0.064 (0.099)
Number of Candidates in Incumbent Primary	0.005 (0.011)	Same Party as Outgoing Governor	−0.011 (0.007)
Number of Candidates in Challenger Primary	−0.005 (0.009)	Same Party as President	−0.022*** (0.007)
Incumbent Scandal	−0.056 (0.080)	Former Governor	0.019 (0.025)
Incumbent Same Party as President	−0.027 (0.026)	Federal Office Experience	0.018 (0.024)
State Political Support for Incumbent's Party	−0.133 (0.158)	Statewide Office Experience	0.009 (0.021)
Challenger Former Governor	−0.038 (0.043)	State Legislative Experience	0.030 (0.024)
Challenger Federal Office Experience	−0.043 (0.051)	City or County Office Experience	−0.015 (0.028)
Challenger Statewide Office Experience	−0.019 (0.027)	Good Occupation	−0.024 (0.026)
Challenger State Legislative Experience	−0.014 (0.023)	Fame	−0.032 (0.024)
Challenger City or County Office Experience	0.065* (0.037)	Opponent is Former Governor	−0.023 (0.025)
Challenger Famous	0.010 (0.034)	Opponent has Federal Office Experience	−0.017 (0.024)
Observations	112	Opponent has Statewide Office Experience	−0.018 (0.021)

(*Continued*)

Table 2.1 (*Continued*)

Variables	Incumbent	Variables	Open Seat
		Opponent has State Legislative Experience	−0.024 (0.023)
		Opponent has City or County Office Experience	0.009 (0.027)
		Opponent has Good Occupation	0.021 (0.026)
		Opponent is Famous	0.025 (0.024)
		Observations	142

Notes: Incumbent model: dependent variable is incumbent percent of two-party vote (from 0 to 1). Open seat model: dependent variable is candidate percentage of two-party vote (from 0 to 1). Cells contain coefficients with standard errors in parentheses.
***$p < .01$, **$p < .05$, *$p < .10$.

hold up in the 2SLS model when candidate quality and other political measures were taken into account. Ansolabehere and Snyder (1995, 28) similarly found that while in an OLS model spending by House incumbents was statistically significant and *negatively* associated with incumbent votes, a 2SLS model correctly showed that incumbent spending was positively associated with incumbent votes.

The coefficients by themselves suggest that incumbent spending has a slightly greater effect than challenger spending. This bears out the intuition of Beyle (1986, xxviii), who noted that incumbents "are generally more effective in translating their spending into votes on election day."

The exact interpretation of the coefficients is not straightforward, as the measures were transformed with natural logs. For the basic equation $y = b(\ln(M))$, where b is the coefficient produced by the second stage of the regression and M is the untransformed expenditure variable, a partial derivative gives $\partial y / \partial M - b/M$. The result of dividing the coefficient by expenditures (which are measured as deflated expenditures divided by state population in thousands) gives the effect on the vote by an increase in the value of 1 in the expenditure measure. The value of 1 is not trivial, as the mean value of M for incumbents is 6.68 and for challengers is 4.40.

For the value of 5, which is between the means of these two types of candidates, the substantive impact of incumbent and challenger spending is very close. For incumbents (0.15/5), the results show that for an M value of 5, the next increment of 1 will increase the incumbent vote by just under 3 percent. For challengers, the same figure leads to a decrease for the incumbent of just over two and one-third percent. These figures nearly cancel themselves out, and one way to test this possibility more rigorously is by an F test. This examines whether the two variables substantively sum to a value of 0; the results show that we cannot reject this possibility with any confidence.

The model also shows that the worse an incumbent does in the primary, the fewer votes that incumbent receives on election day. This is similar to the dynamic Westlye (1991) found for incumbent senators. The substantive interpretation of the impact of the incumbent primary variable on the dependent variable is straightforward, as they are both continuous variables measured as a percentage from 0 to 1. Every 10 percent drop in an incumbent's primary percentage should reduce his or her general election percentage by about two and a half percent. The challenger primary variable is not significant, however.

The only other variable to reach statistical significance is the dummy for challenger experience in city or local office. This is positively correlated with the incumbent vote, suggesting that this type of experience is a disadvantage to challengers. The general election penalty for such candidates is six and a half percent.

Beyle (1997, 198) has pointed out "the considerable difficulty that mayors and former mayors of large cities have in winning the governorships. Over the past 10 elections years, 1987–1996, only two of the 26 mayors and former mayors of a state's larger cities have run and won." Conventional political wisdom has also long claimed that city politics is not a good stepping stone to higher office. While many people who work in politics believe this to be true, it had not been empirically tested.

There are several reasons why mayors might find their office a handicap. First, mayors assume a much greater responsibility for the condition of their constituencies than do legislators. Even if many statewide standard-of-living measures decline during a state legislative session, each legislator is only one of many. A rise in urban unemployment can be more easily laid at a mayor's doorstep, and this connection might provide valuable ammunition to political opponents.

Second, the financial condition of urban areas has been in decline in America, but the ability of mayors to deal with this problem is limited (Peterson 1981). Mayors have thus had responsibility for the most financially troubled part of the federal system while possessing little power to make changes.

Beyle (1997) suggested three other possible explanations for mayors' lack of success in gubernatorial elections: large cities may not provide a broad enough base of support; those living outside large cities may hold an antiurban or anti-big-city bias; and running for statewide office may be qualitatively different from running for mayor. Of course, none of the arguments listed above are mutually exclusive, and more than one may be at work.

None of the other political officeholders appears to hold any advantage or disadvantage over the others. Former governors, state legislators, statewide officials, and federal officeholders hold no particular electoral advantage. The latter are statistically insignificant whether the aggregate variable is used or senators or representatives are separately examined. It might be thought that instead of using multiple experience variables, a single dummy variable should be included instead; no one office may be better than another, but perhaps holding any office is an advantage over being inexperienced. When this measure is substituted in the model for the five experience variables, however, it is statistically insignificant.

Another unimportant variable is state party strength. The model tested two specifications: the first was the average two-party percentage vote for the presidential candidates of the challenger's party over the last four presidential elections, and the second was the Erikson, Wright, and McIver (1993) measure of state partisan identification. Neither approached statistical significance.[18]

The profile of a good challenger is therefore not complicated: he or she should outspend the opposition, not hold local political office, and hope that the incumbent has a difficult primary. This is both good news and bad news for challengers. While there is not much they can realistically do to affect the incumbent's primary vote, they at least will not suffer because of their political background unless they hold the job of mayor. Fundraising is a factor that diligent challengers with good Rolodexes can influence, but they must also worry about how much the incumbent spends.

How do the second-stage regression results compare with those of other specifications? The first column of table 2.2 presents the results for the basic Jacobson model. This simple model suggests that incumbent spending does not play a role in gubernatorial outcomes but that challenger spending does. As such, the results fall in line with Jacobson's findings for congressional elections.

The second column of table 2.2 shows the results for the Patterson (1982) version of the Jacobson model and suggests that incumbent spending is not helpful for the incumbent. When

Table 2.2 OLS gubernatorial election models

Variables	Jacobson[a]	Patterson[b]	A&S[c]
Intercept	0.366*** (0.025)	0.144* (0.082)	–
ln(Incumbent Expenditures) (per voting age individual)	–0.011 (0.015)	–0.007 (0.015)	–
ln(Challenger Expenditures) (per voting age individual)	0.060*** (0.009)	0.063*** (0.008)	–
Party of Incumbent	–0.001 (0.015)	0.008 (0.018)	–
Incumbent State Party Strength	–	0.060 (0.107)	–0.018 (0.082)
ln(State Voting Age Population)	–	0.234*** (0.007)	–0.022*** (0.007)
ln(Incumbent Expenditures) (divided by state population)	–	–	0.016 (0.015)
ln(Challenger Expenditures) (divided by state population)	–	–	–0.059*** (0.008)
Prior Political Experience Dummy	–	–	0.003 (0.015)
Challenger Fame	–	–	0.039 (0.025)
Scandal	–	–	–0.009 (0.043)
Number of Primary Challengers to Incumbent	–	–	0.006 (0.008)
Incumbent Primary Performance	–	–	0.186*** (0.064)
Adjusted R^2	0.36	0.42	0.47
Observations	112	112	112

Note: Cells contain coefficients with standard errors in parentheses.

[a] Replication of Jacobson (1978) Senate OLS model of challenger vote.
[b] Replication of Patterson (1982) gubernatorial OLS model of challenger vote.
[c] Elaborated OLS model on incumbent vote (similar to Abramowitz and Segal approach).

***$p < .01$, **$p < .05$, *$p < .10$.

Patterson (1982) used an adjusted version of this model with 1978 gubernatorial data, he found that none of the variables reached statistical significance.

The third column shows the results from the more elaborated OLS model. These results also support the "profligate incumbent" thesis (Stewart 1989), whereby incumbent spending plays no role in election outcomes but challenger spending is important.

All three OLS models, regardless of the variables used, consistently underestimated the impact of incumbent spending, just as predicted by Ansolabehere and Snyder (1995). To tease out the actual effect required the 2SLS model, which dealt as effectively as is possible with the well-known endogeneity problem in campaign finance studies.

B. Open Seat Elections

As with the incumbent model, the second numerical column of table 2.1 shows that in open seat elections candidate expenditures have a significant and positive influence on candidate election returns. The interpretation of the expenditure variable is straightforward: if a candidate increases the share of expenditures by 10 percent, her general election vote increases by nearly four and one-half points. The primary vote percentage measure is also statistically significant, as it was for incumbents. Substantively, however, it is about two and one-half times less important for open seat candidates than for incumbents.

In addition, the model shows that open seat candidates who are of the same party as the president suffer at the polls by over 2 percent. This is not a midterm dynamic; it affects all elections. This electoral punishment might be explained in two ways. Because presidents become so highly exposed to the public over their terms, they inevitably alienate some constituencies over time through the policy positions they take (Mueller 1973; this is discussed in more detail in Chapter 7). These constituencies may then take out their feelings on a convenient target, and one of these may be an open seat gubernatorial candidate with an easily discernible partisan connection to the president. As mentioned earlier, this is reminiscent of Erikson's (1988) "presidential penalty thesis," whereby voters choose to punish the president by voting against House candidates of his party during midterm elections. Waterman (1990, 101) points out that this dynamic does not apply to Senate elections, but this chapter suggests there may be a somewhat similar effect at the state level.

Another possibility, albeit more speculative, is that some voters want to elect governors of the opposite party of the president in order to create a partisan balance in control over the various levels of the federal system. This argument is similar to the divided government thesis of Fiorina (1992), whereby voters want divided government within the national and the state levels. If this is desired within governmental levels, then why not also between levels? On the other hand, the variable was not significant in the incumbent model, as the presence of an incumbent may give non-open-seat elections an alternative focus to the president and his policies. Overall, the divided government thesis is an interesting but inconclusive possibility in the gubernatorial context.

None of the candidate political experience variables was significant in the open seat election model. As with the incumbent model, the possibility was tested that a dummy variable for political experience was more appropriate. Two such measures were therefore included—one for each candidate—but they were both insignificant. As in the incumbent model, neither the type nor the fact of candidate political experience had an effect on election returns. In addition, the two measures of state party strength were insignificant, as in the incumbent model.

Because the value of a 2SLS approach lies in the quality of the instruments, it is important to note how well they performed in the first stages of the regression. In the first-stage regression on incumbent expenditures, challenger age is statistically significant, but the other instruments are not. F tests reveal that they are not jointly significant (0.19). For the first-stage regression on challenger expenditures, political aide/consultant status and challenger wealth are statistically significant and positive influences. These five instruments are jointly significant at the 0.01 level.

In the open seat regression, the measures for candidate wealth and wealth of the opponent were both statistically significant. An F test also showed that the six instruments were jointly significant at the 0.018 level. Taken together, these results suggest that the instruments are generally working as anticipated in both the incumbent and open seat models.

Conclusions

For almost three decades, two challenges to the campaign finance literature have been (1) to discern whether challenger and incumbent expenditures have the same effect on election outcomes, and (2) to extend research on House elections to other elected offices at different federal levels. This chapter addresses both these issues by studying how money is associated with electoral success in gubernatorial elections. It finds that incumbent and challenger expenditures are both statistically significant influences on gubernatorial election outcomes. Campaign expenditures also play a positive role in open seat elections.

Not only are incumbent expenditures far from being either insignificant or three times less effective than challenger spending (the differential arrived at by some Senate studies), but incumbents may in fact receive slightly more "bang for their buck" than do challengers. The substantive interpretation of the coefficients shows that the magnitude of this difference is not very large, but it does exist. This builds on the previously noted intuition of Beyle (1986, xxviii), who was able to discern, without benefit of regression analysis, that incumbent spending leads to more votes than does spending by their challengers.

These general findings conform to those generated by scholars who have applied this particular 2SLS approach to the study of elections for other offices. Gerber (1998) found similar results for the role of money in Senate elections, and Ansolabehere and Snyder (1995) did so for House elections. The findings in this chapter therefore not only contribute to the study of gubernatorial elections, but also provide evidence toward a general understanding of the effect of money in American elections.

The findings also show that candidates with political experience in city or local offices fare worse against incumbents than do other types of candidates. There is also evidence that incumbents with lower vote percentages in primaries tend to do worse in the general election, and several possible explanations for this are discussed.

Campaign expenditures do not entirely explain election outcomes. Just as Beyle (1986) found that some challengers outspent incumbents and still lost, so this chapter notes that approximately 20 percent of such high-expenditure challengers were unsuccessful. Other factors, such as economic and noneconomic changes in the state and nation, likely play a role in shaping election outcomes. They are the subjects of the next chapter.

3

Election Outcomes: State and National
Economic and Social Conditions

This chapter develops a model of retrospective voting in gubernatorial elections. It examines not only the role of familiar economic change measures, but also the effect of noneconomic factors that have not been examined to date. The campaign expenditure and political variables used in Chapter 2 are also included in the model. This allows for a comprehensive testing of which retrospective factors influence election outcomes, while simultaneously controlling for relevant political factors. Although the elections and retrospective voting literatures have coexisted in the same journals for almost two decades, they have rarely learned from each other in order to answer their joint questions more effectively. This chapter is the first to combine both electoral and retrospective measures in an aggregate model for any elected office.

Even after much academic research, there is no overarching answer to the question of how elections are influenced by preceding economic changes. Scholars have searched for evidence of retrospective voting effects in elections for multiple offices using both aggregate- and individual-level data, but their conclusions vary in several important ways.

For presidential elections, there is strong evidence of retrospective effects at both the aggregate[1] and individual[2] levels. For House elections, there is evidence of national effects at the aggregate level[3], but not at the individual level.[4]

Statewide elections present a more complex problem because both state and national economic conditions must be taken into account.[5] This is certainly true for gubernatorial elections, and constituents might even hold senators responsible for the economic and social conditions within the state. Retrospective economic judgments are a simpler matter in presidential and House elections because the issue of identical constituencies does not have to be taken into account. The next section will discuss both the aggregate- and individual-level findings for all three types of elections.

One of the curious facts in the study of elections is that the two literatures of retrospective voting and campaign finance stand so far apart. To date, only one study (Chressanthis and Shaffer's study of the Senate [1993]) has constructed a model including both candidate expenditures and economic change variables. Most researchers leave out noneconomic variables such as campaign expenditures, even though this may lead to model misspecification. If the purpose of this research is to pinpoint how economic changes affect election outcomes, then other factors that are known to affect the vote should be taken into account. The most important of these are the campaign finance expenditure and candidate quality measures that have been examined by scholars for almost two decades.

One important question to ask at this point is whether governors have real power over their state economies. In other words, is it rational behavior for voters to blame or to credit them for economic conditions? Adams and Kenny (1989, 2), writing in reaction to Peltzman (1987), argued:

> The weakness of the governor as a force in state prosperity strikes us as exaggerated. Governors, because of their veto and appointive powers, have considerable power in state governments. Imperfect factor mobility associated with locational rents gives each state some latitude in setting tax rates and subsidy levels (Epple and Zelenitz 1981; Adams 1986). Moreover, the choice of taxation and expenditure policies is not independent of state prosperity, due in part to its effect on industrial location decisions. Firms are not perfectly immobile, despite their imperfect mobility. Thus, latitude of choice by the governor over state fiscal policies implies at least some ability to influence state prosperity, and contrary to Peltzman (1987, 1988) we regard a degree of accountability of governors as a reasonable position on the part of voters.

Stein (1989, 33) similarly argued:

> State and local governments are not impotent to improve their local economies. The actions of subnational governments are simply

constrained by macroeconomic conditions generally defined by national and international economic policies. Within the context of an exogenously defined economy, state and local governments can engage in taxing, spending, and general marketing strategies to attract and retain productive capital and labor.

Others have thought that because states are able to attract businesses by offering special tax packages and other government benefits,[6] they possess more control over their fate than is commonly thought. Brace (1989, 1991) found that state government had begun to play a larger role in improving state economies as the latter became increasingly detached from national economic conditions. Brace (1993, 122) generally concluded that state government could influence state economic outcomes, but not under all circumstances: "States have again emerged to promote legal and financial inducements to stimulate economic development and the findings reported here show that features of the entrepreneurial state have been associated with growth." Peterson (1995) examined what factors are associated with state economic development expenditures and found fiscal, demographic, and political factors at work.[7]

Scholars have also written about the limited power of cities in the face of mobile capital and corporations and national economic forces.[8] States generally appear to be in better circumstances, although Hendrick and Garand (1991) argued that exogenous national factors are increasingly responsible for state economic growth since 1962.

As discussed in the introduction, the power of the governor's office itself has also increased over the last few decades. Beyle (1990) showed that gubernatorial influence has significantly increased in the areas of appointment power, veto power, and budget power. Sabato (1983) found that not only does the office of governor have more power than in previous decades, but that the quality of governors and the ambition of their policies have dramatically improved. As the power of governors and the range of their undertakings expand, they might well expect to be held accountable by the voters for state conditions.

Owing to this growing role, as well as to their solitary and symbolic position as leaders of the state, governors find it difficult to escape responsibility for policy problems. Dometrius (1999, 54–55) found that "regardless of how an issue gets on the state's agenda, it must be resolved, and the public expects the governor to take the lead in problem resolution. The governor is often blamed for major unresolved state problems, regardless of how the problems developed." Whether or not governors have real power over their economies, there is evidence that the media assume they do. Tidmarch, Hyman, and Sorkin (1984) studied how the press covered congressional and gubernatorial elections; they found that national policy items made up a larger part of House and Senate campaign coverage than gubernatorial campaign coverage. Issues commonly thought to be more susceptible to state control, such as education and crime, were more likely to be covered in gubernatorial elections.

One caveat is that even if the media do cover economic conditions, they may report them incorrectly. Hetherington (1996) pointed out that the failure of voters in 1992 to correctly perceive national economic conditions was largely the fault of the news media. He showed that the more the voters followed the campaign through the media, the worse were their retrospective evaluations of the economy. Patterson (1993) also pointed out that media coverage of the economy in 1992 was almost exclusively negative. In fact, "the networks' portrayal of the economy got worse as the economy improved" (374). Svoboda (1995, 146) also noted that while aggregate economic measures are "objective, these figures may not be consistent with voters' *perceptions* of the state's economy. It is the electorates' perceptions of the economy which determine their voting patterns" (italics in original).

It may therefore be somewhat naive to assume that voters will accurately perceive the state of the economy. Nevertheless, the models will test whether declining or improving economic conditions hurt, help, or have no effect on incumbent governors. This chapter will also test voter rationality by examining whether voters hold governors responsible for changing national conditions (on which the latter have very little influence).

While many noneconomic issues may play a role in elections, there is surprisingly little research on this topic. Much of what exists is normative and found in journalistic accounts of elections. While some researchers have written generally on campaign strategy and the use of issues, most of their analyses have been qualitative in orientation. Only a few political scientists have quantitatively studied the effect of noneconomic issues on election outcomes in a way comparable to the study of economic forces.

Why this lack of research on such an inherently interesting topic? Cook, Jelen, and Wilcox (1994, 188), in their study of the abortion issue in gubernatorial politics, suggested that "previous research may have ignored the role of noneconomic issues because it is difficult to incorporate such variables into aggregate models." This difficulty is an obstacle, but it is not an insurmountable one. This chapter analyzes the effect of two key political issues (crime and education) using data that are publicly available and appropriate for either aggregate- or individual-level research.

A few scholars have argued that issues should be taken more seriously. In his study of presidential public support, Brody (1991, 105) suggested that "a fuller explanation of the dynamics of public support needs to apply this model to noneconomic policy areas as well as to the area of economic policy." More generally, Carmines and Stimson (1989, 3) wrote that "to speak of politics is to speak of political issues, almost invariably. We speak of them as if we knew of them. But we truly do not."

Only a few projects have attempted to understand whether issues affect election outcomes by analyzing individual-level surveys, and none have used aggregate data. The former include the study by Berry and Winters (2001, 1), who found that the abortion issue played a role in the 1990 and 1992 gubernatorial elections: "When Democratic and Republican gubernatorial candidates take predictable and clearly-stated differing positions on the abortion issue, voter preferences on abortion play an important role in explaining individual vote choice." Cook, Jelen, and Wilcox (1994) analyzed exit polls in ten states and found that abortion was a significant predictor of vote choice in nine. In addition, Howell and Sims (1993) analyzed survey data on Louisiana voters. They found that the abortion issue's influence could not be easily generalized, as it depended on specific electoral and contextual factors.

Discussion

The study of how economic conditions affect election outcomes began with studies of the House of Representatives and then expanded to include presidential elections, statewide offices, and even state legislative elections. Bennett and Wiseman (1991) noted that statewide elections are better subjects of study than House or state legislative elections because much more economic data are available at the state level.

A. Previous Retrospective Findings in Gubernatorial Elections

There are two general approaches in the retrospective debate. The first is to use aggregate analysis, whereby aggregate election outcomes and explanatory variables for each state are used. The second approach uses polling data, often American National Elections Study (ANES) or CBS/New York Times data. Studies that use the aggregate approach will be discussed first, and the individual-level research will be discussed next. This section will examine not just the conclusions reached by the authors, but also their data, the specification of dependent variables, and the use of any electoral (or at least noneconomic) variables.

Neither methodology holds a dramatic advantage over the other. This is because research has shown that voters do not need personal experience with economic problems to hold incumbent politicians accountable. In fact, voters often discount their personal experience in favor of how the economy performs more generally. Such behavior is commonly referred to as "sociotropic." For example, Schlozman and Verba (1979) studied unemployment in the 1930s and 1970s and found few political repercussions among those who experienced it. Kinder and Kiewiet (1979, 1981) similarly concluded that personal economic experiences did not affect political evaluations; instead, voters judged the president on the basis of the overall performance of the economy. Aggregate-level studies (such as this one) can therefore contribute to our understanding of how issues affect political outcomes.

Hibbing and Alford (1982, 506) summarized the issues involved in statewide elections when they wrote:

> As past research has amply demonstrated, the impact of economic conditions on House elections is a decidedly partisan phenomenon. It is the party of the president that is blamed or given credit for current economic conditions, and it is through these partisan judgments that individual House races are affected . . . [but] does the greater stature and visibility of the US Senate make a candidate for that office a larger target for the voters' economically-motivated frustration with the incumbent party, or does that same stature and visibility tend to turn the voters toward judgments of individual personality and qualifications and away from blanket partisan judgments?

The same question has been asked of governors, and the literature to date provides a mixed answer.

1. Aggregate–Level Research

Peltzman (1987) found that voters hold governors of the same party as the president responsible for national per capita income growth but not for national inflation rates. The difference between state and national growth rates was also insignificant. He concluded, "They [voters] vote as if they understand that national rather than local policies have the dominant effect on their income . . . Voters are not merely turning the rascals out when their last paycheck is reduced" (296–297).

Chubb (1988) found that measures for presidential responsibility for change in national income growth and gubernatorial responsibility for change in state income growth were both significant, although the national effect was over four times larger than the state effect. He concluded that governors (and also state legislators) have less to fear from state economies than some have suggested and that "gubernatorial elections remain contests of party and personality and not of performance—at least not that of the governor and the state" (150).

Leyden and Borrelli (1995) found that the following variables played a role in gubernatorial elections: (1) the national unemployment rate, (2) the national unemployment rate interacted with a variable for whether the governor was of the same party as the president, and (3) the state unemployment rate interacted with a dummy variable for unified state government. The state unemployment rate by itself had no effect. They argued that this finding was consistent with the responsible-party theorists' claim that parties are more likely to be rewarded or punished by voters when party responsibility for government is clear.

Holbrook-Provow (1987, 481) found that the gross national product (GNP) affected the percentage of gubernatorial victories by candidates of the president's party and concluded that "despite the fact that American governors are not national policymakers, gubernatorial elections are not insulated from the national political and economic climate."

Levernier (1992), however, found that economic conditions had only a weak influence on the vote. Specifically, the growth of state per capita income in the year before the election was only weakly correlated with the election outcome, while the various permutations of state per capita income, national per capita income, state and national unemployment rates, and the difference between state and national per capita income growth were all uncorrelated. He concluded: "The major finding of this study is that state economic conditions exert only a weak influence on the outcome of gubernatorial elections" (189).

Adams and Kenny (1989) found that the growth in state income and the difference between the state income growth rate and the national growth rate were not important. Contrary to Peltzman (1987), they found that an interaction of national income growth with a dummy coded 1 if the governor was of the same party as the president, and −1 if not, was not significant. They argued, however, that two variables intended to isolate the governor's contribution to state personal income growth were significant. This finding assumed that voters were cognizant of how their personal incomes changed over the entire course of the governor's term.

Kenney (1983a) used a different approach by combining incumbent and open seat candidates into one regression. He found that incumbents and candidates of the same party as the incumbent were not affected by changes in state unemployment, inflation, and per capita income from 1946 to 1980.

Kone and Winters (1993) studied over 400 gubernatorial elections and found only weak evidence of the role of taxes. Only changes in general sales taxes appeared to influence outcomes, and while governors were punished for tax increases, they were not rewarded for decreases.

The aggregate studies therefore suggest that only national economic conditions are important in gubernatorial elections. Leyden and Borrelli (1995) found evidence that both state and national effects were important, whereas Levernier (1992) and Kenney (1983a) found no evidence that changes in economic conditions affected election outcomes.

One caveat is that there are almost as many specifications within these aggregate models as there are studies. For example, there are many retrospective economic variables: some measure simple changes, while others are interactions of these changes with factors such as whether the governor is of the same party as the president.

Levernier (1992) tested twelve economic measures, including factors such as state per capita income, national per capita income, and unemployment, some of which measured change while others did not. Adams and Kenny (1989) used six variables, including interactions, based on the growth rate of per capita income in the state, the national growth rate, and the difference between the state and national growth rates. Peltzman (1987) used seven simple and interacted economic variables based on state and national per capita income growth, change in inflation rate, and growth in state revenue.

Chubb (1988) interacted party with variables for the annual change in the growth of national per capita disposable income and with the annual change in the growth of per capita personal income by state.

Leyden and Borrelli (1995) used the percentage change of national and state unemployment in the year before an election, an interaction of state unemployment with a state government unity dummy variable, and an interaction of national unemployment with a dummy variable for whether the candidate of the incumbent's party was of the same party as the president. Holbrook-Provow (1987) used the percentage change in GNP during the election year. While most of these articles test changes in economic measures in the year before the elections, some also test for change over longer periods of time (Adams and Kenny 1989).

There is also a great deal of variety in how the dependent variable is specified. Some studies used the incumbent party vote as the dependent variable[9] which means that both incumbent and open seat elections were included in the same regression. Adams and Kenny (1989) used incumbent party vote alone, while Chubb (1988) used the Democratic percentage of the vote. The percentage of gubernatorial elections won in an election year by candidates of the incumbent presidential party has also been used (Holbrook-Provow 1987).

Even when one study explicitly attempted to replicate another, as Adams and Kenny (1989, 3) did with Peltzman (1987), the authors cautioned: "There are several important differences in samples and dependent variables that must be noted."

Despite these great variations, the literature exhibits the common shortcoming of inadequately controlling for electoral factors. The elections literature is rarely consulted, and a variety of political control variables are inconsistently used.

Adams and Kenny (1989) included the percentage of gubernatorial victories by the incumbent's party in an election year , the percentage of gubernatorial victories by the incumbent's party in the state since the postwar period, a turnout measure, the fraction of the population that was employed by state government, and whether state law restricted the reelection opportunities of the governor. Levernier (1992) used a dummy coded 1 if the presidential candidate representing the incumbent governor's party won and coded 0 if the candidate did not win or if there was no presidential election, a dummy for whether an incumbent governor sought reelection, a dummy for whether a former governor sought election, and the average share of the vote received by the incumbent governor's party in the previous two gubernatorial elections.

Peltzman (1987) used incumbent party's share in the previous election and a dummy for the incumbent. Chubb (1988) included the prior Democratic vote percentage for governor, a dummy for incumbent, the Democrat vote for president, a dummy for presidential election year, the Democratic vote percentage for Senate, a dummy for senatorial election year, and a turnout measure. Leyden and Borrelli (1995) added the state party identification scores calculated by Wright, Erikson, and McIver (1985), a dummy for whether an incumbent was running, and a dummy for a presidential election year. Holbrook-Provow (1987) included the additional measures of a midterm election dummy variation, presidential approval ratings in the months before an election, and the percentage of elections involving governors of the same party as the president.

This chapter will include a large set of political variables so that the effects of economic and noneconomic change variables can be isolated as carefully as possible. In doing so, it creates yet another retrospective voting model, but hopefully, this comprehensive approach will prove to have some merit.

2. Survey Research

The second approach makes use of individual-level public opinion data. Atkeson and Partin (1995) compared the effect of economic conditions in gubernatorial and Senate elections and found evidence that voters act rationally. In Senate races, there were few economic effects on the vote, yet presidential approval had a strong influence on the vote for candidates of the president's party. For governors, state economic evaluations played an important role, while presidential approval did not, suggesting that "despite their similar constituencies, governors and senators are held responsible for different agendas" (106).

Carsey and Wright (1998) replicated Atkeson and Partin (1995), simultaneously taking into account the pooled nature of the ANES data and the misreporting problem of the ANES subpresidential data (which means that too many respondents claim to have voted for the winner). Like Atkeson and Partin (1995), Carsey and Wright (1998) agreed that voting for the two offices differed, but they argued that Senate voting was affected by national economic conditions and that voting in gubernatorial elections was affected by presidential approval.

Atkeson and Partin (1998) replied that Carsey and Wright's research (1998) generally supported their "functional responsibility" theory. They acknowledged that presidential politics may play some role in gubernatorial elections, but they doubted that the data problems were as significant as claimed. Carsey and Wright (1998) responded that two major differences still existed on issues of theoretical significance (mentioned above) because of differences in data and model specification. Both sides agreed that more attention should be paid to collecting better data on such important questions.

Stein (1989) compared economic effects in gubernatorial and Senate elections and found that "not only can voters identify the party and members within that party responsible for current economic conditions, but they can identify the offices and level of government responsible for these economic conditions" (52). Specifically, in 1982 he had found evidence of economic voting in Senate elections, with all Republican incumbents and challengers affected by economic evaluations. In gubernatorial elections, however, incumbents were not held responsible for the economy. Yet some economic effects did occur when voters assigned the incumbent some responsibility for the state economy; in those instances, the incumbent from the president's party was punished more.

Svoboda (1995) argued that retrospective economic evaluations did occur in gubernatorial elections. In 1986, both positive and negative evaluations by voters of the governor's performance were important. This also applied to open seat elections, whereby voters rewarded or punished the candidate of the same party as the outgoing governor. Presidential evaluations—in this case, whether the president was responsible for the economic problems of the state—also affected both open seat and incumbent elections, although the former more than the latter.

The 1982 data also allowed Svoboda (1995) to directly test the Bloom and Price (1975) theory that voters would punish incumbents when their personal financial situations declined but would fail to reward them if there was improvement. He found that this held true for incumbent elections but not for open seat contests.

Howell and Vanderleeuw (1990) found that evaluations of state economic performance strongly affected gubernatorial approval levels. Niemi, Stanley, and Vogel (1995) suggested that a poorly performing state economy, increases in taxation, and worsening personal finances all negatively affected governors and their parties.

Partin (1995) showed that state economic evaluations were significantly correlated with the vote for the incumbent and the open seat candidate from the incumbent's party. Presidential approval was not important. The results also showed that Republican incumbents were less successful than Democrats, although interactions of political party with both perceived and objective economic measures were not significant. National factors were most likely at work in open seat elections; the interaction of open seat elections with presidential approval was positive and significant, while the interaction of open seat elections with state economic evaluations was negative.

These studies are based on a variety of public opinion polls.[10] They also use a variety of dependent variables. In Svoboda (1995), the dependent variable for incumbent elections was the incumbent vote, and for open seat races the dependent variable was the vote for candidates of the outgoing governor's party. Partin (1995) used a dummy for whether or not the incumbent or the candidate from the departing incumbent's party won the election. Howell and Vanderleeuw (1990) used a dependent variable of approval for the incumbent governor. Atkeson and Partin (1995) used the respondents' vote choice for the Republican candidate, while Stein (1989) used three measures: the vote for the Republican candidate and the vote for Democratic and Republican incumbents.

As with the aggregate studies, it is often unclear how the noneconomic variables were chosen. The electoral variables used by Partin (1995) included measures of partisanship, a Republican incumbent dummy, and a dummy for open seat elections. Howell and Vanderleeuw (1990) added ideology and views on property taxes. Atkeson and Partin (1995) included party identification and ideology, while Svoboda (1995) put into the mix party affiliation and respondent ideology. The only noneconomic measure used by Stein (1989) was party affiliation.

What broad conclusions can be drawn from this wide range of research? In contrast to the findings of the aggregate-level research, the individual-level studies tend to support the argument that state economic factors are the most important. Because this chapter will conduct an aggregate examination of retrospective economic voting, it is important to keep in mind these different findings.

B. Previous Retrospective Findings in Senate Elections

Because senators share the same constituencies as governors, the literature on retrospective voting in Senate elections is briefly examined for any insights it might provide.

Bennett and Wiseman (1991) found that none of the state-level economic measures they tested (change in employment, change in per capita real personal income, and real personal income change) had any effect on election results. They did find that incumbent governors were held responsible for national changes in per capita income if they were of the same party as the president.

Chressanthis and Shaffer (1993) critiqued the above study because, among other reasons, it included both incumbent and open seat elections in the same regression analyses and used changes in employment growth rather than the better-publicized factor of changes in the unemployment rate. They found that state-level change in unemployment was a significant factor, although it was overshadowed by political factors such as challenger spending, presidential coattails, and incumbent primary divisiveness.[11]

Hibbing and Alford (1982) found that the effect of changes in real disposable per capita income was much greater in Senate elections than in House elections. Because the ratio was about 3:1, and given that one-third of the Senate comes up for reelection every year, they noted that "the potential for economically-induced turnover in the Senate is very nearly the same as that in the House" (512) in terms of overall proportion of membership. Like Chressanthis and Shaffer (1993), the authors analyzed both incumbent and open seat elections in the same regressions.

Some studies have explored whether ideological proximity between Senate incumbents and voters plays an electoral role.[12] This has been done using measures such as conservative coalition support scores or those of Americans for Democratic Action (ADA) and comparing them with some measure of state ideology, such as the Wright, Erickson, and McIver (1985) data. This measure is unavailable for the study of gubernatorial elections because such groups do not rate incumbent governors.

Other Senate studies have used public opinion polls instead of aggregate state or national data. While most of this research is concerned with retrospective effects, Lockerbie (1991) used ANES data to investigate how prospective evaluations might influence the vote. He found that prospective economic evaluations have a consistently strong influence on vote choice and may even outweigh retrospective evaluations.

Two studies discussed in the section on previous retrospective findings in gubernatorial elections compare results for gubernatorial elections with results for Senate elections. Atkeson and Partin (1995) found that governors were held responsible for voter perceptions of state economic conditions, whereas Senate elections showed a referendum effect whereby candidates of the president's party were either punished or rewarded depending on presidential popularity. Stein (1989, 50) found that while economic voting for governor existed only when voters specifically held the governor entirely or partially responsible for state economic problems, "senatorial voting exhibits clear and unambiguous economic voting, with all Republican senatorial candidates . . . held accountable by voters' simple and mediated retrospective economic evaluations."

Of the Senate and gubernatorial analyses described above, only the Chressanthis and Shaffer Senate study (1993) included any campaign finance measures. In addition, no study included noneconomic factors that the public might take into account at the polls. It therefore appears that some of the problems with gubernatorial retrospective research are also at work in the Senate literature.

The Model

This section builds on the models discussed and tested in Chapter 2 and uses the same data set covering the same time periods. The primary innovation is the addition of retrospective factors and the creation of interaction terms, which will be discussed below.

As before, incumbent and open seat elections are considered separately. This is especially important in this chapter because aside from the president and vice president, the governor is the most well-known political figure in a state.[13] When such a well-known and *accountable* personality is the incumbent, the election dynamics should be different from when two nongovernors are running. The voters may link the nongovernors to the achievements and failures of the outgoing administration through partisanship, but this is not the same as the accolades or blame that will attach to the governor.

All of the retrospective variables measure the percentage change from the year before the election to the election year. This is in accordance with Peltzman's argument (1987, 294):

> Cursory examination of annual real income, inflation, and unemployment series reveal considerable persistence, while growth of real income, change in inflation, and change in unemployment are approximately random walks, and these latter are what voters react to. Another pervasive result is reaffirmation of the voters' short memory.

This chapter agrees that voters' memories are unlikely to reach back four years.

This model will use both state and national economic conditions to test some of the previous studies' findings. The primary economic measure used in the literature, per capita income, is included here. It is specified as the change in per capita income in the year of the election from the previous year. In addition, as Levernier (1992) found that "the literature on gubernatorial elections has so far ignored the impact of unemployment rates on election outcomes" (188), the unemployment rate is also included.

Two noneconomic measures are introduced for the first time in this chapter: specifically, changes in the state crime rate and state SAT scores in the year of the election. These are two of the most significant policy issues that governors must face because they affect so many people and receive so much attention. Dometrius (1999, 60) noted that "the perennial state issues—those likely to show up consistently on the agenda of governors—have been crime, education, highways, and, to a lesser extent, health and welfare." The latter three are not easy to incorporate into regression analysis, but measures of crime and education are available.

The expectation is that rising crime rates and declining SAT scores will lead to less support for the governor who was presiding at the time, while improvements will lead to higher vote percentages. These changes are also single-year measures.

Two national-level economic change variables are also used. These are per capita income and unemployment. They are in turn interacted with a dummy variable measuring whether the incumbent is of the same party as the president. In this way, we will see whether gubernatorial incumbents suffer for national economic changes when they share a party label with the "responsible" president.

The second-stage model (based on the Ansolabehere and Snyder approach [1995]) is therefore the following:

$$
\begin{aligned}
\text{Incumbent Vote} = \; & \alpha + \beta_1 \ln(\text{Incumbent Expenditures}) \\
& + \beta_2 \ln(\text{Challenger Expenditures}) \\
& + \beta_3(\text{Incumbent Primary Margin}) \\
& + \beta_4(\text{Challenger Primary Margin}) \\
& + \beta_5(\text{Number of Candidates in Incumbent Primary}) \\
& + \beta_6(\text{Number of Candidates in Challenger Primary}) \\
& + \beta_7(\text{Incumbent Scandal}) \\
& + \beta_8(\text{Incumbent Same Party as President}) \\
& + \beta_9(\text{State Party Support}) \\
& + \beta_{10}(\text{Challenger Former Governor}) \\
& + \beta_{11}(\text{Challenger Federal Office Experience}) \\
& + \beta_{12}(\text{Challenger Statewide Office Experience}) \\
& + \beta_{13}(\text{Challenger State Legislative Experience})
\end{aligned}
$$

$+ \beta_{14}$(Challenger City or County Office
Experience)
$+ \beta_{15}$(Challenger Famous/Name
Recognition)
$+ \beta_{16}$(Change in State Per Capita Income)
$+ \beta_{17}$(Change in State Crime Rate)
$+ \beta_{18}$(Change in State SAT Scores)
$+ \beta_{19}$(Change in State Unemployment Rate)
$+ \beta_{20}$(National Changes in Per Capita Income
[NCPC])
$+ \beta_{21}$(National Changes in Unemployment
Rate [NCUR])
$+ \beta_{22}$(NCPC) * Same Party as President
$+ \beta_{23}$(NCUR) * Same Party as President
$+ \varepsilon.$

As in Chapter 2, the instrumental variables added to the first-stage model are incumbent age, challenger age, incumbent wealth, challenger wealth, and challenger experience as a political aide or consultant.

Open Seat Model

The open seat model is built on the one used in Chapter 2. Each observation consists of a candidate in an open seat election, and the model covers the same time period and uses the same political variables as those in Chapter 2.

The economic and social change variables were specified somewhat differently from those in the incumbent model. The state measures are now interacted with a dummy variable coded 1 if the candidate was of the same party as the outgoing governor and –1 if the candidate was from the opposite party. The national change measures are also interacted with a 1 if the party of the candidate and the party of the president are the same and with a –1 if they differ. The instrumental variables are the same as those used in the open seat model of Chapter 2.

The second-stage model, also based on Ansolabehere and Snyder (1995), is therefore the following:

Open Seat Candidate Vote $= \alpha + \beta_{1}$(Spending Percent)
$+ \beta_{2}$(Primary Margin)
$+ \beta_{3}$(Number of Candidates in
Primary)

$+ \beta_4$(State Party Support)

$+ \beta_5$(Same Party as Outgoing Governor)

$+ \beta_6$(Same Party as President)

$+ \beta_7$(Former Governor)

$+ \beta_8$(Federal Office Experience)

$+ \beta_9$(Statewide Office Experience)

$+ \beta_{10}$(State Legislative Experience)

$+ \beta_{11}$(City or County Office Experience)

$+ \beta_{12}$(Good Occupation)

$+ \beta_{13}$(Fame)

$+ \beta_{14}$(CSPCI) * Same Party as Departing Governor

$+ \beta_{15}$(CSCR) * Same Party as Departing Governor

$+ \beta_{16}$(CSUR) * Same Party as Departing Governor

$+ \beta_{17}$(CSSS) * Same Party as Departing Governor

$+ \beta_{18}$(NCPC) ** Same Party as President

$+ \beta_{19}$(NCUR) ** Same Party as President

$+ \beta_{20}$(Change in State Per Capita Income [CSPCI])

$+ \beta_{21}$(Change in State Crime Rate [CSCR])

$+ \beta_{22}$(Change in State Unemployment Rate [CSUR])

$+ \beta_{23}$(Change in State SAT Scores [CSSS])

$+ \beta_{24}$(National Change in Per Capita Income)

$+ \beta_{25}$(National Change in Unemployment Rate)

$+ \varepsilon.$

Results

Table 3.1 shows the results of the second stage of the fully specified two-stage least-squares (2SLS) retrospective incumbent and open seat election models.

Table 3.1 Second stage of 2SLS regression for retrospective voting in incumbent elections

Variables	Incumbent	Variables	Open Seat
Constant	0.571*** (0.130)	Constant	0.269*** (0.078)
ln(Incumbent Expenditures)	0.126* (0.065)	Percent of Money Raised	0.349** (0.143)
ln(Challenger Expenditures)	−0.096*** (0.027)	Primary Vote Percent	0.032 (0.034)
Incumbent Primary Vote Percent	0.232** (0.097)	Number of Primary Candidates	−0.000 (0.003)
Challenger Primary Vote Percent	−0.090 (0.062)	State Partisan Support	0.067 (0.092)
Number of Candidates in Incumbent Primary	−0.008 (0.010)	Same Party as Outgoing Governor	−0.007 (0.008)
Number of Candidates in Challenger Primary	0.006 (0.008)	Same Party as President	−0.026** (0.013)
Incumbent Scandal	−0.060 (0.067)	Former Governor	0.014 (0.022)
Incumbent Same Party as President	0.005 (0.042)	Federal Office Experience	0.015 (0.023)
State Political Support for Incumbent's Party	−0.168 (0.146)	Statewide Office Experience	0.011 (0.019)
Challenger Former Governor	−0.026 (0.041)	State Legislative Experience	0.014 (0.024)
Challenger Federal Office Experience	−0.064 (0.044)	City or County Office Experience	−0.021 (0.025)
Challenger Statewide Office Experience	−0.020 (0.025)	Good Occupation	−0.016 (0.025)
Challenger State Legislative Office Experience	−0.018 (0.021)	Fame	−0.020 (0.022)
Challenger City or County Office Experience	0.054 (0.034)	Change in Per Capita Income * Same Party as Outgoing Governor	−0.429 (0.372)
Challenger Famous	0.009 (0.031)	Change in Crime Rate * Same Party as Outgoing Governor	−0.068 (0.083)

(*Continued*)

Table 3.1 (*Continued*)

Variables	Incumbent	Variables	Open Seat
Change in State Per Capita Income	0.067 (0.539)	Change in Unemployment Rate * Same Party as Outgoing Governor	−0.013 (0.040)
Change in State Crime Rate	−0.269* (0.158)	Change in SAT Scores * Same Party as Outgoing Governor	−0.649 (0.791)
Change in State SAT Scores	1.719 (1.333)	Change in National Per Capita Income * Same Party as President	0.253 (0.693)
Change in State Unemployment	−0.078 (0.060)	Change in National Unemployment Rate * Same Party as President	−0.125* (0.072)
National Per Capita Income Change	0.323 (1.339)	Change in State Per Capita Income	−0.045 (0.354)
National Unemployment Change	0.080 (0.137)	Change in State Crime Rate	−0.007 (0.083)
National Per Capita Income Change * Incumbent Same Party as President	−1.173 (1.185)	Change in State Unemployment Rate	0.004 (0.050)
National Unemployment Change * Incumbent Same Party as President	−0.039 (0.114)	Change in State SAT Scores	−0.036 (0.813)
Observations	107	Change in National Per Capita Income	0.019 (0.686)
		Change in National Unemployment Rate	−0.001 (0.087)
		Observations	140

Notes: Incumbent model: dependent variable is incumbent percent of two-party vote (from 0 to 1). Open seat model: dependent variable is candidate percentage of two-party vote (from 0 to 1). Cells contain coefficients with standard errors in parentheses.
***$p < .01$, **$p < .05$, *$p < .10$.

A. Incumbent Model

The regressions show that four independent variables are significant. As in the regression in Chapter 2, both incumbent and challenger expenditures are associated with the general election vote. The substantive significance of the variables is slightly lower than in Chapter 2 but in the same approximate range.

The results also confirm the previous finding that incumbents must worry about their primary election vote percentage; however, the measure for city or county political experience is below conventional levels of statistical significance. This suggests that once the incumbent election model is fully specified, no type of challenger political experience has an impact on election outcomes.

The one retrospective variable that plays a role is the state crime rate. When crime rates increase, an incumbent's share of the two-party vote decreases. The precise effect is easy to calculate, because both variables are continuous measures between 0 and 1. Every 10 percent increase in the crime rate, for example, should lead to an almost 3 percent drop in the general election vote of the incumbent.

There is no precedent in the retrospective literature for such an effect because it has never been tested before. To date, only economic change variables have been examined. Because crime and SAT scores are only two of many potential noneconomic variables that may affect the decisions of voters, future research should attempt to take them into account.

The first thing to notice about the crime variable is that it is a state-level measure. It is also important to note that none of the national-level variables were significant. This suggests that voters have some understanding of what factors governors do and do not have the power to influence.

But why do changes in crime, and not state changes in per capita income, SAT scores, or unemployment, have an impact? This could reflect voter feeling that the other issues are not under the control of the governor. Alternatively, the public might believe that while all these issues are under the control of the governor, only crime is important enough to directly affect their voting decisions.

As noted previously, crime is one of the "perennial" issues facing states (Dometrius 1999, 60). It should come as little surprise that the public and the news media pay attention to increases or decreases in the crime rate. The influence of the media in setting the political agenda should not be underestimated,[14] as research suggests that the media are the primary suppliers of political information to the public.[15] If the media were to focus on crime and do so in a way that attached credit or blame to the governor, then it would come as little surprise to see voters blaming the governor for increased crime rates. There is in fact evidence that the media do exactly this. Tidmarch, Hyman, and Sorkin (1984) found that issues commonly thought to be more susceptible to state control, such as crime and education, were more likely to be covered by the media in gubernatorial elections.

The education variable's lack of significance might mean that SAT scores are a poor proxy for the overall health of the school system, and not that voters do not care about education. Other education variables could be put to the test in future research, especially as education has been one of the most discussed policy issues in the 1980s and 1990s and as more state and local testing data are becoming available because of the No Child Left Behind (NCLB) legislation.

One important concern is the statistical fragility of these findings. When alternative specifications of the model were tried, the results held up well. When all the national and state economic change variables except for the state crime rate were removed, the statistical significance of the latter only increased. When only the national change variables were removed, the state crime rate measure was unharmed. In each of these alternative specifications, the city/county political experience variable increased in statistical significance.

B. Open Seat Model

There are three statistically significant variables in the open seat regression. As in the open seat model in Chapter 2, the comparative measure for campaign expenditures was highly significant ($p < .003$), so money plays a role in both incumbent and open seat elections, even while controlling for multiple candidate quality and retrospective voting measures.

The other two statistically significant variables suggest a referendum effect in open seat elections. When the unemployment rate rises and the candidate is of the same party as the president, the candidate is punished by the voters. In addition, a candidate who is simply of the same party as the president likewise runs into trouble at the polls. This is not a midterm dynamic; it affects all elections. Put together, this is evidence that national political and economic factors may make their way into gubernatorial elections.[16]

It is also important to note that in open seat elections, no state-level measures were significant. Taken together with the findings from incumbent elections, we see that incumbent elections were affected by state conditions, while open seat elections were affected by national conditions.

Substantively, a 10 percent increase in the national unemployment rate leads to a one and a quarter percent decrease in the vote for a candidate of the same party as the president. Independent of this effect, a candidate of the same party as the president will lose almost 3 percent of the general election vote to his or her opponent. These factors could make all the difference in a close election.

Why is the national per capita income rate not a factor, while national unemployment is? The answer may be that the latter is better known than the former. Chressanthis and Shaffer (1993, 266) found that "the unemployment rate is a much more readily available and publicized voting cue on economic performance than income." This could well be due to reporting by the news media, which tend to focus on the unemployment rate, whereas changes in per capita income are noted mostly by economists. While some voters may have a general sense of how deflated per capita income changes from year to year, it is much more likely that the simpler measure of national unemployment comes to their attention.

When alternative specifications of the model were tried, the results again held up well. All the state-level change variables were removed, and then the national per capita income variables were deleted. The only changes were that the statistical significance levels of the inter-acted unemployment variable and the presidential variable increased (both to the $p < .001$ level).

Conclusions

Using a data set of gubernatorial elections from 1980 to 1996, this chapter argues that retrospective voting does take place, although it varies according to the type of election under consideration. In incumbent elections, the state crime rate influences voter decisions: the higher the crime rate, the more the incumbent is punished at the polls. In open seat elections, there is evidence of a national economic effect but not of any state-level dynamics. When the national unemployment rate rises and a candidate is of the same party as the president, then that candidate is punished at the polls. This suggests that open seat elections, which lack the dominating presence of an incumbent, take on some aspects of a national referendum on the president. This possibility is reinforced by the finding that in open seat elections, candidates who are of the same party as the president are also punished.

It is difficult to say how this chapter's findings compare with the literature on gubernatorial retrospective voting described above, because even within the aggregate literature there are several nontrivial differences in the data sets and variables used. This study builds on the earlier work by separately examining incumbent and open seat elections, which makes for clearer analysis, but also for more difficult comparisons.

Some scholars have suggested that voters can hold governors and gubernatorial candidates of the same party as the president accountable for national changes,[17] but aggregate studies have generally found only weak evidence that governors and gubernatorial candidates may be rewarded or punished for state-level economic changes;[18] studies that show evidence of stronger effects use specifications other than those tested here.[19] The findings of this chapter therefore complement the studies that found national effects, but they somewhat contradict those on state findings. The caveat "somewhat" is included because the state-level variable—changes in crime rates—was not tested in the earlier literature.

Some important questions are: Why are crime and unemployment important factors in these contexts, while other issues are not? Why do voters not punish incumbents for declining state per capita income, and why do some open seat candidates not suffer when national income declines? For incumbent elections, the most likely explanation is hypothesized to be the way the news media report stories on gubernatorial elections. The retrospective finding for open seat elections may also reflect media reporting practices, especially the greater attention paid to unemployment statistics than to per capita income data. The other finding, that open seat candidates of the same party as the president suffer at the polls, may reflect the accumulation of constituencies alienated over time by the president. These constituencies then take out their feelings on a convenient target with an easily discernible connection to the president. A more intriguing possibility is that voters may want divided government not only within a particular level of the federal system, as Fiorina (1992) suggested, but also between levels.

Hopefully, this chapter will lead to additional research by political scientists on how noneconomic issues affect election outcomes. One of the difficulties of doing this is that some issues may either not play a national role at all or may affect elections in some states but not others. As Brody (1991, 113) wrote about presidential elections, "The mix of policies entering the performance judgment is likely to differ from president to president." In the same way, different factors may play varying roles in different election cycles and even among different states. Qualitative analysis of particular gubernatorial elections might be fruitfully combined with survey data in order to see whether local or idiosyncratic issues play a statistically and substantively significant role.

A key finding of this chapter is evidence of politically rational behavior by the voting public. Incumbents were not punished for changes in national issues but only for a change in a state condition. Open seat candidates were not affected by state conditions but were affected by two national factors. This is generally reminiscent of the voter accountability arguments developed by Stein (1989), Atkeson and Partin (1995), Carsey and Wright (1998), and others.

If the data showed the opposite, it might suggest that voters were unreasonably blaming or crediting candidates for factors over which they have little control. Instead, this chapter suggests that voters understand how to hold politicians accountable and is therefore in its own small way "a happy event for those who are optimistic about democracy" (Key 1966, vii).

4

Voter Turnout: Competition, Candidates, and Conditions

This chapter tests how demographic and political factors, along with economic and noneconomic changes, affect aggregate voter turnout in gubernatorial elections. There are two ways to study the determinants of voter turnout: the first examines the personal characteristics of voters, and the second focuses on the political mobilization factors they might encounter. This chapter will examine variables in both categories to better understand what brings voters to the polls. Like Chapters 2 and 3, this chapter covers most gubernatorial elections from 1980 to 1996. It builds upon the small body of literature on mobilization factors in gubernatorial elections, which is limited to the 1978–1982 time period. The extended coverage that this chapter provides is especially important because the campaign finance literature shows that regression results can be unstable when limited time periods are examined (see Green and Krasno [1988] for examples), and the same could be true for the study of turnout.

In addition, this chapter introduces some changes to existing turnout models. Most importantly, incumbent and open seat elections are examined separately, as in the two preceding chapters. Although the elections literature has demonstrated that there are fundamentally different dynamics at work in these two types of elections, turnout scholars have not distinguished between them except to note generally that turnout is reduced in incumbent elections. Although an incumbent/open seat dummy variable provides some information, it does not help us to understand how the structure of turnout may vary when the state chief executive is present or absent.

This chapter also tests whether some of the variables examined in the retrospective voting chapter (Chapter 3) might play a role in determining turnout. The models in this chapter therefore include seven economic and social change factors at both the national and state levels. These include yearly changes in state and national employment rates, state and national per capita income, state tax rates, state crime rates, and state SAT scores.

Political variables beyond campaign expenditures might also influence turnout, particularly the political experience of the candidate and the intensity of the campaign. These have rarely been examined in the turnout literature, but this chapter will test the possibility that they influence electoral participation. Factors such as candidate quality, electoral margin, region, and scandals are also included.

Discussion

There are three primary studies relevant to this topic. Two examined gubernatorial turnout (Patterson and Caldeira 1983; Hill and Leighley 1993) and one examined gubernatorial influences on overall turnout (Cox and Munger 1989).

Patterson and Caldeira (1983) examined aggregate data for elections in 1978 and 1980. Their strategy was to test in one model the variables associated with both the socioeconomic and the political mobilization models of turnout. The socioeconomic model included variables such as income, education, and age; the mobilization model examined campaign spending variables, a measure of electoral closeness, the effect of a concurrent Senate election, and a voter registration law measure. They concluded that while income reached a conventional level of statistical significance in a purely sociological model, it joined the other socioeconomic variables in insignificance when mobilization factors were added.

All of the mobilization factors were significant and in the expected direction. Total expenditures, party competitiveness,[1] and the presence of Senate and presidential contests all increased turnout, while electoral closeness and stringent registration laws decreased turnout. One potential shortcoming of their study is that it examined both incumbent and open seat elections in the same regressions and did not differentiate between the two.

Cox and Munger (1989) examined aggregate turnout in 1982 House elections. Their final model showed that the variables for campaign expenditures in House, Senate, and gubernatorial races were significant and positive, although the House expenditure variable had about three times the substantive effect of the Senate or gubernatorial expenditure variables. Unlike the Patterson and Caldeira study

(1983), all of the demographic variables were significant and in the expected direction. Of the four measures indicating the closeness of an election, the simple difference in the number of votes between the winner and the loser was statistically significant, as was the margin percentage in the Senate race. The gubernatorial margin did not affect turnout.

Hill and Leighley (1993) examined the role of party competitiveness, ideology, and party organization in gubernatorial elections from 1980 to 1986. They found that competitiveness and ideology were associated with turnout, although the significance of these variables depended upon the restrictiveness of voter registration requirements. Concurrent presidential elections as well as campaign expenditures were positively related to gubernatorial turnout.

Another line of inquiry in the turnout literature began with Boyd (1981) and is largely concerned with how the number of elections on a ballot may affect turnout. Boyd hypothesized that declining voter participation might be caused by the decision of political elites in many states to insulate state elections from "contamination" by national presidential elections. This was done by enlarging gubernatorial terms to four years and moving contests to nonpresidential election years. Boyd's theory was that the fewer the elections on a ballot, the lower the number of voters who will turn out.

Cohen (1982) and Hansen and Rosenstone (1984) tested these propositions with aggregate data but found no evidence to support them. Boyd (1986) used individual-level data[2] and found evidence for his 1981 hypothesis. Using similar 1976, 1980, and 1984 data, Boyd (1989) found that the presence of gubernatorial elections, but not the presence of Senate elections, in a presidential election year served to increase turnout.

In other research, Wolfinger and Rosenstone (1980) found that the presence of concurrent gubernatorial elections in presidential election years slightly increased turnout, although concurrent Senate elections again did not. Caldeira, Patterson, and Markko (1985), by contrast, argued that contested gubernatorial and Senate elections both increased turnout in off-year elections. This chapter will test for Senate and presidential effects on turnout by including in the models dummy variables noting the presence of these elections.

There are also related literatures on primary turnout in gubernatorial elections[3] and the consequences of turnout on state-level election outcomes,[4] although they are less directly relevant. This chapter will test how primary campaigns may affect turnout in gubernatorial elections, as discussed below.

Data and Variables

The incumbent election data set includes 112 general elections, the same data set used in the previous two chapters. The open seat data set contains 73 elections; instead of each candidate constituting an observation, as in the previous two chapters, each open seat election is now the unit of analysis.

A. Dependent Variable

Patterson and Caldeira (1983) specified turnout as the percentage of the voting age population in a state that voted in the 1978 and 1980 gubernatorial elections. Cox and Munger (1989) also used the total ballots cast (in the 1982 House election) divided by the voting age population of the state. This chapter similarly divides the total number of votes cast for the two general election gubernatorial candidates by the voting age population of the state. It would make little sense to divide the number of votes by total state population, as turnout would appear lower in states with larger populations of children.

B. Campaign Finance Variables

There are two specifications of campaign expenditures in both the open seat and incumbent models. First, the total amount of money spent by both candidates is added together, deflated by the consumer price index (urban) to ensure comparability across the two decades, and then divided by the voting age population of the state. This measure takes into account the fact that the same amount of money will vary in effect depending on the size of the state. It also allows for easy analysis of its relationship with the turnout variable, which is similarly divided by state voting age population. As noted previously, Hill and Leighly (1993) found that per capita total expenditures[5] were positively associated with turnout in states with less-restrictive registration laws, although data were available at that time only for elections from 1984 to 1987.

A simple measure of overall candidate spending may be inadequate. A second measure therefore takes into account the differing expenditures of the two candidates. The money spent by the more spendthrift candidate is divided by the money spent by the other candidate. This is a way to measure the intensity of an election, and it is also used in Chapter 7 for this purpose.[6]

Why are differences in intensity levels important? One reason is that whether a campaign is hard fought or low key has implications for how voters make decisions. As Westlye (1991) argued, hard-fought campaigns bring more information to the attention of voters, while low-key contests lead to an information-poor political environment. This suggests that voters are able to make better-informed decisions in the former, but are often just going through the motions in the latter.

The smaller the expenditure ratio, the closer the election should be.[7] The higher the ratio, the more television, radio, and print advertisements the voters will notice from one candidate than from the other. This may suggest that the election is not going to be close enough to make participation worth the effort. Voting is almost never a useful investment of time and effort for the individual, statistically speaking, but perhaps for those individuals who vote out of a sense of civic duty, an election that does not appear to be close releases them from this self-imposed obligation.

C. Demographic Variables

The individual demographic variables follow those of Wolfinger and Rosenstone (1980). Measures of the average education, income, and age in the various states are included. The expectation is that all three will positively correlate with turnout.

Boyd (1986) found that "as is well known, rootedness in primary groups and the community is consistently related to voting." In this chapter, the rootedness factor is taken into account by the percentage of housing in the state that is owner-occupied. A state of homeowners is more likely to have higher voter turnout than a state of renters, as homeowners do not have to reregister to vote as often as more-mobile apartment dwellers.

D. Other Political Variables

A measure that takes into account the presence and closeness of gubernatorial primaries is also included. It has five values in both incumbent and open seat models: one point for each primary election, and another point if the winner received less than 50 percent of the vote. The range is therefore from zero (no primaries) to four (two closely contested primaries).

There are several reasons to expect that primaries may affect turnout. Boyd (1989, 730) found that "presidential and state primaries divert resources away from the general election" and therefore reduce turnout. Volunteer labor and campaign contributions are scarce resources, he argued, and primaries consume them. Boyd (1986) also pointed out several reasons why primaries might increase a person's likelihood to vote in future elections. Most prominent among them is that voting is not just an instrumental act but also a normative one, often based on a sense of civic obligation. The more one votes, the more likely one is to vote in future elections (Brody and Sniderman 1977).

The general election margin is included because margin has been found to play an important role in turnout for elections at several levels of the federal system. This factor is specified as the difference in the vote percentages of the two major candidates. Because states are of varying sizes, the simple closeness in terms of numbers of votes was not appropriate; a 100,000 vote difference may indicate a squeaker in California but a landslide in Wyoming.

There has been some debate in the literature about how to specify this election expectations measure. Cox (1988) argued that the simple percentage margin measure (the raw vote margin divided by the total number of votes cast in the district) is problematic. This is because the measure of total votes cast can be found both in the margin measure and in the turnout variables: the former in the denominator, the latter in the numerator. On the other hand, there are theoretical problems with using just the raw closeness of the vote, especially when the size of the constituencies varies. Cox and Munger (1989) used both margin and closeness, but this chapter excludes the latter.

The theory behind the margin variable is twofold. First, citizens may be more likely to participate in close elections if they perceive that their vote has a greater likelihood of making a difference. This is seen as a corollary of the work of Downs (1957) and Riker and Ordeshook (1968), who argued that people should vote when expected benefits exceed costs, although their reasoning was disputed by Ferejohn and Fiorina (1974, 1975). The second theory suggests that elites respond to closer elections with greater campaign efforts. This particular effect, however, should be controlled for by the campaign expenditure variable. Another possibility is that the media pay more attention to closer elections, and this increased coverage leads to greater turnout.

This margin variable, however, is not equivalent to the campaign intensity measure discussed above. According to Westlye (1991, 18), "In many instances, a close margin of victory does accompany a high-intensity campaign, and vice versa. But the two concepts are theoretically distinct, and it would be a mistake to characterize the intensity of a campaign solely by the margin of the outcome." He argued that a Republican candidate in a solidly Democratic state may wage a highly intense campaign but still lose by a large margin if the voters retained their party loyalties. "Margin of victory, then, is at best a problematic measure of the intensity of a given campaign. And since achieving a high level of intensity is essential in terms of a campaign's purpose—conveying information to voters—it makes more sense to use a measure that directly taps activities designed to reach voters" (19).

There is also a dummy variable for presidential election years, as turnout should be higher when these highly publicized contests are on the ballot. A measure for Senate elections is included, although prior research is divided on whether these contests increase turnout.

The general level of political contestation in a state may also influence gubernatorial election turnout. As Holbrook and Van Dunk (1993, 955) explained,

> Close elections are likely to generate more interest and information, thereby reducing certain costs associated with voting. Close elections also provide a strong incentive for the candidates and parties to organize and mobilize the electorate (Powell 1986). Most empirical studies have supported the relationship between competition and turnout (Dye 1966; Milbrath 1971; Patterson and Caldeira 1983; Wolfinger and Rosenstone 1983), although there is some evidence to the contrary (Gray 1976).

Holbrook and Van Dunk (1993) therefore created a unique measure based on district-level state legislative election returns from 1982 to 1986. They argued that this measure was "empirically and intuitively superior" to the usual measure, the folded Ranney (1976) index, because the former is based on election returns and not on state government partisan balance. They found that their variable was significantly related to presidential election turnout (the average of 1984 and 1988 returns). This chapter will test the measure in the gubernatorial arena.

Candidate political factors are also included. For incumbent elections, dummy variables measure whether the challenger was famous, whether the challenger had prior experience in an elected office, and whether the incumbent was facing a scandal. It is expected that a more politically experienced candidate is better known and more credible and may therefore draw a greater proportion of people to the polls. A similar dynamic may occur if famous individuals run for governor, and a scandal may attract an unusual level of attention to and interest in the campaign.

In the open seat model, the prior political experience variable is coded 0 if neither candidate had held elective office, 1 if one candidate had, and 2 if both candidates had. Fame is also coded in this three-level manner. The scandal variable is not included because there was only one instance of scandal among all open seat candidates.[8]

The models also include a dummy variable for gubernatorial elections in the south. The Democratic Party dominated this region for many years, and winning the Democratic primary was tantamount to winning the general elections. Although party competition has significantly increased in recent decades, the legacy of historically de-emphasized general elections may lead to lower participation vis-à-vis the rest of the nation.

Also included is a measure of the strictness of state voter registration laws, as some states allow registration on the same day as the general election, while others require voters to register a number of weeks in advance. The more-restrictive registration requirements should lower turnout, as those who do not plan ahead may find themselves unable to vote (for discussion, see King and Wambeam 1995/1996 and King 1994).

Hill and Leighley (1993) tested two measures of party organization and mass–elite ideological differences. Their first measure derived from a 1979–1980 survey of party county chairpersons; the second was based on activist data collected from 1972–1980 and public opinion data from 1976 to 1982. These data were appropriate for a gubernatorial turnout study encompassing elections from 1980 to 1986, but less so for a study including contests up to 1996. As replicating these variables would be a significant undertaking, they are not used in this chapter. While they may still be factors today, it is important to point out that no paper in this literature has included all possible determinants of the gubernatorial vote.

E. Economic and Social Change Variables

Seven such measures are included. They consist of state changes in unemployment, per capita income, taxation, crime, and SAT scores, and national changes in unemployment and per capita income. Political scientists and observers generally expect that worsening conditions increase turnout while improvements lead to complacency. The public is likely to see government, and therefore elections to public office, as more important when there are problems to solve. Such problems may also provide more issues for the candidates to debate and may generate more news coverage. The media are attracted to controversies, and declining economic conditions, rising crime rates, and higher taxes are prime examples. When conditions are good, the public and the media may lose interest in elections. Some political scientists have observed that an improvement in economic conditions may lead to public complacency. As Arnold (1990, 51) noted in his study of Congress:

> Citizens are far more likely to pursue traceability chains when they incur perceptible costs than when they reap an equal measure of benefits. Part of the reason is that costs produce more intense preferences than do benefits. In addition, costs inspire people to search for someone to blame, whereas benefits are usually enjoyed without a corresponding effort to discover whom to reward.

Veteran journalist Hal Bruno similarly noted that "when you have prosperity, you tend to have low turnout, in all elections. When you have economic hard times, people come out and vote because they're angry and they're scared and worried. And that's the greatest motivation for people to get out and vote."[9]

Although the general expectation is that declining conditions will increase turnout, the opposite could also be true. Given the limited research on the effect of conditions on turnout, it is difficult to rule out *a priori* either possibility. According to this alternative argument, worsening conditions might provide convenient political ammunition for one candidate to use against another, especially in incumbent elections, where responsibility for social and economic change is clear. This ammunition might take the form of negative advertising that targets the incumbent, and in open seat races, targets the candidate of the outgoing governor's or president's party. Ansolabehere and Iyengar (1995) and Ansolabehere, Iyengar, and Simon (1999) argued that negative advertising depresses voter turnout. If this is the case[10]—and if negative advertising is more common when conditions are negative—then turnout may be reduced in such contests.

An additional hypothesis involves psychology and neuroscience research on how emotions affect life activities.[11] While positive emotions can lead to increased activity, negative emotions are more likely to lead to withdrawal. If news of improving social and economic conditions generates positive emotions, then one result could be increased political participation.

The Model

Because the dependent variable is continuous, ordinary least-squares (OLS) regression is used. The model is therefore:

$$
\begin{aligned}
\text{Turnout} = \alpha &+ \beta_1(\text{State Population Percent over 65 Years of Age}) \\
&+ \beta_2(\text{State Population Percent with College Experience}) \\
&+ \beta_3(\text{State Population Per Capita Income}) \\
&+ \beta_4(\text{State Population Percent Owner-Occupied Housing}) \\
&+ \beta_5(\text{Total Candidate Expenditures}) \\
&+ \beta_6(\text{Candidate Expenditure Ratio [campaign intensity]}) \\
&+ \beta_7(\text{Candidate Prior Political Experience}) \\
&+ \beta_8(\text{Candidate Fame/Name Recognition}) \\
&+ \beta_9(\text{Candidate Scandal}) + \beta_{10}(\text{Election Margin}) \\
&+ \beta_{11}(\text{Presidential Election}) \\
&+ \beta_{12}(\text{Senate Election}) + \beta_{13}(\text{Gubernatorial Primary}) \\
&+ \beta_{14}(\text{State Political Competition [Holbrook–Van Dunk]}) \\
&+ \beta_{15}(\text{Voter Registration Limit}) + \beta_{16}(\text{South}) \\
&+ \beta_{17}(\text{State Tax Change}) \\
&+ \beta_{18}(\text{State Per Capita Income Change}) \\
&+ \beta_{19}(\text{State Crime Rate Change}) \\
&+ \beta_{20}(\text{State Unemployment Rate Change}) \\
&+ \beta_{21}(\text{State SAT Score Change}) \\
&+ \beta_{22}(\text{National Per Capita Income Change}) \\
&+ \beta_{23}(\text{National Unemployment Change}) \\
&+ \varepsilon.
\end{aligned}
$$

As described previously, the coding of some variables varies depending on whether the open seat or the incumbent data set is used.

Results

Table 4.1 shows the results of the incumbent and open seat turnout models. In the incumbent model, the regressions show that eight variables reached conventional levels of statistical significance.

Of the seven economic and social change measures, it is the change in state tax rates that is significant, with an increase in taxation associated with an increase in turnout. It therefore appears that voters are turning out to express their anxiety over this issue. While it is possible

Table 4.1 Incumbent and open seat election turnout models

Variables	Incumbent	Open Seat
Intercept	0.156	0.115
	(0.137)	(0.160)
State Age	1.438***	0.770*
	(0.316)	(0.402)
Education	0.416***	0.227**
	(0.125)	(0.098)
Per Capita Income	−0.008***	−0.008*
(in thousands)	(0.003)	(0.004)
Home Ownership	0.123	0.242
	(0.128)	(0.179)
Total Expenditures	0.001	0.002**
	(0.001)	(0.001)
Expenditure Ratio	−0.002*	−0.000
	(0.001)	(0.002)
Challenger Elected Office	−0.007	−
Experience	(0.012)	
Elected Office Experience	−	−0.010
		(0.021)
Challenger Famous	−0.000	−
	(0.020)	
Candidate Famous	−	0.004
		(0.012)
Incumbent Scandal	−0.014	−
	(0.038)	
Electoral Margin	0.017	−0.113
	(0.037)	(0.099)
Presidential Election Year	0.148***	0.139***
	(0.015)	(0.018)
Senate Election	0.006	0.004
	(0.007)	(0.008)
Primaries	−0.005	−0.003
	(0.006)	(0.007)
State Political Competition	0.000	0.001*
(Holbrook-Van Dunk measure)	(0.001)	(0.001)

(*Continued*)

Table 4.1 *(Continued)*

Variables	Incumbent	Open Seat
Voter Registration Deadline	−0.002***	−0.002***
	(0.001)	(0.001)
South	−0.041**	−0.065***
	(0.019)	(0.023)
State Tax Change	0.127**	0.115
	(0.062)	(0.118)
State Per Capita Income	−0.085	0.233
Change	(0.301)	(0.475)
State Crime Change	−0.128	0.094
	(0.100)	(0.108)
State Unemployment Change	−0.051	0.147**
	(0.036)	(0.059)
State SAT Change	1.105	−0.272
	(0.702)	(0.973)
National Per Capita Income	0.040	1.761*
Change	(1.212)	(0.946)
National Unemployment	0.072	0.084
Change	(0.130)	(0.110)
Observations	107	65
Adjusted R^2	0.75	0.82

Notes: Dependent variable: gubernatorial election turnout divided by state voting age population, giving a percentage from 0 to 1. Cells contain coefficients with standard errors in parentheses.

***$p < .01$, **$p < .05$, *$p < .10$.

that voters are heading to the polls in order to reward incumbent governors who have overseen tax increases, this scenario seems less likely. It is also important to note that the change in state tax rates is a state-level change. It makes sense that a state change appears to play a role when an incumbent is present. Substantively, for every 10 percent increase in the tax rate, turnout increases by about 1.3 percent.

The spending ratio variable is statistically significant and substantively negative, meaning that less-competitive elections see lower turnout. The maximum value of the ratio variable is about 20, while the mean is 3; the decrease in turnout associated with these two values is about 6 percent and 1 percent, respectively. The overall expenditure measure is not correlated with turnout. This suggests that the total amount of political "noise" a campaign makes is less important than whether the challenger is able to run a credible campaign. Regardless of how much is spent, voters are apparently less motivated to help decide an election that has only been weakly contested.

The traditional margin variable is not significant, which illustrates that this particular measure may be as problematic as some have argued. It might be thought that this contradicts the interpretation of the expenditure ratio variable, but a competitive election is not necessarily the same as a close one. As Westlye (1991) discussed, it is possible for a campaign to be both hard fought and a landslide. The distinction between intensity and closeness is useful because only in a hard-fought campaign will voters receive an adequate range of information with which to make a decision. The voters may still vote overwhelmingly for the incumbent in a hard-fought campaign, but an important point is that they will do so while being aware of the alternative. It therefore makes sense that a competitive election, rather than a close election, affects turnout.

Of the demographic variables, the age and education of state residents correlated positively with turnout, while state per capita income was negatively correlated. This latter finding may seem surprising, but Kenney (1983a) also found that per capita income was negatively correlated with turnout.[12] The substantive effects of these three variables are very similar. A 1 standard deviation increase in the age variable increases turnout by about 3 percent, while similar changes in the other two variables are each associated with 4 percent changes.

The two variables testing the effect of simultaneous presidential and Senate elections on turnout differed in significance. A concurrent presidential election was positively associated with turnout, increasing it by a substantial 15 percent, but the Senate election variable was not significant.

We also see that the length of time required to register to vote in an election is negatively associated with turnout. As expected, and as others have found, states in which it takes longer to register have lower turnout. We also see that southern states generally have lower turnout in gubernatorial general elections, which may be a legacy of the historical importance of primary elections. Whether this dynamic will continue into the future is likely to depend on the strength of two-party contestation in these states.

The second numerical column in Table 4.1 shows the results of the open seat model. Ten factors were statistically significant. Of the economic condition variables, we find that two factors are associated with an increase in turnout—the change in the state unemployment rate and national per capita income. The substantive significance of state unemployment is not very large. A 5 percentage point increase in unemployment, which is approximately the maximum increase in the data set, is associated with a turnout increase of less than 1 percent. The substantive effect for national per capita income is almost ten times larger, however.

As in the previous model, a decline in conditions is associated with an increase in turnout. As before, this may be interpreted as bad news bringing people to the polls or good news keeping them at home, but the result is the same. The open seat model also indicates that an increase in national per capita income is associated with an increase in turnout. This suggests a lack of uniformity in the effect of conditions on turnout; in two cases negative changes lead to higher turnout, but economic good news may also lead to higher turnout.

The effect of national per capita income on turnout is not likely related to changes in voter income, as it is a change in national and not state income. This indicates a sociotropic effect, whereby good national economic conditions are perceived by the public and serve to spur political action. It also suggests that open seat election turnout can be affected by factors originating from outside the state, while incumbent elections are affected only by changes taking place during the governor's tenure. This is consistent with Chapter 3, which found that the vote for incumbent governors was affected by a state condition whereas open seat candidates had to worry about national factors.

The overall spending variable is also significant, but the spending ratio variable is not. This is the opposite of the incumbent model and points out the different dynamics in these two elections. It appears that in open seat elections, the competitiveness of the two candidates may not be important; these elections may receive significant attention regardless of relative campaign expenditures. Overall spending in incumbent races does influence turnout, with greater amounts of money leading to higher levels of turnout. Specifically, the mean value of expenditures is associated with an increased turnout of 4 percent (in comparison to no spending), and a 1 standard deviation increase is associated with an increase of 2 percent.

The presence of a presidential election once again raised turnout, while the presence of a Senate election once again did not. A presidential election led to an additional turnout of 14 percent. Of the demographic variables, the age, education, and income variables were all statistically significant. As in the incumbent model, the first two are positively associated with turnout, while the latter is negatively associated with turnout.

We also see that the Holbrook and Van Dunk (1993) measure of state political contestation is statistically significant in open seat elections but not in incumbent elections. As with the differential statistical significance of total expenditures and expenditure ratios, this suggests that the presence of an incumbent can alter turnout dynamics. The history of state partisan competition does not appear to matter when an incumbent is involved. When an election features open seat candidates, who are generally less well known than incumbents, historic levels of competition are more important.

How do these turnout results compare with the previous research discussed above? Because the differences between incumbent and open seat elections were not taken into account by previous researchers, it is difficult to make direct comparisons.

In the fully specified model of Cox and Munger (1989), all demographic variables were significant. In addition, all the total candidate expenditure variables were positively associated with turnout. The closeness measure for House elections was significant, as was the Senate election margin, although the gubernatorial margin had no impact. Patterson and Caldeira (1983) found that none of the demographic variables were significant, while the expenditure, closeness, and Senate election variables were.

This chapter found that most of the demographic factors were significant. Age, education, and income (although negative) were significant in both models, although home ownership was not. The data also suggest that money and competitiveness played a role in turnout, although there were differences according to the type of election. Concurrent Senate elections and the traditional margin measure were not significant in either model, contrary to previous research.

Earlier research did not take into account economic and social condition variables, so we do not know how such factors would have fared in previous models. This chapter showed that a state-level change in overall taxation was positively associated with turnout in incumbent elections. In addition, both changing state unemployment and changing national per capita income were significant in open seat contests.

Conclusions

This chapter investigated how demographic, political, and retrospective factors affected voter turnout in gubernatorial elections. Instead of just testing how overall turnout was structured by demographic factors, it (1) examined incumbent and open seat elections separately,

(2) expanded the scope of gubernatorial turnout studies from one or two elections to a seventeen-year period, (3) used a complete gubernatorial campaign finance data set from this time period, and (4) tested new variables, especially state and national economic and social change measures, candidate political characteristics, and an overall measure of state political competition.

The regressions show both similar and different factors at work in incumbent and open seat gubernatorial contests. One important difference is the role of campaign expenditures. Overall expenditures contribute to turnout in open seat races, but the ratio of expenditures is significant in incumbent elections. As discussed, this likely reflects the differences between incumbent and open seat elections. Open seat elections usually receive more attention because they lack the defining presence of an incumbent. Money spent by any candidate is likely to draw even more attention and thereby increase turnout. Incumbent elections, however, are only worthy of attention if the challenger can make a go of it. Millions of dollars will not increase turnout, because people have little reason to vote in an election where the outcome is not in doubt.

Economic conditions also played different roles in these two types of contests. Increased state taxation was associated with increased turnout in incumbent elections, while increases in state unemployment and national per capita income stimulated voters in open seat contests. This suggests that when the incumbent is not on the political scene, national influences can play a role in election outcomes.

As noted above, there are also similarities between the two models. These include the statistical insignificance of the candidate variables, the significance of presidential elections in raising turnout, and the role of registration requirements and region. Demographic factors also play a consistent role in both models.

A more general lesson of this chapter is that one literature in the elections subfield can learn from another. In particular, research on turnout may benefit from an examination of the literature on the role of issues in elections. Future research on turnout will hopefully incorporate the types of measures introduced in this study and thereby contribute to a more comprehensive understanding of the turnout phenomenon.

5

Candidate Quality Revisited

This chapter further examines the issue of candidate quality in gubernatorial elections. The earlier chapters found this issue to be a relatively unimportant factor, in sharp contrast to the findings of previous research on House and Senate elections. We will therefore test an additional variable and use new approaches to better understand how candidate quality might affect campaigns, as well as what structures the emergence of quality candidates.

It is thought that one of the most important elements in any electoral campaign is the prior political experience of the candidates. It has been demonstrated in House[1] and Senate campaigns[2] that incumbents are less successful when challenged by a candidate with prior officeholding experience. Krasno (1994, 160) found that "the identity of the challenger is the most immediate answer to the question of what makes for a hard-fought Senate race." In fact, challenger quality is the primary explanation for why Senate incumbents lose more often than House incumbents.[3] Challenger quality therefore has important implications for governance, as politicians who do not face credible tests at the voting booth are generally thought to have less incentive to pay attention to their constituents.[4]

We have already demonstrated in Chapters 2 and 3 that the previous political experience of open seat candidates and challengers to incumbents does not have an effect on vote totals. Given the weight of previous research in the congressional field, the reader might require some additional evidence before concluding that candidate quality is inconsequential. This chapter provides this evidence in two ways, via campaign finance and candidate quality data.

The first regression model tests whether a variety of political factors, state and national economic change variables, and state social issues help determine the quality of the challenger. The results are then compared with previous work on this subject in gubernatorial elections,[5] Senate campaigns,[6] and House campaigns.[7]

As the next chapter will note, the political ambition of House members for governor is not well structured, meaning that fewer factors are statistically significant influences on their decision to run for this office than on their decision to run for Senate. This suggests that such candidates are not acting strategically, which may have implications for their ability to conduct successful campaigns.

This does not mean that the ambition of all potential candidates for governor is unstructured. Schlesinger (1966) provided theoretical reasons why the ambition of some officeholders would be directed to governor and others to senator. Well-structured ambition should therefore exist in the aggregate for both offices. This chapter will test whether or not the political environment structures the emergence of quality candidates in gubernatorial elections. It will show to what degree state politicians respond to environmental stimuli in deciding whether or not to run. If the decision involves a large random element, it would suggest that potential candidates are not behaving with the rationality assumed by ambition theory,[8] which in turn might affect their ability to affect election returns. Even if the reader was not entirely convinced by the regression results from Chapters 2 and 3, such a finding would be additional evidence that gubernatorial challengers were not behaving in a manner likely to maximize their odds of victory.

The second regression model tests one of the key assumptions about high-quality challengers: that they have a substantial fundraising advantage over lower-quality challengers.[9] Specifically, we will see whether or not high-quality challengers are able to spend more money on their campaigns than lower-quality challengers. The results will be compared against those of Squire (1989), who investigated this question in the Senate elections context. This comparison allows further examination of whether challenger quality matters in gubernatorial elections.

The chapter will discuss the concept and specification of challenger quality, previous findings on the two questions discussed above, the models to be tested in this chapter, and the results. The more general questions of how often gubernatorial incumbents face quality challengers and how their experiences compare with the experiences of Senate incumbents will be discussed in Chapter 7.

Discussion

A small body of literature has investigated challenger quality questions in the Senate context. This context is the most relevant to a gubernatorial study because both offices share the same constituency. The first question is, What structures the emergence of quality candidates? Squire (1989) investigated the determinants of quality in Senate elections from 1980 to 1986. He included many of the same measures that will be used in this chapter, such as incumbent seniority, incumbent age, incumbent primary percent, challenger party, a measure of the quality pool, a midterm election dummy, state population, and a measure of challenger party strength. His results showed that only two variables were statistically significant: state population and the quality pool.

Lublin (1994) also investigated this topic for Senate elections, although his time frame was much broader (1952–1990) and his model somewhat different. The independent variables included previous incumbent vote,[10] change in presidential approval, whether the incumbent was of the same party as the president, changes in real state per capita income), changes in real national per capita income,[11] and the number of congressional districts. He found that all these measures were statistically significant with the exception of the last. The significant economic variables indicated that state and national increases in per capita income deterred quality challengers. He did not use campaign expenditures as a dependent variable because this data became available only in the 1970s.

Adams and Squire (1997) used ANES data to test whether incumbent vulnerability affected the emergence of quality challengers. They found that none of the vulnerability measures was important and that only one specification of their challenger pool variable was significant. Squire (1992) examined gubernatorial elections from 1977 to 1989 and found that in incumbent elections only the challenger pool measure and the change in national per capita income were significant (both positive). He did not test state economic data. For open seat elections, he found that only the vote for the other party in the previous election was statistically significant (and substantively in the expected negative direction).

The second question is, Are higher-quality challengers able to spend more money on their campaigns? Not only should more-experienced candidates acquire strong fundraising skills during their years in office, but they would have developed a circle of reliable supporters they could count on for support in future elections. In addition, political elites might be more likely to donate in anticipation of a close election. Donors, especially parties and political action committees (PACs), do not like to waste money on hopeless challengers;[12]

the quality of the challenger is one crucial determinant of which candidates might run competitive campaigns.

Squire (1989) investigated this question for Senate elections and found that candidate quality was both statistically and substantively significant in the context of fundraising. He suggested two reasons why quality challengers might attract more money: "High quality candidates have previous experience at the task and because contributors are more generous with candidates whose prospects seem bright" (538). He also found, in his 1992 gubernatorial study, that quality affected expenditures, but noted that this result should be interpreted with caution because of the very low number (ten) of observations.

Data and Variables

The data are from the same incumbent data set used in Chapters 2, 3, and 4. As discussed previously in the book, the variables, with the exception of the financial expenditure measure, were obtained from standard reference sources.[13]

A. Explaining Candidate Quality

There have been several attempts to quantify challenger quality, although how this factor should be used in a regression model depends upon the specific question under investigation. If the goal is to control for quality in a study primarily interested in how incumbent spending and challenger spending affect electoral outcomes, then a single aggregate measure would be inappropriate. As noted in Chapter 2, Gerber (1998) and Ansolabehere and Snyder (1995) argued that in this context the concept of challenger quality should be divided into its constituent parts and then used in different stages of a two-stage least-squares (2SLS) equation. This does not mean that an aggregate measure of candidate quality is meaningless,[14] but that researchers must be careful how they use it. This chapter uses an aggregate measure of candidate quality because (1) it does not attempt to analyze a highly endogenous elections outcome model and (2) it seeks, for purposes of comparison, to replicate previous statewide models that used a single quality measure.

A number of indices of challenger quality have been developed in the congressional elections literature.[15] However, Lublin (1994, 229–230) noted that most "measures of challenger quality based on the level of prior political office make assumptions about the relative value of prior posts in running for House or Senate that have little empirical foundation." In order to determine which offices might be more helpful launching pads, he tested dummy variables for six types of elected political office in a regression model explaining challenger vote. He used their demonstrated relative importance as the basis for his aggregate quality measure.

Chapters 2 and 3 found that no particular type of prior political experience improved challenger vote totals. Therefore, this investigation needs a measure that does not distinguish between elected offices. It is nevertheless reasonable to assume that elected officeholders bring more to the table than do political amateurs and that the measure should also incorporate other politically relevant factors.

Rather than reinvent the wheel, this chapter adopts a well-known measure that meets these criteria, that of Green and Krasno (1988, appendix 5). Green and Krasno assigned politically experienced challengers a base value of 4 and amateurs a base value of 0. Other politically relevant factors added one additional point each to the base value. For the experienced, these factors included type of office (based on the size of the electoral constituency), current officeholder, previous congressional run, and celebrity status. For amateurs, this included previous runs for any office, previous runs for congressional office, nonelective officeholder, type of nonelective office, political aide or activist, professional job status, and celebrity status.

For the variables used in this chapter, extra points were not assigned for type of office or type of nonelective office, as earlier regressions failed to establish unique electoral values for particular offices. In addition, a point is given only for a previous run for a major statewide (gubernatorial or Senate) office. The value for politically experienced challengers theoretically ranges from 4 to 7, while for amateurs it varies from 0 to 6.

There are four categories of independent variables used in this model: incumbent measures, challenger measures, other state political measures, and economic and social change measures. As will be noted, some were used by previous research, and several are original to this book.

The first of the incumbent measures is age. Squire (1989, 535) noted that older incumbents might draw stronger competition "because they have made enough unpopular decisions over time to arouse opposition, have lost touch with their initial electoral coalition, or have become infirm or less active (Tuckel 1983; see also Hinckley 1970 and Kostroski 1978)."

The incumbent's last electoral vote is included because incumbents who won by narrower margins are more likely to appear vulnerable.[16] Candidates who barely won should, on the whole, be perceived as more vulnerable than those who won by large majorities. Lublin (1994) pointed out that strategic challengers almost certainly examine the last vote of the incumbent in order to determine the odds of winning the next election.[17]

The incumbent's primary vote is also important because stronger opposition may signal weakness to potential challengers. Squire (1989) noted that this is an after-the-fact measure but assumed that it is known ahead of time whether an incumbent will face a tough primary battle. Incumbents with greater seniority might be perceived as more difficult to beat than freshmen, so a measure of tenure is included.[18]

The party strength of the challenger is specified here as the average of the last four vote percentages in the state for the presidential candidate of the same party. A larger percentage suggests a greater baseline of support for the challenger. Bianco (1984) and Squire (1989) also used a measure of party strength. Challenger party is included as well; scholars have found that Democrats have been able to put forth better challengers because they have a larger pool of state and local officials from which to draw.[19]

The Holbrook and Van Dunk (1998) measure of state political competition (discussed in Chapter 4) is included. In states with a history of frequent and competitive elections, quality challengers should be more willing to run for gubernatorial office.

A dummy variable for midterm elections is added and also interacted with a variable for whether the challenger is of the same party as the president. Strong potential challengers might be less likely to run in a midterm election when the president is from their party, anticipating a tougher election. Lublin (1994) included a variable for whether the incumbent was from the same party as the president, and Squire (1989) used a midterm dummy, but no previous research has tried this interaction.

The presence of a concurrent Senate race is also included, as another statewide election might draw away experienced potential candidates. This measure is also unique to this study. The size of the state is included because larger states are likely to have a greater pool of potential quality challengers. Most ambition scholars include a measure of state size in statewide election studies, and here it is specified as the voting age population of the state.

Lublin (1994) tested whether real changes in state and national per capita income affected the emergence of quality challengers. Our model includes not just these measures but adds state and national changes in the unemployment rate and a measure of state-level change in the crime rate. When state and national economic and social factors worsen, we might expect stronger challengers to emerge. This is especially true for gubernatorial elections, as governors can be held accountable for state conditions more easily than a single member of the Senate can be held accountable for national conditions. The unemployment and crime measures have not been tested in any of the research cited.

As Jacobson and Kernell (1983) argued, challengers behave strategically; they run when they perceive the odds of winning to be high and sit tight when the odds are poor. They suggested that one possible cue for potential candidates is the national standing of the political parties. For congressional elections, when incumbents are thought to assume some responsibility for national economic conditions, quality candidates from the party in power are more likely to run when the economy improves. For gubernatorial elections, we should look to the condition of the individual states, as declining state conditions might inspire greater opposition.

National economic conditions might also be relevant because citizens may conflate their evaluations of national and state conditions when they vote (assuming that they vote sociotropically and not with their pocketbooks). Voters might also hold governors responsible for national economic problems if the governors are of the same party as the president, so interaction terms of national unemployment and per capita income with the incumbent presidential party dummy are included. If the national unemployment rate decreases and the incumbent is from the same party as the president, we might expect to see challengers of lower quality emerge.

Two potentially important factors cannot be taken into account. The first is the financial war chest of the incumbent. Goldenberg, Traugott, and Baumgartner (1986) and Box-Steffensmeier (1996) argued that early fundraising and expenditures were able to preempt quality challengers. Krasno and Green (1988) and Ansolabehere and Snyder (1996), however, found this had little impact. Although interesting, this hypothesis cannot be tested here because such detailed financial data are not available for gubernatorial candidates.[20] Second, the ideological-distance factor tested by Adams and Squire (1992) and Lublin (1994) cannot be taken into account in this chapter because ideological ratings are not available for governors. The first model is therefore specified as:

Challenger Quality = α + β_1(Incumbent Age) + β_2(Incumbent Primary Percent)
+ β_3(Incumbent Party) + β_4(Incumbent Tenure)
+ β_5(Incumbent Last Vote)
+ β_6(Incumbent State Party Strength)
+ β_7(Challenger from Party of President [CPP])
+ β_8(State Political Competition)
+ β_9(State VAP) + β_{10}(Midterm Year)
+ β_{11}(Midterm Year) * (CPP)
+ β_{12}(Concurrent Senate Race)
+ β_{13}(Per Capita Income-State)
+ β_{14}(Crime-State) + β_{15}(SAT-State)
+ β_{16}(Unemployment-State)
+ β_{17}(PCI-National)
+ β_{18}(Unemployment-National)
+ β_{19}(PCI-National) * (CPP)
+ β_{20}(Unemployment-National) * (CPP)
+ ε.

B. Explaining Challenger Finances

The second dependent variable is the total amount of money spent in the election by the gubernatorial challenger. This is deflated using the consumer price index (urban) and transformed using the natural log to reduce potential bias by outliers.[21] It is also divided by state voting age population because of the substantial variation in state size.

One possible alternative specification is the percentage of money spent by the challenger in the general election. However, this introduces the conflating factor of incumbent spending into the denominator. If the challenger is able to raise a good deal of money, then the incumbent may respond by raising more, and a significant element of endogeneity is thereby introduced. Using the total amount of money raised avoids this problem; it also follows the precedent set by Squire (1989). Squire (1989) also theorized that several variables are associated with both quality challengers and candidate finances, and the second model in this chapter likewise includes several variables used in the first model.

The most important independent variable is the challenger quality measure discussed in the previous section. This will test whether higher-quality challengers are able to attract more money to their campaigns and whether lower-quality challengers are passed over by individuals, PACs, and party contributors.

Several incumbent measures are also included, as signs of incumbent weakness might suggest that money donated to the challenger is not wasted. Foremost among these is the primary percentage, as an incumbent's doing poorly in the primary signals significant weakness. The last general election percentage of the candidate is important, as a lower number in that election similarly suggests a weaker base of support among the public. This is probably a less important signal than the primary percentage, as in most cases the information the former conveys is four years old.[22] Finally, the younger an incumbent, the more likely he or she might excel at fundraising.[23]

For variables relevant to challengers, the first is the challenger's primary percentage. Those who faced difficult primaries and received a lower vote percentage might be seen as less likely to win. Not only does a difficult primary experience signify less support within their own parties, but negative accusations generated in a difficult primary may carry over into the general election. In addition, those who faced a difficult primary may have been forced to spend a large amount of money in the primary and therefore spent more money overall than those candidates who did not face a primary. For these reasons, the challenger's primary percentage variable should be positively correlated with the amount of money raised.[24]

On the other hand, a hard-fought primary might suggest that the nomination is worth fighting for and would therefore correlate with larger amounts of money raised in the general election. The number of candidates in the challenger primary and in the incumbent primary is also included as two separate variables. This is necessary because a 40 percent primary percentage has a different meaning if there were two rather than seven candidates.

The model includes challenger age because Ansolabehere and Snyder (1995) found that it correlated positively with expenditures in House elections. Challenger party strength, specified as the average state vote for the presidential candidate of the challenger's party over the last four elections, should be positively related to fundraising.

Political party is included because Republicans are typically wealthier than Democrats.

The gender of the challenger is noted because male candidates may be able to raise and therefore spend more money than their female counterparts. Squire (1989, 538) hypothesized that "women candidates may find it more difficult to be taken as serious challengers by contributors," and his regression found that male candidates were statistically associated with greater expenditures. He noted that Uhlaner and Schlozman (1986) did not find this to be true for House elections.

In addition, a challenger who runs in a midterm election year and is of the same party as the president might be expected to raise less money than his or her opponent, as the election is likely to be more difficult under these conditions. A dummy variable for midterm year, a variable for whether the challenger is of the same party as the president,[25] and an interaction of the two are therefore included.

A dummy variable for independently wealthy challengers was constructed by consulting the reporting of *CQ Weekly*. Wealth should be associated with money raised, as the Supreme Court has ruled that candidates may spend an unlimited amount of their own money on their own campaign.

A dummy for whether or not a Senate election took place concurrently is included, as this might reduce the amount of money available to the gubernatorial challenger. Although Senate and gubernatorial candidates often have different fundraising sources,[26] two major statewide elections in the same year may tax the willingness and ability of the politically active people within the state to contribute.

The Holbrook and Van Dunk (1998) party competition measure is included, as a state political system with stronger competition for elected offices might be a good source of the money necessary to run a strong campaign. A challenger in a state with less contestation might find fundraising more difficult.

Lastly, the same national and state economic and social change measures from the first model are tested, as improved conditions should dampen enthusiasm for a challenger, while declining conditions would suggest an opportunity for running. The national variables are interacted with the dummy for whether the challenger is from the same party as the president, as discussed in the candidate quality model.

The second model is therefore:

Challenger expenditures
(deflated, per capita) $= \alpha + \beta_1$(Incumbent Age)
$+ \beta_2$(Incumbent Primary Percentage)
$+ \beta_3$(Incumbent Party)
$+ \beta_4$(Incumbent Tenure)
$+ \beta_5$(Incumbent Last Vote)
$+ \beta_6$(Incumbent State Party Strength)
$+ \beta_7$(Challenger from Party of President [CPP]) $+ \beta_8$(State Party Competition)
$+ \beta_9$(Midterm Year)
$+ \beta_{10}$(Midterm Year) * CPP
$+ \beta_{11}$(Concurrent Senate Race)
$+ \beta_{12}$(PCI-State)
$+ \beta_{13}$(Crime-State) $+ \beta_{14}$(SAT-State)
$+ \beta_{15}$(Unemployment-State)
$+ \beta_{16}$(PCI-National)
$+ \beta_{17}$(Unemployment-National)
$+ \beta_{18}$(PCI-National) * (CPP)
$+ \beta_{19}$(Unemployment-National) * (CPP)
$+ \beta_{20}$(Challenger Quality)
$+ \beta_{21}$(Incumbent Primary Number)
$+ \beta_{22}$(Challenger Primary Number)
$+ \beta_{23}$(Challenger Wealth)
$+ \beta_{24}$(Challenger Gender)
$+ \beta_{25}$(Challenger Age)
$+ \beta_{26}$(Challenger Primary Vote)
$+ \varepsilon.$

This model is similar to that of the first-stage model on challenger expenditures from Chapter 3, although it differs because it includes some of the measures tested by Squire (1989) and Lublin (1994). These were not all included in the models in Chapter 3 because their justification did not seem sufficient.[27] As will be shown, the regression results do not significantly differ; the variables that were included in both models[28] do or do not reach conventional levels of statistical significance in each.

Results

Table 5.1 shows the models for the aggregate quality of gubernatorial challengers and their expenditures.

A. Determinants of Quality

In the first numerical column of table 5.1, four independent variables reached conventional levels of statistical significance. One key finding is that a rise in the national unemployment rate is associated with higher-quality challengers. This suggests that when the national unemployment rate rises, potential challengers view their chances of victory more positively. Relatedly, Lublin (1994) found that declines in both state and national per capita income were associated with quality Senate challengers, while Squire (1992) found that increases in per capita income the previous year were positively associated with quality gubernatorial challengers.

Why is there no evidence that state-level changes (such as changes in the state unemployment rate) affect candidate quality? Perhaps this is due to the influence of national party officials in recruiting candidates. As parties struggled to recover political relevance in the wake of the various 1970 party reforms, they began to offer political services to candidates and also to help recruit (and sometimes discourage) potential candidates. National soft money often found its way to state parties, and national party advice may have followed. Also, candidates may believe that they will be aided by national economic problems regardless of incumbent party, although the results from Chapter 3 suggest otherwise.

Jacobson and Kernell (1983) argued that stronger candidates are more likely to run when national conditions appear favorable and that they are less likely to do so when the converse holds. The economy is part of this decision calculus, but it is thought to be mediated by party; high-quality Republicans, for example, are more likely to run if the economy performs poorly under a Democratic president. This chapter provides no evidence for this theory.

The challenger party measure indicates that when the incumbent is a Democrat, a lower-quality candidate is likely to run against him or her. This bears out previous research on the generally larger pool of high-quality Democratic candidates,[29] although Squire (1989) did not find this factor to play a role in Senate elections. State party strength was not significant, regardless of how it was specified.[30]

Table 5.1 Models of challenger quality and challenger expenditures

Variable	Challenger Quality	Challenger Expenditures
Constant	6.034**	0.146
	(2.402)	(2.206)
Incumbent Age	−0.035	0.000
	(0.022)	(0.013)
Incumbent Primary Percent	0.054	−0.130
	(0.975)	(1.088)
Incumbent Party	−0.938*	−0.263
	(0.505)	(0.319)
Incumbent Tenure	0.143	0.135**
	(0.101)	(0.065)
Incumbent Last Vote	−3.990	−2.010
	(2.955)	(1.959)
Incumbent's State Party Strength	−1.387	0.125
	(2.703)	(1.696)
Challenger Same Party as President	0.273	0.733
	(0.655)	(0.690)
State Party Competition	0.034**	0.002
(Holbrook-Van Dunk measure)	(0.014)	(0.009)
Voting Age Population of State	0.012***	–
(in thousands)	(0.004)	
Midterm Dummy	0.178	−0.323
	(0.595)	(0.389)
Midterm *Challenger Same Party	−1.329	0.047
as President	(0.804)	(0.520)
Concurrent Senate Race	−0.056	0.022
	(0.336)	(0.214)
State Per Capita Income Change	1.807	3.647
	(8.446)	(5.861)
State Crime Change	−0.956	−0.880
	(2.927)	(1.893)
State SAT Score Change	−6.979	−14.203
	(20.936)	(13.383)
State Unemployment Change	−1.578	−0.337
	(1.146)	(0.737)
National Per Capita Income Change	43.491	17.228
	(31.575)	(20.501)

(*Continued*)

Table 5.1 (*Continued*)

Variable	Challenger Quality	Challenger Expenditures
National Unemployment Change	7.167**	3.171
	(3.395)	(2.152)
National Per Capita Income Change	−31.763	−25.278
* Challenger Same Party as President	(49.612)	(30.837)
National Unemployment Change	−2.194	−1.775***
* Challenger Same Party as President	(4.639)	(0.009)
Challenger Quality	–	−0.003
		(2.206)
Number of Candidates in	–	0.052
Incumbent Primary		(0.126)
Number of Candidates in	–	0.140*
Challenger Primary		(0.076)
Challenger Wealth	–	0.989***
		(0.339)
Challenger Gender	–	0.300
		(0.349)
Challenger Age	–	0.016
		(0.011)
Challenger Primary Vote	–	−0.162
		(0.619)
Observations	105	120
Adjusted R^2	0.18	0.24

Note: Cells contain coefficients with standard errors in parentheses.
***$p < .01$, **$p < .05$, *$p < .10$.

The state party competition measure is positive and significant, meaning that a state with greater political competition is more likely to find more experienced political challengers in gubernatorial elections. The size of the state is also positively correlated with higher-quality challengers, as larger states have larger talent pools.

It is also useful to discuss some variables that were not significant. First, the tenure variable was insignificant, suggesting that longer-serving incumbents do not attract more daunting opposition. Squire (1989) similarly found that previous margin was not important in Senate elections and that neither previous margin nor term length was important in gubernatorial elections (1992). He noted that "higher quality challengers appear to make their decisions about running without giving great weight to an incumbent's apparent vulnerability" (544), and Adams and Squire (1997) agreed.

As mentioned previously, Lublin (1994) showed that in Senate elections, candidate quality increases when the incumbent is from the same party as the president. This dynamic was not found to be at work in the gubernatorial context. In addition, the interaction variable, consisting of the midterm dummy and the dummy for copartisanship with the president, was insignificant in gubernatorial elections, suggesting that this national effect does not influence the decisions of challengers; there is little previous research to suggest whether this is to be expected or not.

Overall, this suggests that the emergence of quality challengers is only partially structured by the political environment. Only four measures are significant, while a much larger number of independent variables are not.

B. Challenger Expenditures

The second column of Table 5.1 shows which variables are associated with the amount of money spent by a challenger. The data show that four variables are statistically significant and that one key variable is insignificant. The most important finding is that the challenger quality measure is not associated with the amount of expenditures. Squire (1989) found that it was both statistically and substantively significant in Senate elections, but the dynamics of gubernatorial and Senate elections appear to differ in this important respect.

Squire (1989, 538) suggested two reasons why quality challengers might attract more money: "high quality candidates have previous experience at the task and because contributors are more generous with candidates whose prospects seem bright." These factors are apparently not at work in gubernatorial contests. The fact that the simple correlation between challenger quality and expenditures is only 0.094 suggests that county executives, members of Congress, and political amateurs may raise similar amounts of money once they reach a gubernatorial general election. This is also shown by the first-stage regressions on challenger expenditures in the fully specified model in Chapter 3, where no particular office experience is statistically significant.

Why the lack of association between challenger experience and challenger expenditures? Perhaps gubernatorial elections are so important to most major statewide political actors that they make every effort to fund the candidates of their party regardless of their prior political experience. A particular interest group might prefer a higher-quality challenger to run, but if one does not, this may not dissuade the group from making its usual contribution. The political stakes within a state may be too high to ignore any gubernatorial election. In contrast, federally focused interest groups often ignore hopeless races in favor of tighter elections, thereby maximizing the impact of their donations by strategic giving. This is much less a factor in state elections. A Nebraska interest group, for example, is unlikely to ignore its local gubernatorial contest and instead contribute to the Alaska gubernatorial race just because its preferred Alaskan candidate has a better chance of winning than its favorite Nebraska candidate.

State political actors may also believe that if a vigorous gubernatorial campaign is not waged, then the campaigns of state legislative and statewide candidates of their party may be harmed. This means that regardless of the quality of the nominee, other elected officials have an incentive to make sure that the candidate is relatively well funded.

The data also show that challengers appear to spend more money when the incumbent has longer tenure. This may reflect the fact that even in states without term limits, governors rarely make careers out of their office. As expected, wealthier challengers spend more money than challengers who are not wealthy, and the more candidates who contest a primary, the more money the eventual winner will spend.

The relatively few statistically significant variables recall Squire's (1992) results, which showed that only four of ten measures were statistically significant. His four were challenger quality, challenger gender, challenger party strength, and state population. This chapter, in contrast, did not find the first three significant and did not use the fourth because it was incorporated into the dependent variable.

Conclusions

The emergence of quality challengers and challengers' ability to raise money are generally thought to have important consequences for political campaigns. This chapter examined which factors are associated with the rise of quality challengers to incumbents and whether these candidates are able to do better in the fundraising game. It arrives at conclusions different from those found in Senate studies and in the only other gubernatorial study of these topics.

Most importantly, there is no evidence that higher-quality challengers are able to spend more money in their electoral campaigns. In light of previous research on challengers in Senate elections, this chapter points out another way in which the dynamics of gubernatorial and Senate elections differ. Whereas Squire (1989, 544) concluded that "the level of challenger quality matters because it influences how much money can be raised," this chapter finds that challenger quality matters less in elections for governor. This finding also differs from the findings of Squire's (1992) gubernatorial study, which argued that candidate profile was related to expenditures.

The role of economic factors in candidate emergence, as described in this study, is different from that in previous statewide election studies. Lublin (1994) found that declines in state and national per capita income were associated with higher-quality challengers. This chapter found that while a national factor does play a similar role, it is the unemployment rate, not per capita income. Squire (1992) found in his gubernatorial study that an increase in per capita disposable income in the year before the election was positively associated with higher-quality challengers, which was a counterintuitive result.

Do incumbents of a particular party scare away higher-quality challengers? Squire (1989) found no evidence for this and Squire (1992) did not test it, but table 5.1 shows that when the incumbent is a Democrat, a lower-quality challenger is more likely to run. This could be a result of the quality pool rather than ideology, as other scholars have found that the pool of potential Democratic candidates is larger than that of Republican candidates. If so, this dynamic might change over time if Republicans continue to do well in state and local elections.

There are some similarities between this study and previous research. Squire (1989, 544) noted that "higher quality challengers appear to make their decisions about running [for Senate] without giving great weight to an incumbent's apparent vulnerability," although House research has come to the opposite conclusion.[31] This chapter agrees that vulnerability does not play a role in the emergence of quality candidates. Squire's (1992) gubernatorial study similarly found that length of tenure and the last vote percentage of the incumbent were not factors.

It is also important to note that only four variables out of twenty tested were associated with the entry of quality challengers to incumbent governors. One of the statistically significant variables, the decline in the national unemployment rate, may even be a misleading indicator of an optimal time to run.

The findings suggest that the decision to run for governor is poorly structured, an argument that will also be made in the following chapter on the progressive ambition of House members for gubernatorial and Senate office. Once again, this could mean that there is some underlying logic that regression models cannot detect, or it could mean that candidates are running for office in ways that do not maximize their chances of victory. Consider a few of the factors *not* guiding their decision: the vulnerability of the incumbent, the overall strength of the party in their state, whether it is a midterm year and the governor is of the same party as the president, and all of the state economic and social change factors.

On a final note, it must be pointed out that while the candidate quality variable is not appropriate for highly endogenous election models, it remains a useful measure for assessing candidates in the world of politics and in political science models such as the two in this chapter. Simultaneity is not an issue in either model, which further suggests that the results of this chapter are reliable guides to the dynamics of statewide elections.

6

Gubernatorial versus Senate Election Dynamics: Progressive Ambition

This chapter continues the discussion of candidate emergence in gubernatorial elections, although from a different perspective than that of the previous chapters. Chapter 5 examined the factors structuring the emergence of high-quality challengers in gubernatorial elections. This chapter investigates the variables associated with the entry of U.S. representatives into gubernatorial and Senate races. House members are chosen because theirs is a key political office common to all states and the one most often studied by the political ambition literature. This chapter also begins the direct comparison of gubernatorial and Senate electoral data, whereas previous chapters compared their findings with the extant literature on Senate elections.

In America, political ambition has traditionally been looked upon with some suspicion. With much public opposition to political careerism and a widespread cynicism about the motives of those in politics, some would rather criticize politicians than try to understand their actions and motivations. At both the state and federal levels, "ambition" is an honorary four-letter word in American politics. Schlesinger (1966), however, pointed out that

> to slight the role of ambition in politics, then, or to treat it as a human failing to be suppressed, is to miss the central function of ambition in a political system. A political system unable to kindle ambition for office is as much in danger of breaking down as one unable to restrain ambitions . . . No more irresponsible government is imaginable than one of high-minded men unconcerned for their political futures.

The more concerned America is with the state of its democracy, the more important the study of ambition must be.

Schlesinger's book was the first comprehensive attempt to better understand the nature of political ambition and its consequences for governance. He developed three categories of ambition and argued that a politician's behavior in office depended on which was operative. His work spawned a subfield of research, much of which seeks to quantitatively model the factors shaping the quest for higher office.

As will be discussed in more detail in the next section, there are essentially two types of previous research on this topic: the first finds different ambition structures for gubernatorial and Senate candidates, and the second makes little distinction between ambition for the two offices in their regression models. This chapter uses the insights of the former to rework the models used by the latter.

Specifically, two models will separately analyze the decisions to run for governor and for the Senate. This is different from the usual single-model research on political ambition, where the dependent variable is coded 0 if a member runs for reelection but 1 if a member runs for *either* the Senate or gubernatorial office. This is a problem because the literature may incorrectly attribute to gubernatorial ambition factors that are associated only with ambition for the Senate. This chapter will determine which political and personal variables are associated with progressive ambition by House members for which office, thereby bringing to light long-overlooked factors unique to gubernatorial ambition. In addition, a third model will use the usual aggregate dependent variable for purposes of comparison.

House members are examined for two reasons. First, they are among the most prominent politicians below the offices of governor and senator. They have already demonstrated successful ambition for a major office, their job provides various political resources that may be useful in a campaign (such as staff, a fundraising base, name recognition, and coverage by home state media), and their constituencies provide a potential electoral base. Previous research has argued that House members are among the strongest candidates in Senate elections, although Chapters 2 and 3 show that they are not advantaged in campaigns for governor, a point that will be further explored in subsequent chapters. We therefore care more about their ambition than that of other state officials, who are not as numerous, generally not as powerful, not always present in every state, and not always elected officials.

Second, the ambition of House members is the focus of analysis of the extant political ambition literature. This is due to the large number of House members available for study as well as to their prominence, as mentioned above. While one might examine the progressive ambition of lieutenant governors, the findings would not be comparable to prior research, and the number of observations would be limited. Finally, there are several methodological reasons why this chapter is a useful contribution to the ambition literature. Not only does it include several new variables that have not been previously tested, but it also reexamines and respecifies several commonly used measures. The most recent research ends at the 1986 elections, but this chapter includes elections up to 1996, extending the field into a previously untouched decade of ambitions and elections.

Discussion

Schlesinger (1966) described three types of ambition: static, discrete, and progressive. Static ambition is found when a politician is content to hold the office currently occupied. Studies in this field take the form of examining the decision either to retire from office or run for reelection (Levine and Hyde 1977; Frantzich 1978; Hibbing 1982; Brace 1985; Moore and Hibbing 1992; Groseclose and Krehbiel 1994; Jacobson and Dimock 1994; Hall and van Houweling 1995). Discrete ambition is exemplified by a politician seeking election to an office with no desire to run for reelection or for higher office. This category is rarely noted except in academic discussions such as this.

Progressive ambition, the subject of this chapter, is concerned with the attempt by a politician in office to seek a higher office. In the literature on this subject, the main question is, What factors influence whether a member seeks higher office or runs for reelection (Brace 1984; Copeland 1989; Kiewiet and Zeng 1993)? This follows the theories of Rohde (1979), who argued that progressive ambition was shaped by the associated risks and costs of running for higher office. He assumed, for example, that all House members would accept an offer to be senator or governor if there were little or no cost, but would be much more cautious if they had to give up their current office to run for such office. He also argued that some politicians are more risk-averse than others, which, in addition to other political factors, influences decisions.

The ambition literature is useful for several reasons. Most importantly, it tells us about the people who run for higher office and the institutional and personal factors that help structure their decision. Thus we learn more about the people who occupy some of the highest political jobs in the land, particularly whether they behaved strategically in their decision to run. In addition, much of the turnover in the House of Representatives is generated by the voluntary resignation of incumbents, either to retire or to run for higher office (Ornstein et al. 1996). The factors that lead members to resign from relatively safe seats and run for higher office therefore help determine the level of political contestation in the congressional arena. As Schlesinger (1966, 116) noted: "My rationale for seeking order in American political careers derives from the inference that, if progressive ambitions are to act as a control upon the behavior of politicians, there must be some focus or pattern in political careers."

Schlesinger (1966) found that in general, representatives were less likely to run for governor than for Senate. He argued that the logic of functions and of arenas is a likely explanation for the difference. The logic of functions states that skills learned in the House are easily transferred to the Senate, while the decision-making skills of a statewide officeholder or a judge can best be applied to the job of governor. The logic of arenas suggests that because state legislators interact often with governors and House members with senators, it is little wonder that they begin to think of holding those jobs themselves. (The logic of electorates does not apply to this chapter because a House district provides the same constituent base for a run for governor as for senator.)

It is not clear whether the decision making of candidates who run for governor and of those who run for senator is different. Because the decision to run for either office is usually treated as an equivalent decision in the literature, we know little about how House members or any other gubernatorial candidates arrive at it. To date, the literature finds that candidates are "acting strategically" (Copeland 1989, 563) when they run for Senate or for higher office. This is because multiple independent variables measuring the risk and the likelihood of winning have been shown to be associated with both decisions.

Ambition for governor, as noted previously, has not been tested in this way. Only in rare cases has progressive ambition for the two offices been considered separately (Schlesinger 1966; Black 1972), and these were the very earliest studies. This chapter will therefore test an ambition model for gubernatorial, Senate, and aggregate higher-office ambition. By doing so, it will examine whether representatives are acting strategically when they run for governor. If not, this raises the question of what their motivations might be and how this might affect the effectiveness of their electoral campaigns.

Data

The data include all members who served in the U.S. House of Representatives in the 99th to 104th congresses, covering elections from 1984 to 1996. Following the lead of Schlesinger (1966), the unit of observation is each member in each election year when there is an opportunity to run for higher office.

Several scholars have pointed out that while a Republican (or Democratic) House member is theoretically free to challenge an incumbent Republican (or Democratic) senator, this happens in practice only in the most unusual cases. "Opportunity" is therefore defined as an open seat election or an election where the incumbent is from the opposing party. As Rohde (1979, 13) specified in his seminal article, "We consider a member to have an opportunity to run for higher office . . . when the office in question is either held by an incumbent of the other party or has no incumbent seeking election." In this data set, only one House member challenged an incumbent governor of the same party and only two challenged senators of the same party.

Not considered are gubernatorial elections held in odd-numbered years, as members were not required to give up their seats to run for the office (Rohde 1979; Brace 1984).[1] Because this study consists of those who ran either for higher office or for reelection, it follows precedent and excludes those who voluntarily retired[2] or ran for a lower office.[3] In this time period, the total number of House members who gave up their office to run for governor is 28 and for senator is 85.

Variables

A. Dependent Variables

Three specifications of the dependent variable—whether a member ran for higher office—are used. The first measures whether a House member ran for the Senate or for reelection, and the second whether he or she ran for governor or for reelection. A third measure collapses the first two measures into one and will be referred to as the "aggregate" variable in this chapter. This third variable allows for comparison with the other two variables and with the typical dependent variable in the ambition literature. Members were coded so that those who sought higher office were assigned the value 1, while those who ran for reelection were coded 0.

As mentioned in the previous section, the ambition literature treats ambition for the governorship as a separate phenomenon only in a limited way. While Schlesinger (1966) differentiated between the paths that ambitious politicians took for gubernatorial and Senate office, subsequent research did not. He argued that "the route to the Senate is more sharply defined than the route to the governorship" (97). In addition, he found that "while my data show that state and federal careers are sometimes intertwined, they also reveal distinct routes to the states' two major elective positions: the state-office route for governors, the federal-office route for senators" (117).

The implication of this distinction is that separate regression models might be useful for testing ambition for each office. Yet only Rohde (1979) clearly differentiated between the two. He argued that politicians would accept fewer opportunities to run for governor than for the Senate. He also argued that two-year gubernatorial seats would be even less attractive than four-year seats. Because this study did not use regression analysis, it was not possible to check for the effect of any particular variable while controlling for others.

Rohde (1979) also discussed why politicians perceive the value of these two offices differently. The governor is an executive and has constitutional powers that allow for more direct authority to design and execute policy. Senators have a six-year term, while most governors in this data set were limited to four-year terms. Senators can be reelected an unlimited number of times, while many governors are restricted to one or two terms. This means senators have a better chance of making politics their entire career, as there are few jobs beyond senator and governor. The job of the senator is also closely related to that of the representative, while the job of governor is quite different.

Brace (1984) included four dummy variables in his aggregate regression model in order to take into account some factors influencing the decision to run specifically for governor. The first was a dummy variable for Senate versus gubernatorial opportunity, the second was a dummy for two-year gubernatorial term, and the third and fourth were dummy variables for gubernatorial incumbents in their first term and those in their second or later terms, respectively. He expected that candidates would be less likely to run when the office is for governor rather than senator, when the gubernatorial term is for two years, or when the incumbent is beyond his or her first reelection campaign.

Brace found all these variables to be statistically significant, although the third variable pointed in an unexpected direction. The significance of the first variable indicated differences between ambition for the two offices, a finding upon which this chapter builds. The nature of the dependent variables in this chapter explains why multinomial logit analysis (mlogit) should not be used. In order for an observation to be included in an mlogit, all choices must be simultaneously available. This was the case in previous political ambition research that used it (Kiewiet and Zeng 1993), but it is not the case here. While this data set has three options—run for reelection, run for governor, or run for Senate—they are not simultaneously available in most election years. Gubernatorial elections take place on average once every two election cycles and Senate elections twice every three, so that the fraction of elections where both take place is one-third, meaning that two-thirds of the data set would have to be dropped from the start. In addition, many other observations must be dropped because either the senator or governor was from the same party as the representative, as discussed elsewhere in this chapter.

In addition, mlogit does not allow for the state-specific measures, such as gubernatorial power and partisanship of the state legislatures. While these might be hypothesized to influence ambition for governor, they should have no role in ambition for Senate office.

B. Independent Variables

The independent variables for the three models are explained below, along with their sources and an expectation of how they should perform in the regressions.

1. Measures of Ambition

One factor curiously missing from political ambition research is a convincing measure of ambition. Ambition is usually found only in the dependent variable—it is what most models seek to explain. Yet some have argued that one of the crucial factors encouraging individuals to seek office is their own personal drive for success in politics (Fowler and McClure 1989; Ehrenhalt 1992). It is unusual that no independent variable measuring this kind of ambition is found in a literature on political ambition.

The variable in previous research that comes nearest to measuring ambition is a measure of candidate risk-aversion (which is also included in our models and is described below). This is quantified as whether the member came to Congress by defeating an incumbent or by running for an open seat where the opposition party won the last three elections by a margin of 57 percent or more (Rohde 1979; Brace 1984). Black (1972) noted that "the study of political ambition is the study of the motivations of politicians and hence requires data on individuals." The measure of risk-aversion satisfies the requirement for personal data, but it is not the same thing as ambition.

Ambitious aspiring politicians may certainly take some risks, but they may also quietly bide their time in their current office until a reasonable opportunity to move up presents itself. Because the loss of a current office may end a political career (Fowler 1979), risks are not to be taken lightly.

However, the risk-taking measure quantified by Rohde (1979) and Brace (1984) may encompass many of the candidates Canon (1990) referred to as "amateurs" or "the hopeless." If these people run for Congress against long odds, the Rohde (1979) measure may include some of them; but if they run for open seats or against weak incumbents, it will not. Therefore, the traditional risk-averse variable is to some degree a dummy measure of those who, for a variety of reasons, run against long odds and are lucky enough to win.

This measure, in itself, may have implications for future behavior, as such winners may be encouraged to take greater risks in future elections. Fenno (1989), for example, describes this factor at work in Dan Quayle's career. Because he won against long odds in his first congressional race, a race many people told him not to run, he discounted negative advice when he considered challenging Senator Birch Bayh in 1980. In this study, ambition is quantified as the members' age when they entered the House. We thus follow the lead of Schlesinger (1966, 182), who argued that the younger a member is on entry, the more ambition is revealed: "The evidence does seem to support the inference that the early starter is the true career politician." Subsequent ambition literature, however, did not explore this idea.

By definition, everyone who is elected to the House is politically ambitious. Only in political mythology are people pulled into political office by popular acclaim or talked into running, as was the character portrayed by Jimmy Stewart in *The Man Who Shot Liberty Valence*. As Schlesinger (1966, 4) wrote, "No man is likely to obtain a major political office unless he wants it." Nevertheless, an interesting question is, Who among this pool of ambitious people is most ambitious? Those who enter the House earliest might be the most interested in winning major political offices. Members who worked in another career, or in other offices, for twenty years before entering congressional politics show by their actions that they are less single-mindedly focused on politics. They may be ambitious, but are less so than the person who successfully ran for the House before the age of thirty. This age-at-entry measure is also closer to Canon's (1990) definition of the ambitious.

Kiewiet and Zeng (1993, 933) interpreted the age-at-entry variable as meaning that "the increase in utility between their current office and the office they aspire to is especially large." This may be true, but there are other important facets to this measure. The age/ambition variable should therefore be negatively correlated with running for higher office, as those who enter at an older age are less likely to try to move up the ladder.[4]

Despite these concerns about the traditional way of measuring ambition, it is included in this study. As specified by Brace (1984), who sought to follow as closely as possible the lead of Schlesinger (1966), ambition is coded 1 if "when first running for the House the representative challenged an incumbent or ran in a district carried by the other party by 57 percent or more in the previous three elections." Brace (1984) obtained this data from the *Guide to US Elections,* but this source does not contain data on primary elections. Therefore, his variable measured only those who defeated an incumbent in the general election but not in a primary election.

The variable in this study is operationalized in a similar way. Although Brace (1984) does not directly make the claim, there may be good reasons for not worrying about primary elections. Any House incumbent who manages to lose in a primary election is probably badly damaged by some other factor, such as scandal or redistricting. This means that the challenger is not undertaking the same type of daunting activity as challenging an unblemished incumbent.

Of course, any incumbent who is defeated may have already been weakened by scandal. None of the ambition research takes this into account. Therefore, for every instance of a House member who defeated an incumbent, various years of *The Almanac of American Politics (AAP)* are checked. These reference guides describe the circumstances surrounding the election of an incumbent, and in not a few cases, a scandal by the previous incumbent plays a prominent role. The variable therefore does not code as "ambitious" any incumbent who took advantage of scandal or of some exceptional circumstance to win office, as this does not measure ambition as Schlesinger (1966) and Brace (1984) defined it.[5] The simple correlation between the variable adjusted for scandal and the regular specification is 0.87.

2. Tenure

The tenure variable measures the amount of time served in office until the date of the election in question. This is an important factor because it measures seniority and, therefore, the influence members put at risk when they seek higher office. Long-serving members are more likely to have settled into their roles and grown to see House membership as their career, and they have higher opportunity costs than do members with fewer years of service.

This study departs from most research because it does not include a variable for the age of the members. Kiewiet and Zeng (1993, 933) pointed out that "exactly how age enters potentially ambitious House members' utility calculus has never been well specified." They nevertheless included the variable for age of the member and discussed several other researchers' justifications for including it.

In previous studies, the age variable must have picked up several different effects. First, it took into account factors relating purely to years alive. Age in this sense measures personal factors such as physical endurance, flexibility, and the settling into (or just settling for) a comfortable routine. Hain (1974, 274) is the one exception to this lack of interest in the age variable. He found that the relationship between age and ambition was not linear, but that "the patterns in the data reported here and elsewhere support the generalization that politicians undergo a 'middle-age crisis.'"

The age variable may also correlate with the tenure measure. Rohde (1979) argued that older members are generally likely to have served more terms than younger members and therefore have a greater opportunity cost if they run for higher office. Kiewiet and Zeng (1993) followed this logic in including the variable.[6]

To avoid this conflation of theories in the age variable, the age-at-entry variable and a length of House service measure were used instead. Both have the important benefit of being causally prior to the members' age at the time a decision to run for higher office must be made.

3. Majority Party

This is a familiar variable in the literature, but in this chapter it is not as simple to quantify as in previous studies. Until the 1994 elections, Democrats were in the majority for all the election years under consideration. Their job satisfaction was assumed to be higher than that of members of the Republican minority, but Republicans in the

Senate and in governors' mansions were often in a more advantageous political position. Brace (1984) and Copeland (1989),[7] for example, found that Republicans were more likely than Democrats to seek higher office because of their minority status. Kiewiet and Zeng (1993), however, found that party affiliation did not explain the decision to seek higher office.

In this chapter, the party variable was replaced with a measure for member of the majority party. Democrats are so coded for elections from 1984 to 1994, while Republicans are so coded for the 1996 election.

4. Distance from Home State to Washington, D.C.

This variable is derived from one of the common assumptions of the ambition literature—that the decision to run for higher office reflects a complex calculus of the relative costs and benefits of running or standing pat. One cost of House membership is the constant travel to and from the district. Although member travel reached a peak in 1980 (Hibbing 1991), the amount of time spent on the road over the last few decades is still substantial.[8] The travel time is determined in large part by the distance of the home district from Washington, D.C.: the farther away the district, the longer the travel time. The expectation is that the farther the district, the more likely the House member is to run for higher office. This is because higher office reduces the amount of travel time and is therefore more attractive to those who must travel the most.

Distance may influence the decision to run for Senate or for state office differently. A job in state politics eliminates the necessity of this travel. Some travel between the state capital and the hometown may be unavoidable, but this is trivial compared with the frequent flier lifestyle of a representative.

Home states are the same distance from Washington, D.C., for senators and for representatives, but senators travel home less often than do representatives (Parker 1986, 18, 103) because of the six-year election cycle. In addition, it may occur to a representative based in a distant state to think: "If I have to travel this far, I might as well be a senator." Such reasoning would be only one small part of the complicated decision to run, but it may reflect the fatigue brought on by a grueling travel schedule.

Most services that incumbents take advantage of are personally cost-free. Using the frank to mail newsletters or respond to mail, buying office furniture, and hiring staff members do not exact much wear and tear on the member. But travel takes a physical toll and is one job that cannot be effectively delegated to staff. Therefore, travel may affect the decision to stay in the job or move to a higher office; it is part of the costs and benefits calculus that members must make about their current job and potential jobs. As Black (1972, 158) argued, "the structure of the political systems may play a significant role in shaping the ambitions of the men who occupy offices within the system." Much has been written about the district travel that members undertake as part of their incumbency advantage (Fenno 1978; Parker 1986; Hibbing 1991), but the consequences of using official benefits have not been studied in this way.

The travel factor was quantified by measuring the distance from Washington, D.C., to the state capital of the member's home state. This "as the crow flies" measure is not accurate for all districts, but it avoids other problems. Many districts are as lengthy as the state or are the size of the state. Choosing a point in those districts would be equally arbitrary.

This variable is also useful because of time zone changes. The rule of thumb is that for every time zone change, a traveler requires one day to recover fully. The representative who leaves for the west coast from Washington, D.C., on Thursday night, for example, may not fully regain mental and physical strength until Sunday, at which point it is almost time to return.. Although political science has not considered the effect of this variable before, there are some indications that it is seen as politically consequential in the "real world" of politics. Barone and Ujifusa (1993), in their biennial *AAP*, noted that "the 4th District [of Oregon] used to be a marginal district, because it is farther in flight time from the US Capitol than any other in the continental United States."

Another possible way of quantifying the travel variable is to measure the number of trips made by each member. As Hibbing (1991) pointed out, this may be done by examining requests for reimbursement from the *Report of the Clerk of the House*. One problem is that members from the six nearest states often do not bother to seek reimbursements for their small expenses. This means that this specification of the travel variable would be systematically biased by the very factor we wish to measure: distance from Washington, D.C.[9]

5. Number of House Seats per State

This variable simply reflects the fact that members from states with smaller populations are more likely to run for statewide office than members from states with larger populations because their constituencies make up a larger percentage of the state population. Hibbing (1991) found that this was especially true for members from the smallest states, those with only one House seat. This variable is common to the literature, and the expectation is that it will negatively correlate with running for higher office.

6. Opportunity for Other Office

Sometimes the opportunity arises to run for either a Senate seat or a gubernatorial seat. A dummy variable is therefore included in each of the separate office regressions that notes whether the other office is also available. One might expect that representatives would be less likely to run for governor when there is a concurrent chance to run for Senate. Another variable was added to the Senate model to measure whether both Senate seats were available for a particular incumbent at the same time. For example, in 1992 there were elections for two open Senate seats in California, so the dummy variable was coded 1 for House members of both parties. In the model, a variable measures how many total opportunities to run for higher office existed at the time.

7. Divided State Government

Because this model considers the decisions to run for the Senate or for governor separately, factors relevant to these two different decisions are included. For the member considering a run for the governor's office, the possible political context to be faced should be taken into account. A three-level variable is therefore included that assigns a 3 to a unified state legislature of the member's party, a 2 to a divided legislature, and a 1 to a hostile unified state legislature. Democrats might be less willing to run for governor if the legislature is controlled by Republicans but more willing to work with a friendly or even a divided legislature. Of course, members cannot predict the partisanship of a state legislature after the election, but they probably look to the present as the best available guide to the future.[10]

8. Other Gubernatorial Factors

Also included are three variables that take into account various institutional arrangements in the state executive branch. The first two are dummy variables, the first measuring whether the office is term limited and the second whether the term of office is two or four years. The third is a three-level variable measuring whether the governor has relatively strong powers, average powers, or weak powers. The measure of the governor's power is derived from the governor's formal budgetary and veto powers, as defined by the *Book of the States* for various years. Two points are assigned if the governor is described as having full budgetary power and one point if the governor's power is shared. One point is added to this number if the governor has a line item veto, and no points are added if not.

The hypothesis is that members will be less likely to run for gubernatorial office if the office is term limited, is limited to two years, or has only weak powers. Ambitious individuals may be more likely to wait for an opportune time to run for a Senate seat instead.[11]

Models

The first model tests which factors influence the decision to run for higher office, defined as both gubernatorial offices and Senate seats:

$$\text{Higher Office} = \alpha + \beta_1(\text{Age Enter House})$$
$$+ \beta_2(\text{House Tenure})$$
$$+ \beta_3(\text{Cleaned ``Risk Averse''})$$
$$+ \beta_4(\text{Majority Party}) + \beta_5(\text{Miles}) + \beta_6(\text{Seats})$$
$$+ \beta_7(\text{Extra Opportunities}) + \varepsilon.$$

The second model examines the factors relevant to the decision to run for the Senate:

$$\text{Senate Office} = \alpha + \beta_1(\text{Age Enter House})$$
$$+ \beta_2(\text{House Tenure})$$
$$+ \beta_3(\text{Cleaned ``Risk Averse''})$$
$$+ \beta_4(\text{Majority Party}) + \beta_5(\text{Miles}) + \beta_6(\text{Seats})$$
$$+ \beta_7(\text{Gub. Opportunity})$$
$$+ \beta_8(\text{Two Senate Seats Up}) + \varepsilon.$$

The third and fourth models examine the factors relevant to the decision to run for governor. For purposes of comparison, the third model is similar to that used for the Senate decision, except that there were never two gubernatorial elections at the same time:

$$\text{Gubernatorial Office} = \alpha + \beta_1(\text{Age Enter House})$$
$$+ \beta_2(\text{House Tenure})$$
$$+ \beta_3(\text{Cleaned ``Risk Averse''})$$
$$+ \beta_4(\text{Majority Party}) + \beta_5(\text{Miles})$$
$$+ \beta_6(\text{Seats}) + \beta_7(\text{Senate Opportunity})$$
$$+ \varepsilon.$$

The fourth model includes variables that take into account the four political and institutional factors a new governor would face:

$$
\begin{aligned}
\text{Gubernatorial Office} = \alpha &+ \beta_1(\text{Age Enter House}) \\
&+ \beta_2(\text{House Tenure}) \\
&+ \beta_3(\text{Cleaned "Risk Averse"}) \\
&+ \beta_4(\text{Majority Party}) + \beta_5(\text{Miles}) \\
&+ \beta_6(\text{Seats}) + \beta_7(\text{Senate Opportunity}) \\
&+ \beta_8(\text{Gub. Power}) + \beta_9(\text{Term Limits}) \\
&+ \beta_{10}(\text{Two Year Term}) \\
&+ \beta_{11}(\text{State Leg. Partisanship}) + \varepsilon.
\end{aligned}
$$

This study therefore includes variables not previously tested in the contemporary ambition literature, including distance of district from Washington, D.C., age of entry into the House, tenure of service in the House, partisan context of the state legislature, and gubernatorial power. In addition, the traditional measure of risk aversion has been reexamined and respecified. It also includes familiar variables, such as political party and number of seats per state. The party variable is adjusted so that it now reflects majority party status. But it does not include one common measure—age of member at the time of election—because it is broken down into its constituent and causally prior components of age at entry and number of years served.

Findings

Rohde (1979) found that from 1954 to 1975, House members took only 3.7 percent of opportunities to run for higher office. Copeland (1989), who examined decisions to run for the Senate, found that from 1980 to 1986 the percentage increased from 2.5 to 5.4 percent. This chapter, which covers the elections from 1984 to 1996, found that House members took 7.6 percent of opportunities to run for the Senate but only 3 percent of opportunities to run for governor. This confirms Rohde's (1979) finding that House members are more likely to run for the Senate than for the executive mansion. It also suggests that House members differ in how they see the two offices; thus, it would be a mistake to aggregate them into one dependent variable.

Why are House members less likely to accept the chance to become governor? As discussed previously, Schlesinger (1966, 117) found that there were "distinct routes to the states' two major elective positions." Gubernatorial candidates were more likely to have recently served in statewide office, the state legislature, and law enforcement (including the judiciary). Senatorial candidates, on the other hand, were more likely to have come from the House and from statewide office. Schlesinger argued that the logic of functions and the logic of arenas are likely explanations for this difference.

Sabato (1983, 33) asked governors what they considered the ideal background for their job to be and found that

> almost all governors agreed that experience in the state legislature just prior to election as governor is invaluable, because it affords the governor a broad view of current problems faced by the state, a comprehension of the governmental structure and operation, expertise in a few specific areas, and the opportunity to develop personal relationships with legislative and administrative officials who will be serving concurrently.

This does not mean, of course, that members of the House do not run for governor. Sabato (1983, 41) also found that "twenty-eight states have had at least one governor come from Congress since 1950, which is a surprisingly broad-based total."

The results from all four models are displayed in Table 6.1.

The first model shows that all variables were statistically significant explanatory factors of the decision to run for higher office (either Senate or governor), with the exception of the adjusted measure of risk aversion.

Some of these findings are in line with previous research into progressive ambition. Several scholars have already found that Republican (i.e., minority) party membership is correlated with an increased willingness to run for higher office.[12] The fewer number of House districts per state has also been shown to have an encouraging effect on ambition.[13]

In addition to these well-known factors, some of the variables unique to this study are also shown to be significant to the decision-making process of House members. The distance of the home state from Washington, D.C., is positively related to the decision to run for higher office. As discussed previously, it was expected that distance would have a positive effect on interest in running for higher office. The higher personal costs of constant travel back to the district, an especially necessary state of affairs when faced with biennial elections, apparently help motivate members to seek less physically grueling positions. This effect holds up even when the outlier state of Hawaii is excluded from the data set.[14]

The age at which a member is elected to the House is also significant. Earlier entry is associated with a greater likelihood of an

Table 6.1 Models of political ambition

Variables	Higher Office[a]	Senate[b]	Gov[c]	Gov[d]
Constant	−0.449	0.536	−0.064	1.830
	(0.713)	(0.801)	(1.321)	(1.816)
Age Enter House	−0.056***	−0.066***	−0.019	−0.016
	(0.015)	(0.018)	(0.029)	(0.030)
Tenure	−0.036**	−0.040**	−0.013	−0.009
	(0.016)	(0.019)	(0.033)	(0.033)
Cleaned "Risk-Averse"	−0.080	−0.061	−0.161	−0.330
	(0.240)	(0.280)	(0.523)	(0.531)
Majority Party	−0.432**	−0.437*	−0.849*	−0.598
	(0.212)	(0.257)	(0.455)	(0.508)
Miles (in hundreds)	0.046***	0.067***	−0.050	−0.035
	(0.013)	(0.016)	(0.033)	(0.037)
Seats	−0.047***	−0.040***	−0.140***	−0.157***
	(0.009)	(0.010)	(0.039)	(0.043)
Opportunity	0.735***	–	–	–
	(0.223)			
Gubernatorial Opportunity	–	0.235	–	–
		(0.273)		
Two Senate Seats Up	–	1.386**	–	–
		(0.630)		
Senate Opportunity	–	–	−0.680	−0.675
			(0.484)	(0.493)
Gubernatorial Power	–	–	–	−0.553
				(0.374)
Gubernatorial Term Limits	–	–	–	−0.280
				(0.524)
Two-Year Term for Governor	–	–	–	−0.695
				(1.002)
Partisanship of State Legislature	–	–	–	−0.321
				(0.275)
χ^2	70.74	49.09	32.36	37.00
Probability > χ^2	0.000	0.000	0.000	0.001
Pseudo R^2	0.09	0.09	0.15	0.17
Observations	1615	1081	798	792

[a] Decision to run for higher office vs. run for reelection.
[b] Decision to run for senate vs. run for reelection.
[c] Decision to run for governor vs. run for reelection.
[d] Decision to run for governor vs. run for reelection (expanded model).
***$p < .01$, **$p < .05$, *$p < .10$.

attempted run for higher office. As discussed earlier, this variable is a better measure of political ambition than the usual risk-averse measure. Members who enter the House earlier are more likely to be single-mindedly striving toward national-level political power and are therefore more likely to accept the risks inherent in running for higher office. Their ambition does not allow them to remain comfortable in their current jobs for long, just as they apparently found it difficult to wait before running for a House seat.

The longer a member stays in office, the less likely he or she is to exhibit progressive ambition. This was expected, as the more time a member invests in a House career, the less likely the member will put it at risk. More years in office often result in leadership positions on committees and subcommittees, as well as formal and informal leadership roles within the party. In addition, the longer a member serves, the more this particular job comes to resemble a career. A longer career also puts the member's previous career further into the past, thus making the transition back to normal life more difficult in case of defeat. Some members may become lobbyists, but those with other job skills, or those who do not wish to lobby their former colleagues, may find it more difficult to return to their previous worlds (Leal 2002). In other words, members have more to lose by running for higher office as the duration of their tenure increases.

The traditional measures of risk aversion—winning against an incumbent or winning an open seat where the opposing party won the last three elections by at least 57 percent—are not significant. The results are identical whether this factor is specified in the traditional or the adjusted format. This finding stands in contrast to those of Rohde (1979) and Brace (1984).

The larger the state, as measured by the number of House districts, the less likely it is that the member will run for the Senate. This was expected, as the greater the percentage of the state that is included in a member's constituency, the better the odds of victory.

The second column of table 6.1 shows that the model for progressive ambition toward the Senate closely reflects the previous aggregate ambition model. All the variables are significant, except for two. The opportunity to run for governor does not tempt members away from running for the Senate; this is not entirely surprising, as members are more than twice as willing to run for Senate as for governor. The new risk-averse variable is also insignificant, just as in the aggregate model. The extra variable in this model, the presence of two open Senate seats, also has a positive effect on the willingness to run.

The third column of table 6.1, however, shows that most of the factors that help channel House members' ambition toward the Senate do not apply to the decision to run for governor. The only two statistically significant factors are the overlap of constituencies (the number of House seats per state) and majority party status. The age at entry into the House, length of tenure, risk aversion, distance from Washington, D.C., and presence of Senate opportunities are statistically insignificant.

The more elaborated gubernatorial model in the fourth column of table 6.1 suggests that only one factor is significant—the number of seats per state. The four new measures are all insignificant, suggesting that the specific personal, partisan, and institutional contexts of the gubernatorial job are not important.

Conclusions

This chapter separately examined the decision of House members to run for the two major statewide offices: governor and senator. The previous regression-based ambition literature did not clearly distinguish between the two, even though the seminal work of Schlesinger (1966) suggested that progressive ambition for these two offices should vary among lower officeholders.

The most important finding is that almost no variables structure the progressive ambition of House members for gubernatorial office, whereas many variables are at work for Senate ambition. Only one measure, the size of the state, was clearly associated with the decision to run for governor. In contrast, five measures were influential in senatorial, but not in gubernatorial, decision making; House members were unlikely to take into account their personal ambition, their tenure in office, their membership in the minority or majority party, the distance of their state from Washington, D.C., and the presence of a concurrent statewide election while making the decision to run for governor.

The aggregate model, in which the dependent variable consists of a decision to run for either governor or senator versus not running for such offices, mirrored almost exactly the Senate model.[15] This means that previous research, which did not always differentiate between the two offices, incorrectly attributed many factors relevant only to progressive Senate ambition to progressive gubernatorial ambition.

These results show that representatives do not see gubernatorial and Senate office as interchangeable, as two largely equivalent promotions. They are not just running for the two offices at different rates, but are basing their decisions to run on different criteria. This is similar to Schlesinger's (1966) point that representatives would see the two offices differently in part because of their varying institutional roles. The results again highlight the differences between elections for these two offices.

This leads to the question of which criteria House members are using when they decide whether or not to run for governor. According to Black (1972, 145), the theory of ambition argues that "office seekers attempt to behave in a rational manner in selecting among alternative offices." The finding that representatives largely did not weigh the political and personal factors tested in this chapter when they ran for governor suggests a lack of strategic thinking. It would also appear to imply a lack of rationality (as it is defined by the ambition literature). Representatives are most likely basing their decisions on some criteria, but these may not be easy to measure or discern.

There are two possible explanations for this: House members are basing their decisions to run on strategic factors that cannot be easily measured or on personal reasons unrelated to the objective political environment. As representatives largely ignore most elementary political factors, it is difficult to make the first argument. As for the second, we can only speculate what reasons might be operative. Perhaps some representatives run when they conclude that they dislike legislative work but are not ready to retire from politics. They may also be on the verge of leaving Congress and decide that they have little to lose by running for governor. If true, these decisions would not correlate with any of the independent variables in this study. We would need to find and test a measure of members' frustration level or unhappiness with their job, but there are few obvious proxies for this.

This finding has implications for the study of candidate quality, because nonstrategic decision-making processes may be related to the inability of representatives to do well in gubernatorial elections. On the other hand, it could be a coincidence that strategic House members do well in Senate elections, while their nonstrategic colleagues do not in state campaigns. Previous research provides little guidance. Perhaps House members who run for governor are not doing so at an optimal time, are not running for an office for which they are professionally well suited, or are otherwise through their decision-making processes (and not because of the advantages and disadvantages of the House office itself) minimizing their electoral impact.

In addition, this chapter has examined several variables not previously included in the contemporary ambition literature, such as distance of districts from Washington, D.C., age of entry into the House, tenure of service in the House, partisanship of the state legislature, and gubernatorial power. The first three were important in the Senate model; the special gubernatorial variables were insignificant, but it is nevertheless useful to know this. In addition, the traditional measure of risk aversion has been reexamined, respecified, and proven insignificant in this revised form in all three models.

Some familiar variables were included, such as political party and the number of seats per state, although the party variable was adjusted to reflect majority party status. Not included in this chapter is one common measure, age of member at the time of election, because it was broken down into its constituent and causally prior components of age at entry and number of years served.

Overall, this chapter adds to the evidence that despite having the same constituencies, gubernatorial and Senate elections cannot be assumed to have the same dynamics. This will become clearer over the next three chapters, which will find very few similarities. In fact, the results from Chapter 2 on the effect of expenditures on election outcomes will be the only evidence of important parallel properties.

7

Gubernatorial versus Senate Election Dynamics: Electoral Competition and Campaign Intensity

This chapter examines and compares electoral competition in gubernatorial and Senate contests. In particular, it focuses on campaign expenditure and candidate quality data to learn more about the differing nature of competition in these elections. This is not only the first time electoral competition has been examined in such detail in gubernatorial elections, but it is also the first comprehensive comparison of the role of candidate expenditures and quality in both offices.

As mentioned previously, governors and senators are unique among important political officeholders because they share the same constituencies and frequently hold concurrent elections. While one might guess that many of the electoral dynamics for these two offices are similar, there is surprisingly little evidence in the literature to suggest whether or not this is correct.

The comparisons in this chapter are different from those found in most of the previous chapters, which discussed how their findings compared to the conclusions drawn in the extant Senate elections literature. In the absence of Senate studies to compare with the gubernatorial findings, this chapter directly presents and compares gubernatorial and Senate competition data.

To do this, a new data set (the third in this book) was assembled. It contains candidate expenditure and candidate background data for Senate elections from 1980 to 1996. These were obtained through Federal Election Commission (FEC) reports and election descriptions in various issues of *Congressional Quarterly Weekly Reports* (*CQ*) and the *Almanac of American Politics* (*AAP*). In this respect, the chapter most resembles Chapter 6, which assembled and compared gubernatorial and Senate ambition data because no previous research had separately examined and compared ambition for each office. A newcomer to the elections literature might assume that there are many books and articles comparing contests across institutions. In fact, there are surprisingly few. Only a small number of books compare Senate and House elections, and only one article has contrasted competition in gubernatorial and Senate elections. These works will be briefly discussed because they have developed and tested hypotheses for why electoral competition might differ between institutions, hypotheses that might help explain differences between gubernatorial and Senate elections.

Krasno (1994) studied why senators are more likely to suffer defeat than representatives. He critiqued much of the conventional wisdom about Senate and House elections. One of his first findings was:

> Analysis of the 1988 Senate Study supplies scant evidence that the public thinks that members of the House and Senate do different jobs. In theory people believe that senators and congressmen are responsible for the same activities, and in practice they interact with and assess their legislators in similar ways. (33)

Krasno's findings also contradict the theory that the larger size of Senate constituencies leads to greater electoral difficulties.[1] He also disproved the theory that state diversity, not size per se, is what makes reelection difficult for incumbent senators.[2]

How did Krasno (1994) explain the different competition levels in gubernatorial and Senate elections? In his own words, "Senators lose more often because they are more likely to face formidable challengers who manage to wage intense campaigns" (154). Key to this explanation is the competition that senators face. Senators do "not start off more vulnerable than representatives, but by election day their challengers have made them more vulnerable" (156). He further noted that "the story behind Senate and House reelection rates is more than anything else the story of strategic politicians" (164), with high-quality candidates being more likely to challenge sitting senators than sitting representatives.

Although state size cannot be an explanation for differential reelection success rates for governors and senators, the insight about the role of challengers might apply to gubernatorial elections. This chapter explores the point but arrives at different conclusions.

One of the few other comparisons of House and Senate elections is found in Abramowitz and Segal (1992).[3] Although they focused largely on the Senate, one of their central findings was the greater level of competition in Senate elections vis-à-vis House elections. They pointed out that this causes senators to be more responsive than representatives to the public, contrary to the intent of the constitutional designers. They found several reasons for this senatorial electoral insecurity: the candidacies of a large number of quality challengers attracted to the office (similar to Krasno [1994]), the growth of two-party competition in many previously one-party states, an increase in campaign spending, and a related increase in television advertising.

The only previous quantitative comparison of gubernatorial and Senate elections was conducted by Squire and Fastnow (1994), who examined a variety of electoral and public opinion data. First, they examined incumbent reelection rates from 1980 to 1992, a time period covering all but two election cycles of the period covered in this book. They found that the average incumbent governor received about 4 percent fewer votes than did incumbent senators.

Next, they pointed out that governors were much better known by their constituents than were senators. By counting stories in six newspapers in 1989 they found that "in that nonelection year the amount of coverage each governor got swamped that for both senators combined. Governors were routine news stories; senators only appeared in the headlines now and then" (708–709). They investigated whether this increased familiarity led to higher public support[4] and found that during election years senators were rated higher than governors, a difference that is even larger in nonelection years. It is not clear whether this was due to greater media coverage of governors or to some other factor.

Finally, they showed that governors and senators were about equally likely to face high-quality challengers (defined as former governors, members of Congress, and statewide elected officials).[5] This is significant in light of Krasno's finding (1994) that the presence of quality challengers explained the discrepancy between Senate and House reelection rates.[6] By the end of campaigns, the feeling thermometer differential between governors and their challengers was seven points larger than the difference between senators and their challengers. Why this might be was not easy to answer with their data. The study was therefore a groundbreaking examination of electoral and public opinion data for these two offices, but the authors were not able to fully explain the findings.

This chapter will also go beyond win and loss ratios to understand the competitive nature of gubernatorial elections and how it compares to that of Senate elections. The most comprehensive work on competition is Westlye's *Senate Elections and Campaign Intensity* (1991). He noticed that although every two years political analysts devised reasonable explanations for party gains and losses, there were always anomalous elections belying these explanations. He pointed out that in 1980, for instance, when Ronald Reagan won the presidency and Republicans won control of the Senate, partly by defeating many liberal Democrats, the "triumph of conservatism" argument could not account for many easy wins by liberal Democrats.

He argued that not only had previous research failed to notice this, but that an incorrect conventional wisdom had developed, noting:

> The widespread assumption arose that in Senate elections challengers are nearly as well known as incumbents. As Jones (1981, 99) put it, "Senate races are between the known and the slightly better known." This assumption is inaccurate, however, and has led to a number of other erroneous conclusions and generalizations about Senate elections (see also Mann and Wolfinger 1980; Hinckley 1981; Luttbeg 1983). (11)

Westlye's insight was that while some Senate elections resembled the stereotypical hard-fought campaign of two well-known and well-funded candidates, many others were low-key contests that better resembled a lopsided House race. Sometimes, a hard-fought campaign in a state was followed by a low-key campaign two years later.

Why are distinctions in competition levels important? One reason is that whether a campaign is hard fought or low key has implications for how voters make decisions. As Westlye (1991) argued, hard-fought campaigns bring more information to the attention of voters, while low-key contests lead to an information-poor political environment.[7] This means that voters are able to make better informed decisions in the former. (Whether intensity affects voter turnout has already been discussed in Chapter 4, although Westlye did not address this question.)

One of the key questions this chapter will therefore investigate is, How many gubernatorial elections are hard fought and how many are low key, and how does this compares with Senate elections? Aside from contributing toward an understanding of election dynamics *per se*, this chapter also has important implications for representation. First, democracy is enhanced when voters have more information. Second, without hard-fought elections, gubernatorial incumbents may have less incentive to listen carefully to their constituents.

The first section of this chapter will discuss the basic facts of incumbent success rates in elections for governor and senator. The next section will explore how well the Westlye paradigm applies to gubernatorial elections. The chapter will then compare factors such as campaign expenditures and candidate quality in gubernatorial and Senate elections. It will also consider campaign spending ratios in incumbent and open seat elections; competition trends over time; candidate quality in incumbent and open seat elections; partisan success rates; and partisan and electoral intensity measures in states with simultaneous gubernatorial and Senate elections.

The conclusion will not just review all these findings but will also attempt to explain why governors are more likely to be defeated than are senators. It will in particular ask whether Krasno's (1994) conclusions apply here, or whether some other explanation is more consistent with the gubernatorial data—specifically, an explanation based on the executive nature of the governor's office.

Incumbent Success in Gubernatorial Elections

This section will examine the incumbent success rate in gubernatorial elections and compare it with that in Senate and House elections. As mentioned above; Abramowitz and Segal (1992), Westlye (1991), and Krasno (1994) found that Senate incumbents were more likely to be defeated than House incumbents. Ornstein, Mann, and Malbin (1998) pointed out that only 6.5 percent of House incumbents from 1980 to 1996 were booted out, while 12 percent of senators suffered the same indignity.[8]

For governors, of the 129 incumbents[9] in the main data set, 29 went down in defeat; 23 lost in the general elections, while 6 were defeated in primaries. Overall, this means that 22.5 percent of governors lost their reelection campaigns, a figure almost twice that of senators and three and one-half times that of House members. This is similar to the findings of Squire and Fastnow (1994), who used data from 1980 to 1992 to show that governors lost more often than senators (24 percent vs. 15 percent).

Having established this point, we will explore the percentages in more detail. If we remove those defeated in primaries and examine incumbent success in general elections, the incumbent defeat rate is approximately 19 percent, which is greater than the equivalent figure for senators—about 10 percent. What about the percentage of incumbents who lost in the primaries? We just noted that six governors were dumped by their own party's voters during our time period,[10] whereas only four senators were so removed from office.[11] Six governors defeated in this way is a 5 percent primary defeat rate, while the four senators sent home[12] is a much lower rate of 2 percent. So whether we measure incumbent insecurity in the general or in the primary election, governors have a lot more to worry about than senators.

Electoral Competition

This section will examine whether Westlye's (1991) insights on competition levels in Senate elections apply to gubernatorial elections. That gubernatorial campaigns are harder fought might help to explain the relatively high incumbent defeat rate. This section therefore compares the number of hard-fought and low-key races in both contests. Open seat elections will also be examined to see whether these usually competitive contests are more or less competitive in the gubernatorial context. Expenditures for both incumbent and open seat races will also be compared to see how large any such differences between expenditures in the two statewide elections might be.

As discussed above, Westlye (1991) found that most Senate races fall into one of two intensity categories. The first question to ask is, How did he define "intensity"? One variable he explicitly rejected was electoral margin:

> In many instances, a close margin of victory does accompany a high-intensity campaign, and vice versa. But the two concepts are theoretically distinct, and it would be a mistake to characterize the intensity of a campaign solely by the margin of the outcome. (18)

He argued that a Republican candidate in a solidly Democratic state may wage a highly intense campaign but still lose by a large margin if the voters retained their party loyalties. While such an election might see the Republican do better than Republicans usually do, the simple use of victory margin would not completely reflect that.

> Margin of victory, then, is at best a problematic measure of the intensity of a given campaign. And since achieving a high level of intensity is essential in terms of a campaign's purpose—conveying information to voters—it makes more sense to use a measure that directly taps activities designed to reach voters. (19)

Westlye's main measure of campaign intensity was the description of each Senate contest in *CQ*. These descriptions allowed him to classify about 90 percent of Senate campaigns as either hard fought or low key. The remaining 10 percent were either only briefly described in the *CQ* reports or did not give any information about the intensity of the campaign; for those cases he used campaign expenditures as a proxy for electoral intensity. He used spending ratios (the difference between the top and bottom spender), not differences in absolute or per capita dollars. Races in which one candidate outspent the other by a 2:1 ratio or greater were considered low key, while all others were considered hard fought. While he acknowledged that the 2:1 breakpoint was somewhat arbitrary, he argued that "it is a reasonable way to distinguish in the absence of other information. . . It also removes the problem of varying state populations and numbers of media markets, since both candidates are running in the same state" (22).

Westlye (1991) noted that the *CQ* reports and the expenditure ratio method were highly correlated. For 81 percent of the elections the two methods gave identical classifications, and in the cases where they conflicted, the *CQ* reports were given precedence. He later analyzed four of those elections in some detail and argued that the *CQ* classification was the correct one.

This study uses the campaign spending ratio because the sources Westlye used to classify Senate elections are not as comprehensive for gubernatorial campaigns. He used election previews usually found in an early to mid-October issue of *CQ*, but such detailed descriptions of upcoming gubernatorial elections are not uniformly available.

By 1996, *CQ* had gone through four stages in its preelection coverage of gubernatorial elections. First, from 1980 to 1984 it described elections for Senate and governor in equal measure in the yearly state-by-state preview. In 1986 and 1988 it devoted a single article to all upcoming elections for governor, although they were published at the early dates of August 30 and September 24, respectively. In 1990, there were no detailed descriptions of gubernatorial elections, but from 1992 to 1996 *CQ* began to classify incumbents through gradations such as "vulnerable," "safe," and so on (in one article that described gubernatorial elections across the country).

The problem with this gradation system is that it does not tell us how intense the election was. An incumbent may be "safe," but the challenger could still put up a good fight. As Westlye pointed out, it is possible for a campaign to be both hard fought and a landslide. The distinction between intensity and closeness is useful because only in a hard-fought campaign will the voters receive an adequate range of information on which to make a decision. The voters may still vote overwhelmingly for the incumbent in a hard-fought campaign, but an important point is that they do so while being aware of the alternative.

The *CQ* measures from 1992 to 1996 are therefore inadequate for the task at hand, there are no 1990 data, and the 1986–1988 descriptions are minimally adequate. However, the 1980–1984 accounts are excellent.

Are there any acceptable alternatives to *CQ?* Some brief descriptions of gubernatorial elections are found in various editions of the *AAP*, but they are written after elections, so there is the possibility that knowledge of the electoral outcome may bias the campaign description. Postgame analyses could emphasize why the winner won and downplay the factors in favor of the challenger, thus giving the impression of a lower-key election than in fact took place. *AAP* descriptions also devote relatively little space to losing candidates, which makes it somewhat difficult to gain a complete understanding of the campaigns. These descriptions also seem to focus more on the horse race than on intensity *per se.*

One might also use the Rothenberg Political Report or the Cook Political Report, although the later did not begin until 1984. It might take some extra effort to find back issues, however, as libraries often do not subscribe to such newsletters. Other possible sources of information on elections for governor might include newspapers found through Lexis-Nexis, Dow Jones News Search, or even on microfilm. Not only is this laborious, but it is difficult to find newspapers from many of the states, especially the smaller ones. These alternatives also interfere with the goal of using a single, clear standard of classification instead of multiple sources that are coded by the author, whose judgment must therefore be trusted even more than is usual. Given these problems, and given the close association Westlye (1991) found between expenditure ratios and his codings of *CQ* descriptions, this chapter will use expenditure ratios as the measure of campaign intensity.

The findings of Chapters 2 and 3 also support the view that the expenditure ratios are meaningful. Westlye did not empirically test whether incumbent and challenger expenditures were equally important in Senate elections, nor was there any consensus in the Senate elections literature. As discussed previously, several authors thought that every incumbent dollar spent was only one-third as effective as a dollar spent by a challenger. This means that the expenditure ratio might not necessarily provide any information about how competitive a race was. In this study, however, we know from Chapters 2 and 3 that incumbent and challenger expenditures have approximately equal impact, and recent work by Gerber (1998) shows the same for Senate elections. The spending ratios are therefore meaningful for both elections.

Using this approach, 53 percent of incumbent gubernatorial elections were found to be hard fought, while 47 percent were low key. In incumbent Senate elections, the ratios show that 41 percent of these contests were hard fought and 59 percent were low key.[13]

Table 7.1 demonstrates that the level of contestation in gubernatorial elections is higher than in Senate elections, which is no doubt reflected in the higher defeat rates for incumbent governors. In gubernatorial elections, the average ratio of highest to lowest amount spent was 3.2, in favor of incumbents. The highest ratio was approximately 21, when incumbent William Schaefer easily beat Republican William Shepard in Maryland in 1990. The lowest ratio was almost exactly even at 1.01, when incumbent Robert List lost to Democratic challenger Richard Bryan in Nevada in 1982.

For Senate incumbent contests, the figures need some adjustment because of the frequent occurrence of elections in which one candidate spent almost no money, thus creating ratio values in the hundreds and even up to infinity. If the nine "infinity" campaigns are excluded, the average ratio of highest to lowest expenditures is 26.2, far higher than the 3.2 ratio for gubernatorial elections. When the top ratio is capped at 20 (admittedly a somewhat arbitrary number, but one that represents a very low level of competition),[14] the new ratio

Table 7.1 Comparison of ratios for gubernatorial and Senate incumbent and open seat races

Ratio	I-Gov	I-Senate	O-Gov	O-Senate
1.0–1.1	18	32	24	11
1.2–1.4	21	29	23	19
1.5–1.9	21	33	15	11
2.0–2.4	16	24	2	5
2.5–2.9	3	14	3	2
3.0–3.9	12	16	2	6
4.0–4.9	8	13	1	1
5.0–5.9	3	9	0	0
6.0–6.9	2	7	0	0
7.0–7.9	1	2	0	0
8.0–8.9	1	4	0	0
9.0–9.9	1	7	0	0
10+	6	41	1	4
Total < 2	60 (53%)	94 (41%)	62 (87%)	41 (69%)
Total ≥ 2	53 (47%)	137 (59%)	9 (13%)	18 (31%)

is 5.2. Although smaller than 26.2, this ratio is still higher than the 3.2 gubernatorial ratio.

The lowest ratio in Senate elections was 1.004, belonging to the 1988 Connecticut contest between maverick liberal Republican Senator Lowell Weicker and Democrat Joseph Lieberman, the Attorney General of Connecticut. Weicker lost only by 10,045 votes out of almost 1.4 million cast. Perhaps this close defeat encouraged him to run again for statewide office in Connecticut. Chapter 8 examines his successful run for governor in 1990 as a member of an independent political party of his own creation.

The highest noninfinity value was found in the 1990 Alaska race, where incumbent Ted Stevens spent over $1.25 million, while his opponent Michael Beasley, a Democrat who reported his occupation as "laborer," spent only $1,000. The spending ratio was therefore 1,274, or eighty-five times the average. Stevens easily won.

While 87 percent of open seat gubernatorial elections were hard fought just 13 percent were low key. This is, of course, far higher than the 53 percent hard-fought incumbent gubernatorial elections. It also recalls Westlye's (1991) finding that incumbent and open seat Senate elections had different levels of competition.

The second column of table 7.1 shows that 69 percent of Senate open seat elections were hard fought while 31 percent were low key.[15] Once again, we see that more gubernatorial elections were hard fought than were their equivalents in the Senate.

In gubernatorial elections, the average spending ratio for open seat elections was 1.82. The highest ratio was 23.89, when Democratic businessman Wallace Wilkerson outspent and easily defeated Republican state representative John Harper in the 1987 Kentucky race. Even the *AAP*, which does not routinely note the expenditures of gubernatorial candidates (but does list those of Senate and House candidates), mentioned that Harper was "underfinanced."

The smallest spending ratio (1.005) was found in the 1982 Michigan contest between Democrat Jim Blanchard, a member of the U.S. House, and Republican Richard Headlee, an insurance executive. The *AAP 1984* described Blanchard as "an overwhelming favorite against Republican Richard Headlee" (570). He ended up winning with 51 percent.

In Senate open seat elections, the average spending ratio was 2.08, which was once again greater than the figure for gubernatorial contests. We therefore see that the level of contestation is greater in both types of gubernatorial elections, incumbent and open seat.

The highest spending ratio in Senate open seat elections was 10.51, in the 1984 West Virginia race between Democrat John D. Rockefeller IV and Republican John Raese. Despite the huge spending advantage, Rockefeller won by only 4 percent. This illustrates the point that campaign intensity does not always correlate with votes.

The lowest ratio in Senate open seat elections was 1.0004, in the 1986 Colorado contest between Democrat Tim Wirth and Republican Ken Kramer. Wirth had served for twelve years as a U.S. Representative, while Kramer was a member of the Colorado legislature. The *AAP 1988* called the election "breathtakingly close" (185), and indeed Wirth won by just over 16,000 votes out of over a million cast.

Is there any time trend for levels of competition? Table 7.2 examines the number of hard-fought and low-key gubernatorial incumbent and open seat elections from 1980 to 1996.

Table 7.2 Number of hard-fought and low-key gubernatorial elections, 1980–1996

Election Year	Type of Race	Incumbent Races	Open Seat Races	Total
1996	Hard fought	2	5	7
	Low key	4	0	3
1994	Hard fought	13	7	20
	Low key	7	1	8
1992	Hard fought	1	7	8
	Low key	4	1	5
1990	Hard fought	7	10	17
	Low key	15	1	16
1988	Hard fought	4	4	8
	Low key	3	1	4
1986	Hard fought	9	13	22
	Low key	7	2	9
1984	Hard fought	3	7	10
	Low key	2	1	3
1982	Hard fought	15	7	22
	Low key	7	3	10
1980	Hard fought	6	1	7
	Low key	4	0	4
	Total hard fought	60 (53%)	61 (86%)	121 (66%)
	Total low key	53 (47%)	10 (14%)	62 (34%)

Note: Elections in odd-numbered years are counted in the total for the next even-numbered election.

There seems to be no pattern for incumbent open seat elections, which were largely hard fought regardless of year. Incumbent races, however, became less competitive over time. From 1980 to 1988, the average percentage of hard-fought races was about 60, but this dropped by half for three of the four subsequent election years. It appears that while incumbents generally had to worry about vigorous general election challenges, they were able to rest somewhat easier in later years.

How does this compare with Senate elections? Table 7.3 compares the number of gubernatorial and senatorial hard-fought and low-key elections for incumbent and open seat contests, respectively.

For Senate open seat elections, there is no clear pattern. The percentage of hard-fought Senate elections fluctuates more than in gubernatorial elections, and in no single direction. Senate incumbent elections show no certain pattern either; while 1980 and 1982 had

Table 7.3 Comparing hard-fought and low-key gubernatorial and Senate incumbent and open seat elections, 1980–1996

Election Year	Type of Race	I-Governor	I-Senate	O-Governor	O-Senate
1996	Hard fought	2	9	5	10
	Low key	4	10	0	4
1994	Hard fought	13	7	7	8
	Low key	7	18	1	1
1992	Hard fought	1	8	7	6
	Low key	4	15	1	1
1990	Hard fought	7	12	10	1
	Low key	15	16	1	4
1988	Hard fought	4	9	4	4
	Low key	3	18	1	2
1986	Hard fought	9	10	13	5
	Low key	7	17	2	1
1984	Hard fought	3	8	7	2
	Low key	2	20	1	2
1982	Hard fought	15	18	7	2
	Low key	7	12	3	1
1980	Hard fought	6	13	1	3
	Low key	4	11	0	2
	Total hard fought	60 (53%)	94 (41%)	61 (86%)	41 (69%)
	Total low key	53 (47%)	137 (59%)	10 (14%)	18 (31%)

more hard-fought elections than subsequent years, it would be premature to declare a trend on the basis of only two election cycles.

Comparing Campaign Expenditures

This section will examine overall and per capita campaign expenditures by gubernatorial and Senate candidates. It will also examine the expenditures of incumbents, challengers, and open seat candidates. Additional ratios[16] for all incumbent and open seat expenditures in both gubernatorial and Senate elections will also be compared. As expenditures are an important element of both gubernatorial and Senate campaigns—which Chapters 2 and 3 have already demonstrated—these figures and ratios will help us further understand the competitive nature of gubernatorial elections and whether they are more or less competitive than Senate elections.

In gubernatorial incumbent elections, the average amount of deflated (in 1996 dollars) dollars spent by gubernatorial incumbents was $5,246,551.33, while challengers spent $3,265,303.45. These figures indicate that gubernatorial incumbents spent 1.6 times as much as their opponents.

States vary considerably in size, so spending must also be calculated in terms of dollars per person.[17] A million dollars spent in a New Hampshire election is certainly not the equivalent of a million dollars spent in California. For gubernatorial incumbents, the average cost per person in 1996 dollars was $1.95, whereas challengers spent $1.23. Thus, the spending ratio is 1.59 in favor of incumbents, or almost exactly the same as the 1.6 ratio noted above.

In open seat elections, the average deflated amount of money spent by candidates was $5,440,239.62, which is similar in proportion to the above calculations of spending in incumbent elections (now 66 percent greater than challenger spending and still almost exactly equal to incumbent spending). Per person, open seat candidates spent $1.73. This is less than what incumbents spent, but is quite a bit higher than the amount spent by challengers.

In Senate incumbent elections, the average senator seeking another six years spent $5,158,336 in 1996 dollars. Their challengers managed to spend on average only $2,825,783, resulting in a spending ratio of 1.83. When we take into account state size, the ratio does not change very much (just as we found with gubernatorial incumbent elections). While incumbents spent on average $2.67 per vote, challengers spent $1.39. This leads to a ratio of 1.92, which is only slightly larger than the ratio of 1.83.

Senate open seat candidates spent substantially more than challengers, but did not quite reach the incumbent level. The former spent on average $4,561,392 (in 1996 dollars), which suggests a high level of competition for these seats. Taking state size into account provides a dollars-per-person amount of $1.67, which is slightly less than the 1.73 figure from gubernatorial open seat elections. Table 7.4 more clearly presents these figures and allows for easy comparison between institutions.

How do gubernatorial and Senate incumbent elections compare in terms of expenditures? First, the spending ratios for gubernatorial elections are much smaller than the ratios for Senate elections, regardless of whether the ratios are calculated from total deflated expenditures or dollars per person.

Upon inspection, table 7.4 contains an interesting distinction: while governors outspent senators and gubernatorial challengers outspent senatorial challengers (in terms of total deflated dollars spent), these gubernatorial candidates spent less than the corresponding Senate candidates in terms of average dollars per person. Senate candidates, especially incumbents, therefore appear to spend less overall money but spend more per person.

One likely explanation of these results is the national implications of these two types of elections. For an interest group, political party, or other potential donor, all senators are of roughly equal value. Regardless of whether a senator represents New Mexico or New York, the vote of each senator is the same. This may encourage some donors to contribute to candidates running in smaller states under the logic that this will provide more "bang for their buck."

While governors are able to raise some money from out-of-state sources, there are few groups with a gubernatorial contribution

Table 7.4 Average campaign finance expenditures for gubernatorial and Senate candidates in incumbent elections

Candidates	Average Dollars Per Person . . .	. . . Ratio	Average Total Expenditures . . .	. . . Ratio
Governors	1.95		$5,246,551	
		1.59		1.61
Gub. challengers	1.23		$3,265,303	
Senators	2.67		$5,158,336	
		1.92		1.83
Sen. challengers	1.39		$2,825,783	

Note: Figures deflated in 1996 dollars.

budget trying to decide in which state to invest. Former senator and former governor Lowell Weicker found that "the nation's capital is not much of a place for gubernatorial fund-raising under any circumstances" (Weicker 1995, 184). These donors are focused on national legislation, and while some state policymaking may serve as a testing ground for particular ideas, states are not usually seen as key players in everyday national policy. The small-state fundraising dynamic therefore does not apply to gubernatorial elections, even as it affects senatorial fundraising and therefore Senate elections. This is another way in which the dynamics of gubernatorial and Senate races are different.

The executive/legislative difference may also play a role. Just as national interest groups have important reasons to pay more attention to Senate elections, state interest groups are similarly motivated to influence gubernatorial elections. As executives, governors have a great deal of power in their states. Although some have greater formal powers than others, they are all at the center of state policy debates and often have appointive powers for bureaucratic, state commission, and judicial positions. If governors spend more money overall than do senators, it may reflect the importance of each individual governor to the various interest groups within the state.

Few gubernatorial elections can be easily ignored, not just because of the gubernatorial outcome itself but because the governor is the head of the ticket. A lack of effort in support of a gubernatorial candidate, especially a weak candidate, may have electoral implications down the ticket if party voters stay at home. Voters may also come to consider not just the opposing party gubernatorial candidate but also other state candidates from that party. An underfunded and undersupported gubernatorial campaign may therefore lead to losses in the state legislature or for other statewide offices. Even if party and other political elites do not expect their gubernatorial candidate to win, it is important that the most vigorous effort possible be made.

The finding that gubernatorial elections are much more competitive than Senate elections reinforces the argument that the stakes are higher in any given executive election than in any given legislative election. If these elections were equally competitive and equally funded, we might conclude that state and national political actors do not differentiate between them, but this is not the case.

One possible rejoinder to this argument is that the types of states in the two pools may differ in terms of size. If the gubernatorial election states were on average larger than the senatorial ones, then gubernatorial candidates would naturally outspend Senate candidates.

However, the data show that this is not the case. The average size of a state with a gubernatorial election in this data set was about 3.4 million people, while the average Senate election state contained about 3.6 million people. This is very close to equivalency, and we would expect senatorial candidates to outspend gubernatorial candidates on the basis of size alone. This suggests that the dynamics discussed above were not caused by any mathematical quirk in the sample.

Candidate Quality

One of the few aspects of gubernatorial elections to attract attention over the years is the prior political experience of the candidates. However, it is possible to argue that no discussion of candidate experience is necessary because these variables were statistically insignificant in Chapters 2 and 3.[18] This might not satisfy those who worry that regression analysis does not tell the whole story. It might be thought that clearer patterns showing which types of candidates do better in gubernatorial elections can be found in tabular data.

In addition, there is a well-established literature (Schlesinger 1957, 1966; Sabato 1983; Squire 1992) seeking to make sense of the career paths of governors (and senators). As this work does not extend to 1996, it makes sense to continue it to see if previous trends continue.

Schlesinger (1957) was the first to classify the various career paths to governor. He was also the first (1966) to use "career trees" to illustrate graphically the penultimate and complete political experience of both governors and senators and also defeated candidates for these offices. Sabato (1983) used the same approach to examine the penultimate and prior offices held by governors in most of the twentieth century.

Schlesinger examined the careers of gubernatorial candidates from 1900 to 1958 and of Senate candidates from 1914 to 1958. Sabato's gubernatorial data are divided into two categories: governors serving from 1900 to 1949 and then from 1950 to 1980. This chapter continues this line of research by investigating the penultimate office of governors elected from 1980 to 1996. It differs in one major and one minor way from previous research. First, Schlesinger and Sabato did not differentiate between incumbent and open seat candidates, while this chapter looks for differences in the penultimate office experience of candidates in both types of elections.

The second difference is in the way political experience is classified. Schlesinger and Sabato both used seven categories: state legislative, law enforcement, statewide elective, congressional, administrative, local elective, and none. Squire (1992) used eight slightly different categories: ex-governor, U.S. House, statewide office, state legislative leader, state legislator, local, other, and none. This study borrows from both approaches, using former governor, statewide elected office, state legislator, U.S. House, U.S. Senate, state administrative, local government, law enforcement, political aides/staff, and none. In doing so it disaggregates "congressional" into House and Senate members, which makes better sense owing to the members' different constituencies and different positions in the political hierarchy. It also includes the new category of political aides/staff because there were a number of people with significant nonelectoral political experience who would otherwise have been placed in the "none" category.

One potentially important question is how candidate backgrounds have changed over time. One way to understand this is to see how the figures in the modern time period compare to those from earlier periods. Sabato found that from 1900 to 1949, 8.4 percent of governors had no prior political experience, while from 1950 to 1980, 10.2 percent did not. Our figures show that 25 percent of successful challengers had none, while only 6 percent of successful open seat candidates did. The combined percentage is 10.4, a figure nearly identical to the figure from Sabato's second time period, but one that masks important differences by type of election.

Sabato found that members or former members of Congress constituted 9.6 percent of winners in his first time period and 9.3 percent in the second. In recent years, fourteen winners of open seat contests were from Congress, while only one out of twenty-four winners in incumbent elections had Capitol Hill experience. This means that 14 percent of governors have came from Congress between 1980 and 1996, which is almost a 50 percent increase over the earlier figures.

Sabato found law enforcement to be in decline from 1900 to 1980 as the penultimate job for governor: "While 18.8 percent of all governors from 1900 to 1949 last held a law enforcement post before the governorship, only 13.5 percent of governors since 1970 have" (35). He also noted that these figures would have been even smaller had he not included state attorneys general in the category (they are classified as "statewide elected offices" in the tables in this chapter). From 1980 to 1996, there were no law enforcement officials among the twenty-four victorious challengers in incumbent elections, and there were only two among the eighty-two winners of open seat contests. This means that only about 2 percent of governors elected during this period had a penultimate law enforcement experience, continuing the decline noticed by Sabato.

Administrative office as a stepping stone to the governor's mansion also saw a steep decline. Sabato reported a decline from 13.8 percent to 10.2 percent over his two time periods . From 1980 to 1996, only one winning candidate—or just under 1 percent—had this penultimate experience.

Table 7.5 shows the political experience of successful and unsuccessful challengers to governors from 1980 to 1996. This is similar to table 1 in Squire (1992), although these categories are somewhat different and the time period is more contemporary.[19]

The largest job category was state legislator, followed by no experience, statewide elected office, and local government office. There were also eight former governors, eight political aides/staff, four House members, three state administrators, and two former or current U.S. senators. There were no challengers from a law enforcement background.

Eleven candidates were local political officeholders, but only two won. Even though state legislator was the most common penultimate job, all but five lost. Of the twenty-seven politically inexperienced candidates, six managed to defeat an incumbent. Just because they had no political experience does not mean that they were all retired teachers or young lawyers. Many were accomplished in other fields, particularly business, and sometimes brought a large bank account to the political table.

A surprisingly large number of political aides/staff ran for gubernatorial office (eight), but all lost. While such candidates may possess valuable political skills, as discussed in Chapter 2, their lack of public awareness may prove a tough obstacle. It is also possible that they run only when more credible candidates decline to enter.

Table 7.5 Challenger profile in incumbent gubernatorial elections, 1980–1996

Type of Race	Total	Challenger Won	Challenger Lost
Former governor	8	5	3
Statewide elected office	19	4	15
State legislative	40	5	35
House	4	0	4
Senate	2	1	1
State administrative	3	1	2
Political hacks	8	0	8
Local government	11	2	9
Law enforcement	0	0	0
None	27	6	21
Total	122	24	98

Of all the incumbent challengers during this time period, the only people who seem to have had an advantage over the others are former governors. So for those suspicious of regression results, the lesson from this table is that political background was apparently neither a positive nor a negative factor in their campaigns of most candidates (except perhaps for former governors).

Table 7.6 shows the candidate background for winning and losing open seat candidates from 1980 to 1996. For open seat elections, the greatest number of candidates was from statewide elected office, the state legislature, the House of Representatives, no experience, and local experience. There were also ten former governors. By contrast, there were only a handful of former or current senators, state administrators, political aides/staff, or law enforcement personnel. Former governors won eight out of ten times, and statewide elected officials and House members also did well. The state legislature once again proved a relatively poor training ground, as did law enforcement, state administration, and political aides/staff. So of the ten job categories in open seat elections, this table suggests that three had some advantage over the other seven, depending again on whether or not the reader believes the regression results.

The next question is whether particular political backgrounds are associated with hard-fought or low-key incumbent elections. This is different from asking whether these backgrounds lead to greater vote percentages, as not every hard-fought race is necessarily close and not every low-key race is a loss for the challenger.[20]

This is an important point because Krasno (1994, 161) found that "the background of the challenger remains far and away the most important predictor of campaign intensity. And it stands to

Table 7.6 Challenger profile in open seat gubernatorial races, 1980–1996

Type of Race	Total	Challenger Won	Challenger Lost
Former governor	10	8	2
Statewide elected office	60	34	26
State legislative	31	11	20
House	18	12	6
Senate	2	2	0
State administrative	2	0	2
Political hacks	4	1	3
Local government	15	7	8
Law enforcement	6	2	4
None	16	5	11
Total	164	82	82

reason: challenger quality has a substantial impact on the vote." Just because challenger quality does not appear to affect the vote in gubernatorial elections does not mean that candidate background is irrelevant to campaign intensity. Since this latter point is central to Krasno's argument for why senators have higher defeat rates than representatives, this section will examine its relevance in the gubernatorial context.

The Green and Krasno (1988) aggregate challenger quality measure (which was calculated in Chapter 5) is therefore regressed on the electoral competition measure. The results tell us that the challenger quality variable is not associated ($p < .35$) with our electoral intensity measure. In addition, Chapter 5 showed that the same aggregate challenger variable was not associated with levels of challenger expenditures. So Krasno's argument, while relevant to congressional elections, is another factor that does not apply to gubernatorial races.

The final question is, How do the prior political experiences of gubernatorial candidates compare to those of Senate candidates? Schlesinger (1966) compared previous penultimate offices for both governors and senators and for defeated gubernatorial and senatorial candidates. He found "distinct career lines for the states' two major elective offices" (98). For example, the penultimate office for governors was state legislator about 19 percent of the time, while for senators it was state legislator only 9 percent of the time. Congress was the penultimate job for senators 27 percent of the time, compared to 10 percent for governors.

These general trends were also true for defeated candidates for each office. This was discussed in more detail in Chapter 6. In sum, Schlesinger explained these findings in terms of a theory of "manifest office" (99). "The first is the theory of electorates . . . the second manifest tie between offices is the similarity of functions" (99). Politicians are likely to move from one office to another when they have similar constituencies, and the same is true when the nature of the job itself requires similar skills. A third condition is a similarity in a shared political arena. State legislators interact regularly with governors, so it makes sense that the former would consider themselves natural candidates for governor.

Schlesinger's data included elections from 1900 to 1958 for governors and 1914 to 1958 for senators. Now we will examine whether his findings hold true for elections held more than three decades later. Table 7.7 compares the backgrounds of successful and unsuccessful candidates for both governor and senator for incumbent elections, while table 7.8 does the same for open seat elections.

Table 7.7 Comparing challenger profile in incumbent gubernatorial and Senate races, 1980–1996

Type of Race	Governor Won	Senator Won	Governor Lost	Senator Lost
Former governor	3	3	5	4
Statewide elected office	15	4	4	17
State legislative	35	2	5	37
House	4	13	0	29
Senate	1	0	1	1
State administrative	2	2	1	12
Political hacks	8	2	0	14
Local government	9	2	2	13
Law enforcement	0	1	0	4
None	21	2	6	64
Total	98	31	24	191

Table 7.8 Comparing challenger profile in open seat gubernatorial and Senate races, 1980–1996

Type of Race	Gov. Win	Senate Win	Gov. Loss	Senate Loss
Former governor	8	6	2	3
Statewide elected office	34	6	26	6
State legislative	11	3	20	12
House	12	32	6	17
Senate	2	1	0	2
State administrative	0	0	2	1
Political hacks	1	1	3	1
Local government	7	2	8	4
Law enforcement	2	1	4	2
None	5	6	11	10
Total	82	58	82	58

These data almost entirely uphold the "manifest office" theory. While only 5 percent of victorious gubernatorial challengers were members of Congress, 42 percent of Senate challengers had been elected to this body. And while only 4 percent of losing gubernatorial challengers had this background, 16 percent of losing senatorial challengers did. These general results hold for open seat elections, too. Seventeen percent of winning gubernatorial candidates were from Congress, while the figure for Senate winners was 57 percent. And while 7 percent of those who won the governor's mansion had served in Congress, one-third of those who made it to the Senate had this experience.

In this regard, not much has changed in three decades. Even though governor and senator are the most important statewide offices, they are not approached in the same way by ambitious politicians. In this way, tables 7.7 and 7.8 thus reflect the findings of Chapter 6, which argued that ambition for these two offices was very different and therefore deserving of separate examination.

In other words, we have further evidence that the role of candidate quality in gubernatorial elections is different along multiple dimensions than it is in elections for other offices. These varying candidate quality dynamics will be brought together more comprehensively in Chapter 9.

State Size

Some analysts have argued that state size is responsible for the "defeat differential" of senators and representatives. While it is clear that this cannot be the case when comparing gubernatorial and senatorial elections, it would be interesting to know whether state size makes reelection more difficult for incumbent governors and also whether it is correlated with a greater ability of challengers or incumbents to raise money.

Simple regression analysis shows that state size is not associated with any electoral trouble for incumbent governors. The measure for voting age population was regressed on the incumbent two-party vote and was statistically insignificant ($p < .16$). When the three largest states were dropped, the statistical significance improved only slightly ($p < .14$).

Scholars have previously noted that per capita spending in Senate election campaigns is much higher in smaller states. Because of this, Magleby (1989) called small states the "battlegrounds for control of the Senate." One hypothesis for why small states may have higher per capita expenditures is the lower cost of campaigning in those states, as they do not generally contain expensive media markets. As discussed earlier, politically active groups, individuals, and parties may therefore try to make their contributions go further by donating to campaigns in those states. Ten thousand dollars will not buy much television time in a New York Senate campaign, but will pay for more commercials in New Mexico.

As discussed above, this is a likely phenomenon in elections to a national legislature where every vote counts equally, but does it hold true for state executive elections? Once again, the data used in this book can easily test this proposition. A simple regression of state voting age population on deflated gubernatorial per capita incumbent expenditures shows that the latter is not statistically significant ($p < .16$). If the above theory were true, we might expect to see incumbent per capita expenditures decrease with state size. Yet it may be that challengers are the ones who benefit from size dynamics. The data show that regressing state size on deflated per capita challenger expenditures produces results consistent with those listed above. State size is statistically insignificant ($p < .14$). A further test is whether state size is related to the ratio between incumbent and challenger spending. Even if smaller states do not bring any more money to either the challenger or the incumbent, perhaps they are the scene of more closely contested gubernatorial elections as measured by expenditure ratios. A simple regression shows that state size is not statistically associated ($p < .54$) with competition.

These findings also address the previously discussed finding that while governors outspent senators and gubernatorial challengers outspent senatorial challengers, both types of Senate candidates exceeded their gubernatorial equivalents in per capita expenditures. The heavy concentration of money in Senate elections in relatively small states, and the absence of this dynamic in gubernatorial elections, shows how national forces can affect these two offices differently.

Partisan Outcomes

The next step is to examine how well the two major parties have done from 1980 to 1996 in open seat gubernatorial and Senate elections. Table 7.9 gives the percentage of Democratic candidates who won in each year, followed by the number of Democratic and Republican candidates. Some caveats should be discussed. The low number of observations (particularly for Senate elections) means that in some years a change in a single outcome would significantly alter the percentage of seats won by a party. Similarly, particular election years feature particular elections in particular states; the unique context of each contest may lead to outcomes unrelated to national trends.

It appears that in Senate elections, Democratic Party victories were not related to presidential midterms. While Democrats did poorly in the Clinton midterm of 1994, they also did poorly in the Bush midterm of 1990 and failed to do well in 1982 and 1986, years when Reagan was not at his most popular.

Gubernatorial elections fit the midterm pattern better . Democratic candidates did very well in 1982, their 1986 victory percentage was much better than in 1984, they did poorly in 1994, but they broke even in the 1990 Bush midterm.

Table 7.9 Success of Democratic gubernatorial and Senate open seat candidates, 1980–1996

Year	Gub-Open	Sen-Open
1996	66% (4D/2R)	43% (6D/8R)
1994	25% (2D/6R)	0% (0D/9R)
1992	66% (6D/3R)	57% (4D/3R)
1990	54% (7D/6R)	0% (0D/5R)
1988	60% (3D/2R)	33% (2D/4R)
1986	53% (9D/8R)	66% (4D/2R)
1984	30% (3D/7R)	75% (3D/1R)
1982	75% (9D/3R)	33% (1D/2R)
1980	0% (0D/1R)	40% (2D/3R)
Total	53% (43D/38R)	37% (22D/37R)

One might suggest that open seat elections are not meaningful partisan choices; if some states have a strong tendency to repeatedly elect governors of the same party, the explanation for any midterm gubernatorial outcome is better found in the nature of those particular states that are holding an election that year.

An examination of the governors who served from 1980 to 1996 allows a test of this party continuity thesis. Only eight states elected governors exclusively from the same party during this entire period.[21] This suggests that the voters of most states are quite capable of electing candidates from either party, as would suit an electorate that increasingly claims to vote for the person, not the party.[22]

A further point is that Democrats did better in gubernatorial open seat elections than in Senate open seat elections. While 53 percent of Democratic open seat gubernatorial candidates won, only 37 percent of their Senate equivalents did. Even in 1994, when no open seat Democratic Senate candidate saw victory, 25 percent of such Democratic gubernatorial candidates won.

Simultaneous Gubernatorial and Senate Elections

Westlye (1991) compared consecutive Senate elections to check for partisan and competitive consistencies. He found that "over the last nine election years every one of the fifty states has had one closely contested Senate race back to back with a Senate race that was not at all close" (8). Voters were also quite willing to elect a candidate from one party in one election and a candidate from another party in the next election, a pattern that held in all regions of the country.

This section compares gubernatorial and Senate elections taking place in the same year in the same state. It will examine two questions: To what extent are candidates from the same party simultaneously elected? and How often is the electoral intensity of such campaigns similar? This is yet another way of examining how distinct the elections for these two offices may be. If there is a tendency for simultaneous elections to be either hard fought or low key, or for the same party to win both elections, then perhaps there are some electoral dynamics connecting the two offices that have not yet been discussed in this book.

Figures 7.1 and 7.2 use a two-by-two matrix to illustrate the partisan outcomes of these dual elections in open seat and incumbent contests. Because these races are so different, it makes little sense to aggregate the data.

For open seat elections in figure 7.1, some caution must be used when interpreting the data because of the relatively low number of observations; only twelve concurrent sets of elections took place for which data are available. Keeping this in mind, a pattern emerges whereby nine out of twelve times the winners were from the same party. In only three elections was there a split decision. So while this finding is tentative, it is suggestive.

GOVERNORS

	Democrat	Republican	
Democratic	3	2	SENATORS
Republican	1	6	

Figure 7.1 Comparison of partisan outcomes in states with simultaneous open seat gubernatorial and Senate elections

GOVERNORS

```
         Democrat        Republican


            23         |      17
                       |
                       |             Democrat
                       |
                       |                          SENATORS
        _____|_____
                       |
                       |
            13         |      12        Republican
                       |
                       |
                       |
                       |
```

Figure 7.2 Comparison of partisan outcomes in states with simultaneous incumbent gubernatorial and Senate elections

Figure 7.2 for incumbent elections shows that despite more observations the pattern is less clear. Thirty-five pairs of concurrent elections gave the same party a victory, while thirty resulted in one of each. This is just two state elections removed from being nearly even, which is not enough evidence to support the partisan hypothesis.

Taken together, the data suggest a slight tendency on the part of voters to see elections in partisan terms. Future researchers might be interested in expanding the time frames, not only to add more observations, but also to see whether these patterns change over the decades.

Figures 7.3 and 7.4 use a two-by-two matrix to discern the simultaneity of electoral intensity. Figure 7.3 shows an even smaller number of observations for open seat elections than figure 7.1. This is because gubernatorial expenditure figures were not available for some elections. Once again, despite the limited data, a pattern emerges: concurrent gubernatorial and Senate elections were largely hard fought. Six pairs of elections were hard fought, while only one contained a hard-fought and a low-key election. On the other hand, the data in figure 7.4 for incumbent elections are less clear. Thirty elections had similar electoral intensities, while twenty-six did not.

	GOVERNORS: Hard-Fought	GOVERNORS: Low-Key
SENATORS: Hard-Fought	6	0
SENATORS: Low-Key	1	0

Figure 7.3 Comparison of electoral intensity in states with simultaneous open seat gubernatorial and Senate elections

	GOVERNORS: Hard-Fought	GOVERNORS: Low-Key
SENATORS: Hard-Fought	15	12
SENATORS: Low-Key	14	15

Figure 7.4 Comparison of electoral intensity in states with simultaneous incumbent gubernatorial and Senate elections

One tentative but possible hypothesis is that there is a spillover or contagion effect at work in open seat elections. Perhaps once a statewide hard-fought election stimulates political elites into action, these same actors turn some of their attention to the concurrent campaign. Campaigns could share volunteer networks and hold rallies featuring visits by well-regarded out-of-state politicians. Television advertising by one Democrat, for example, may help the other Democrat. Perhaps generic "issue advertising" by political parties or interest groups serve all candidates of that party.

It might further be thought that when donors contribute to one campaign, they may be more likely to give to the candidate of the same party in the other election. The financial impact of a concurrent Senate election has already been tested for gubernatorial challengers in Chapter 5 and found insignificant. Regressions similarly show that a concurrent Senate election does not increase the total amount of money raised in open seat gubernatorial elections. If there is a spillover effect, it may operate in the manner discussed in the above paragraphs, but not financially.

Conclusions

This chapter directly compared gubernatorial and Senate elections and found substantial evidence of different competitive dynamics. Although both offices share the same constituencies, it would be a mistake to assume that the path to one office resembles the path to the other.

First, governors are almost twice as likely to lose their reelection campaigns as are senators, although this chapter is not the first study to note this difference. Second, for the first time we see that gubernatorial elections are more likely to be hard fought than are Senate elections. This is true for both incumbent and open seat elections. Similarly, whether calculated as an aggregate or a per capita figure, the average candidate expenditure ratio is much lower in gubernatorial incumbent elections than in Senate incumbent elections, and likewise lower in gubernatorial than in Senate open seat elections.

The chapter also discusses how well candidates for either office did during presidential and midterm election years. It found that gubernatorial elections better fit the midterm pattern[23] than did Senate elections, as Democratic victories in elections since 1980 show. In addition, previous theories of penultimate office developed by Schlesinger and Sabato are shown to apply in the 1980s and 1990s to both governor and senator; however, the path to each office remains considerably different.

Preliminary data on levels of competition in concurrent statewide elections were also discussed. Although the number of observations was small, the chapter noted a tendency on the part of voters to elect governors and senators from the same party when there were simultaneous open seat elections, but this dynamic occurred only marginally in incumbent elections. When electoral competition was compared in gubernatorial and Senate elections, the data again suggest the possibility of a similar dynamic in open seat elections, but only slightly so in incumbent contests. As discussed in the concluding chapter, these are among the very few instances of political "spillover" in concurrent gubernatorial and Senate elections.

The most important question to answer is the one mentioned in the introduction: What explains the relatively large defeat rate for incumbent governors? Do any of the reasons given for the greater likelihood of senators than representatives to lose apply to the state electoral arena? As mentioned above, Squire and Fastnow (1994) found that the feeling thermometer differential between governors and their challengers was larger than that between senators and their challengers, but they did not explain this interesting finding.

The lack of quality challengers to House incumbents is a commonly offered explanation for the high reelection rate of the latter vis-à-vis senators. To explain why senators were more likely to lose than representatives in any given election, Krasno (1994) focused on challengers and the intensity of their campaigns, while Abramowitz and Segal (1992) mentioned challenger intensity as one of several explanations.[24]

This does not apply to gubernatorial elections. The evidence from this chapter, as well as from Chapters 2 and 3, strongly suggests that the political experience of a challenger adds little to his or her general election vote. No type of candidate had any advantage over any other, which makes the challenger quality argument very difficult.

Regression results in this chapter also indicated that the Green and Krasno (1988) measure of aggregate political experience did not explain campaign intensity. This is an important contrast to Krasno's (1994, 161) finding that "the background of the challenger remains far and away the most important predictor of campaign intensity." In addition, the regression results in Chapter 5 showed that the Green and Krasno (1988) variable did not explain levels of challenger campaign expenditures, further evidence against the challenger-centered explanation.

Various other potential explanations are also shown to be inadequate. The state size argument cannot explain differences between gubernatorial and Senate election outcomes.[25] Length of term might be relevant because senators and governors serve for different periods, and shorter terms have been thought to be a net advantage for House members.[26] By this logic, the typical four-year terms of governors should contribute to their electoral security vis-à-vis senators. This effect is either not taking place or is overwhelmed by other forces, so another possible explanation from the congressional elections literature does not apply.

We might look instead to the executive nature of the governor to better understand this dynamic. Some possible explanations can be drawn from the presidency literature, while others are inferred from the nature of the job and its relationship to other state political actors.

A. Lonely at the Top: The Solitary Executive

The governor is a single individual who is easily held responsible for state problems. We have already seen how voters blame or credit governors for state crime rates, and it is no stretch of the imagination to argue that some voters may hold them responsible for other issues less easy to quantify. These could include the quality of the state university system, the condition of state parks, the state response to natural disasters,[27] or a myriad of other factors.

It is also possible that governors are held responsible for events out of their control. Americans assign significant responsibility to presidents,[28] so state voters may hold their state executives similarly accountable. There are many public policy issues where the governor may be constrained by state, federal, or local actors but nevertheless held responsible as the most prominent state politician. In addition, a governor could be held responsible for actions taken by local politicians. Voters might blame the governor if the local public library closes, for example. There is no law mandating rational accountability by the public, and political science knows so little about noneconomic electoral accountability that almost no dynamic can be confidently ruled out.

Senators, as members of a hundred-member body that depends on decisions made in the House of Representatives and White House, are less accountable. As one well-known political observer noted during the 1998 meeting of the Republican Governors Association:

> A senator is just one of 100 and therefore not personally accountable for what the Senate does or fails to do. The governor is judged by very different standards . . . Senators raise issues and make tough speeches; governors frequently have to raise taxes and make tough decisions.[29]

As Schlesinger (1966, 69) wrote over thirty years ago:

> Even if the legislature has been obstructionist and "do-nothing," the group aspect of legislative office helps protect the individual legislator from voter reaction in a way in which the governor or President, alone and conspicuous, can never be protected . . . This is not to say that legislators are immune to changes in voter attitudes; American political history easily demonstrates the contrary. But American politics also demonstrates that revulsion against the legislator must penetrate the electorate more deeply.

The level of electoral security for governors, senators, and representatives is possibly related to this issue of accountability. House members are most numerous and most secure in any given election, senators are second in both categories, while governors have no peer in their states but are the most likely to be fired by the voters. Similarly, presidents are the focus of intense national attention and are therefore in the greatest electoral jeopardy.

We might briefly consider whether executives—gubernatorial or presidential—possess the power to meet public expectations. Neustadt (1990) wrote the classic study of presidential power, arguing that the president has few formal powers and cannot easily give commands to others in Washington. He discussed how presidents must guard their reputation to maximize their role in the policy process. Nevertheless, Neustadt understood that presidents are "the focal point of politics and policy" (3) in their political universe.

Are governors state versions of Neustadt's presidents? Similar to Neustadt, Rosenthal (1990) noted that the picture of gubernatorial power is sometimes exaggerated. State legislatures, just like Congress, have much to say about the executive's agenda. Like Neustadt's presidents, governors do not simply give orders to the legislature or the bureaucracy; "They anticipate what leaders and members would like, they consult and negotiate, they compromise their positions, and they trim their proposals" (199). Governors are still the center of state political life; but like presidents, it is easy to exaggerate their power and therefore their level of responsibility.

B. Declining Approval over Time: An Executive Office Phenomenon?

Over the course of their terms, governors must make decisions on controversial and complex state issues and may thereby alienate a growing number of people. Unlike senators, governors cannot limit their responses to speeches or appeals to ideology, and every decision may add another group to the list of the unhappy. As former senator and governor Chuck Robb (D-VA) noted, governors can take immediate action on problems while senators are more likely to take rhetorical action.[30] Governors are therefore more likely to create political enemies, or at least to cause disappointment, than are senators. During the next campaign, these alienated groups and individuals may well remember the affront and sit out the race or support a primary or even a general election opponent.

Some scholars believe that this dynamic helps explain why presidents almost always see their approval ratings decline over time during their first and second terms. As King (1999, 166) noted, each president "experiences a decline in popularity during his term of office, although for some the fall from grace is more extreme."[31]

Mueller (1973) was the first to quantitatively study this phenomenon, which he called the "coalition of minorities" effect. His work was built on the theories of Downs (1957), who argued that even if a president acted on each issue with the majority of the voters on his side, he might gradually alienate a significant number of people. These people might coalesce into a majority in the next election and defeat the incumbent. As Mueller (1973, 205) put it,

> This concept would predict that a president's popularity would show an overall downward trend as he is forced on a variety of issues to act and thus to create intense, unforgiving opponents of former supporters. It is quite easy to point to cases where this may have occurred.

Brody (1991, 120) thought this theory unrealistic because Mueller "appears to apply a 'single-issue' standard . . . but there is no evidence that any sizable fraction of the public is, in this sense, ineluctably 'single-issue.'"[32] There is no reason why this is just a one-step phenomenon, where voters are irreconcilably alienated by a presidential action. It could be that important political, social, economic, or other elite groups are unhappy with presidential policy and let their membership know. Such groups could also sit out the next election or redirect their political resources toward the opposition. Voters might also be alienated not by one but by multiple decisions made by an executive over the course of a term.

Mueller suggested some corollaries of his theory:

> From time to time there arise bitter dilemmas in which the president must act and in which he will tend to alienate *both* sides no matter what

he does, a phenomenon related to what Aaron Wildavsky (1968) has called a "minus sum" game. (1973, 205–206, italics in original)

He also noted that a general sense of disillusionment might work against the incumbent, whereby the president overpromises during his election campaign and then gradually loses support as he fails to deliver.

He found that the average decline for a president's popularity was about 5 percent per year, even taking into account economic performance (unemployment) and foreign crises (the "rally round the flag" effect). Some might point to Eisenhower as an exception, as he did not experience any such gradual decline. Mueller explained that because Ike took very little action as president, a coalition of minorities did not form.

Stimson (1976) similarly argued that presidential popularity is subject to an almost inevitable decline. In his account, this is not the president's fault, but is caused by the unrealistic expectations of the public and their lack of knowledge about the difficulty of the job: "early naïve expectations lead to later cynicism" (9–10). He argues that while presidential candidates may overpromise in the campaign, the public should know better.

Brace and Hinckley (1992) updated Mueller (1973) and confirmed this decay of popular support in both the first and second terms: "The polls decline over time, in what we call a decay curve, independently of anything a president does" (44). Their explanation is "the inflated initial support. The time curve is central to understanding a feature of the office, which continually renews expectations that cannot be fulfilled. All presidents, quite literally, are set up for a fall" (44). One of the few forces to positively influence poll numbers is international crises, which worried Brace and Hinckley as well as previous scholars (Lowi 1985) because it suggested that presidents might start conflicts abroad for the sake of polls at home. The international dynamic is not available to governors, so we might expect their popularity to be more likely to fall than that of presidents.

Overall, the weight of the evidence suggests that there is a temporal component to presidential popularity outside of political and economic events. It is not unreasonable to assume that the combination of inflated public expectations, inflated candidate rhetoric, general public disillusionment, and anger over particular policy decisions may combine to lower approval over time, in either a direct or mediated manner. The decline itself is so clear and consistent that it cannot be ignored, and it suggests a way in which the executive nature of the governor may similarly lead to less support than that received by senators on election day.

There is some evidence to support this hypothesis. Rosenthal (1990, 33) found that

> not only do circumstances tend to eat into a governor's popularity, but the passage of time may be erosive as well. It may be part of the natural cycle of political life, as the office becomes diminished in the eyes of the public by their familiarity with the incumbent. Moreover, the governor may trade in some popularity in order to achieve objectives.

Schlesinger (1966, 69) made a similar argument and suggested that the dynamic may apply to all executive officeholders: "The governor and the President are most vulnerable to the accumulated grievances of voters which produce the rejection of incumbents."

C. Media Coverage

A related dynamic is that governors are covered differently than senators by the state news media. First, governors are much more extensively covered than are senators (Squire and Fastnow 1994). In fact, House members receive the least coverage, senators somewhat more, governors even more, and presidents the most, a pattern that corresponds with incumbent security. Researchers have also shown that presidents receive far more media coverage than does Congress (Graber 1997), and governors more than state legislatures (Rosenthal 1990). This executive attention may prove to be a double-edged sword, especially when social and economic conditions decline.

Brace and Hinckley (1992) noted that the public assigns much policy responsibility to the presidency: "These public attitudes are reinforced by news coverage. Journalists equate the president with the government in their reporting of complex policy making; furthermore, they imply that presidents can solve major problems" (22). Presidential candidates themselves often reinforce these views, and "we thus find an idealized portrait of the office that contrasts sharply with real-world events" (23). Given the parallel institutional placement of the governor as well as the extensive media attention, a similar dynamic may affect governors whereby responsibility for policy outcomes is laid at the doorstep of the governor but not the state legislature.

D. State Political Dynamics

Table 7.4 showed that when the ratios of incumbent and challenger spending are compared—either per capita or total expenditures—it is clear that senators are much better able to outspend their opponents than are governors. This is especially true for per capita expenditures, which is the more meaningful statistic of the two.

Why are incumbent governors much less able to outspend their challengers—or from another perspective, why are gubernatorial challengers such successful fundraisers? There are several explanations that, like those above, are related to the role of the governor in the state political system.

Challengers may raise significant funds because from the perspective of state political elites, the stakes are higher than are those in a U.S. Senate race. The political needs of other state politicians may be one reason. Just as a presidential campaign that ignores a state because of Electoral College considerations may hurt congressional candidates of that party, so state and local politicians may fear that an underfunded campaign by their gubernatorial nominee will reduce their odds of victory. Politically active people and groups may therefore make more strenuous efforts to keep their gubernatorial rather than Senate challengers competitive, regardless of whether they believe the candidate will win.

State political elites may also believe that the office of governor is too important to cede without a fight to the other party, even if the nominee is not a strong candidate or the person they preferred. At stake are not just policy outcomes but jobs in the bureaucracy, state contracts, and sometimes judicial appointments. This may mean gubernatorial candidates have more reliable access to campaign contributions, volunteers, get-out-the-vote efforts, and other politically important resources.

As mentioned previously, federally focused interest groups often ignore weaker Senate candidates in favor of those in closer races, thereby maximizing the impact of their donations. This is much less a factor in state elections. A state association is unlikely to ignore a gubernatorial contest in its own backyard and instead contribute to a candidate running in another state who has a better chance of winning.

In addition, many of the executive arguments discussed previously would help explain this relatively close financial margin. For example, the greater public accountability assumed by governors vis-à-vis senators may explain why they do not more greatly outspend their opponents. If, by making difficult decisions, they have alienated some people or groups who might have otherwise supported them, this may lead to reduced incumbent revenues and increased funding for challengers.

8

Gubernatorial versus Senate Election Dynamics: Third-Party and Independent Campaigns

One of the most unique features of gubernatorial elections is that candidates without a major-party affiliation sometimes win and frequently do well. Although there was much discussion in the 1990s about third-party presidential candidates, it was at the state executive level where independent and third-party candidacies were most successful. That these two executive offices—the governorship and presidency—are both attractive to third-party efforts is infrequently noted. This chapter will discuss why the governorship and presidency have this feature in common.

Senators, by contrast, are almost exclusively major party creatures. No independent or third-party Senate candidates have won in recent times, and such candidates are less likely to post respectable losing efforts than their counterparts in gubernatorial elections. This is not to say that life is easy for "nonaligned" candidates who want to live in a governor's mansion. Their chances of victory are low, but they are better off than nonaligned Senate candidates, who face almost impossible odds.

From 1980 to 1996, three governors were elected without winning Democratic or Republican nominations, and one governor was similarly elected in 1998. During this time period, all senators have worn a major-party label. In fact, only one member of Congress— Representative Bernie Sanders of Vermont (who "has actually functioned as a liberal Democrat")[1]—was elected as an independent.

Before 1980, only a small number of nonaligned governors had held office since the turn of the nineteenth century. The most recent was James B. Longley of Maine, who was elected in 1974 and served for one term. To find others, we must go back to the Depression years, which saw the election of independents William Langler of North Dakota (1937–1939) and Julius L. Meier of Oregon (1931–1935).

Counting from the Reconstruction era, Beck (1997, 47) found that "of more than a thousand governors elected since 1875, only seventeen ran solely on a third-party ticket; another six, all since 1921, were independents." Going back even further to the founding era, there have been a fair number of parties contesting gubernatorial elections. From 1787 to 1998, governors were elected solely on the tickets of fifty parties, and candidates contested general elections either entirely or jointly (in the case of "fusion" systems) on the tickets of 210 parties.

How many candidates without major-party labels seriously contested for the two major statewide offices from 1980 to 1996? In Senate elections during these decades, only five received more than 10 percent of the general election vote. Nonaligned candidates did much better in gubernatorial elections. Three candidates won their bids (not including Jesse Ventura of Minnesota, who won in 1998) and eighteen received over 10 percent of the vote. As will be discussed, the parties ranged from the familiar, such as the Green and Libertarian parties, to personal parties created for the moment, such as the Best Party (BP) and the Illinois Solidarity Party. Many candidates ran without any party label, and one of these served two terms as governor of Maine.

There are some differences within the nonaligned category, but they are often not as important as might be thought. Some nonaligned candidates are entirely independent of any party affiliation, while others are the nominees of minor parties. In some cases, a third party is just a vehicle created by a local candidate for his or her try for office. To call these entities "parties" may be technically correct according to the laws of the state in which they originate, but they have little in common with the two major parties or the minor parties that attempt to build national organizations, like the Libertarian and Green parties.[2]

One point worth mentioning is that not all third parties are unconnected to the major parties. In New York, the small parties operating under the "fusion" system may be officially separate from the major parties but frequently endorse major-party candidates. Under the fusion system, candidates can be endorsed by several parties and appear on the ballot as the candidate of all the endorsing parties, but all votes for a particular candidate contribute toward that candidate's total. The small parties can officially nominate their own gubernatorial and Senate candidates, but in practice they often endorse a major-party candidate.[3] Such parties are not considered true third parties in this chapter, except in the two cases when candidates ran solely and with some limited success on one of these tickets. In addition, in Minnesota, the Democratic–Farmer–Labor party was the local name for the Democratic Party, while the Independent Republican party was the Republican affiliate. These are not counted as third parties.

This chapter examines third-party and independent candidates and their campaigns from 1980 and 1996. It focuses on gubernatorial campaigns but also discusses nonaligned Senate campaigns for comparative purposes.

The first section will briefly examine the eighteen nonaligned gubernatorial candidates who ran respectable but losing efforts. "Respectable" is defined as a general election vote percentage of 10 or more. This section will check for commonalities among their campaigns and ask what might explain their relatively good showings. It will also examine three candidates who confounded the skeptics and won their races. Because of widespread interest in his campaign, Jesse Ventura's victory in 1998 will also be briefly examined, although it falls just slightly outside the time period of this book.

Ten percent may be a somewhat arbitrary number, but establishing a cutoff at the border of single- and double-digit vote percentages seems more reasonable than any alternative. There is also some precedent for this figure in the gubernatorial elections literature. Morehouse (1998, 11) interviewed only gubernatorial candidates who were anticipated by political observers to receive 10 percent or more of the vote in a direct primary or a primary convention. The other candidates were considered "hopeless."

The second section will discuss the five independent Senate candidates who won over 10 percent of the vote. It will try to understand why these candidates did relatively well in an arena where none won and all others failed more resoundingly.

The third section studies the role of campaign finance in gubernatorial elections. It will show how much nonaligned candidates spent per capita in the important election year of 1994 and how this compared to the expenditures of the major-party candidates. The percentage of nonaligned candidates' election expenditures will also be examined, and there will be a preliminary examination of how expenditures correspond with votes.

The fourth section examines time trends in nonaligned campaigns. This will illustrate the aggregate vote percentages gained by all nonaligned candidates in all states from 1980 to 1996. It will also compare elections taking place during presidential election years with those taking place during midterm years, which is when most gubernatorial elections take place.

The conclusion will then examine what lessons can be drawn about gubernatorial nonaligned candidacies, as well as why they have experienced more success than their counterparts in Senate elections. It will be seen that the former have much in common with their major party colleagues. They are not naïve babes-in-the-woods who ran with little political experience or few important politically relevant skills. In two cases, the winning candidate had significant major party electoral experience, and two others had extensive backgrounds in the broadcasting and entertainment businesses and began their campaigns with high name recognition. If some hope that independent and third-party candidacies mean an influx of "average citizens" into electoral politics, they will be disappointed by the cast of characters in this chapter.

Respectable Nonaligned Gubernatorial Candidacies

As mentioned above, eighteen candidates for governor (not including the four victors) won over 10 percent of the general election vote without having a contemporaneous affiliation with Democrats or Republicans. Twelve of them ran in open seat elections, while six were in contests featuring an incumbent.

This section will briefly discuss these contests to understand better the dynamics of independent candidacies. The goal of this chapter is not to give detailed blow-by-blow descriptions of the campaigns, but to create an overview of the most successful nonaligned candidates in recent gubernatorial history. The analysis will first consider the 1994 Alaska contest and then move in reverse chronological order until it ends in 1982, in Alaska, where it began, at which point conclusions will be drawn.[4]

A. Alaska 1994

The 1994 Alaskan gubernatorial race was open because the incumbent, Walter Hickel, declined to run again. Hickel first served as governor from 1966 to 1967 as a Republican and was elected in 1990 as the candidate of the Alaskan Independence Party (AIP) (his campaign is discussed later in the chapter). Hickel's lieutenant governor, Jack Coghill, ran on the AIP ticket[5] and would seem to have been well positioned to run a strong campaign. Very few third-party candidates have the luxury of running a campaign that builds on previous party success.

Coghill received 13 percent of the votes, and his campaign may have been affected by Hickel's decision near the end of his term to return to the Republican Party. Another problem might have been financial: the Alaskan election commission reported that Coghill spent no money. His loss may also reflect the hard-fought contest between the two experienced major-party candidates: Democrat Tony Knowles, the former mayor of Anchorage who placed second in the 1990 gubernatorial general election; and Republican Jim Campbell, who lost the 1990 gubernatorial primary. The election was decided by just over 500 votes. Such a close contest may have diverted attention away from Coghill, but it also meant that the outcome might have been different without Coghill on the ballot.

B. Connecticut 1994

As mentioned above, it is rare for a third-party candidate for governor to run in the shadow of a retiring governor from that party. Not only did Coghill do so in 1994, but another lieutenant governor of a third-party governor tried to build on the incumbent's success in 1994. This was Eunice Groark, the candidate of Lowell Weicker's A Connecticut Party (ACP), who fared six percentage points better than Coghill.

Groark had been elected as a Republican to the Hartford Common Council for two years and in 1985 lost a race for mayor of Hartford. She next worked as the city's corporation counsel until becoming the lieutenant governor.[6]

Weicker's success may have hurt Groark by encouraging another nonaligned candidate to run in 1994. Tom Scott was a former state legislator who at the time hosted a radio talk show. He was the candidate of the Independence Party, which was formed three months before the party filing deadline,[7] and ran as an anti–income tax advocate. Implementing a state income tax had been one of Weicker's most difficult and controversial actions. Scott won 11 percent of the vote, and the *Almanac of American Politics (AAP) 1996* reported that Scott took most of his votes from Republican nominee, and eventual winner, John Rowland.

Al Gore stumped for the Democratic nominee in Hartford and made a traditional criticism of third-party candidacies: "Let's be clear: a vote for Groark is a vote for the Republicans."[8] In November,

Groark started using the slogan, "Remember: a vote for me is a vote for me and not somebody else,"[9] reflecting a concern that low poll standings might lead some of her supporters to vote for Curry in an attempt to bring about Rowland's defeat.

As the *AAP 1992* noted, third parties often "prove to be vehicles for one well-known politician who occupies a niche left vacant in an unusual year" (214). Some critics said that ACP stood for "A Cult of Personality,"[10] but clearly Groark hoped it would stand on its own. She won 19 percent of the vote, which was disappointing not only because she lost, but because ACP thereby missed the 20 percent mark that Connecticut parties must receive in order to obtain major-party status. Weicker predicted that a Groark loss would mean "good-bye Connecticut Party,"[11] and there was indeed no ACP candidate for governor in 1998.

C. Hawaii 1994

The state of Hawaii was the scene of the most successful losing third-party candidate in 1994—Frank Fasi. The victor was Ben Cayetano, a Democrat and former lieutenant governor and member of the Hawaiian state senate and legislature. According to the *AAP 1998* (389), his win "was due less to the strength of his Democratic machine and more to the weakness and division of his opponents." Cayetano won 37 percent of the vote, just 6 percentage points higher than the next candidate. The Republican was Patricia Saiki, the loser of the 1990 Senate election to Daniel Akaka and a former member of the U.S. House. She came in third in the 1994 elections with 29 percent.

The second place finisher was Frank Fasi, the mayor of Honolulu from 1968 to 1994 (with a four-year break), who won 31 percent of the vote. Fasi formed his own party, the BP, and "combatively stressed his get-things-done record as mayor."[12] Fasi previously ran as a candidate for governor several times as both a Democrat and a Republican. In 1998, he ran for office again, but not on the BP ticket. Instead, he ran in the Republican gubernatorial primary but lost to Linda Lingle, the former mayor of Maui. He received 31 percent of the vote, while Lingle won the other 69 percent.

D. New Mexico 1994

Hawaii was not the only state with a majority-minority population to field a third-party candidate in 1994. New Mexico was the scene of a Green Party candidacy by Roberto Mondragon, a former Democratic lieutenant governor. He won 10 percent of the vote, which was enough to establish the Greens as a major party in the next election.[13] To many Greens, this meant that his campaign, although a losing effort, was a partial success.

The winner, by ten percentage points, was Republican Gary Johnson, a businessman with no previous office-holding experience. This election raises a question frequently asked when nonaligned candidate run relatively strong races: Might one of the major party candidates (in this case the incumbent governor, Democrat Bruce King) have won in the absence of nonaligned competition? While this is impossible to ascertain, Greens pointed to polls showing that one-third of Mondragon voters would have stayed home without the Green alternative, and one-quarter would have voted for Johnson.[14] In general, some nonaligned supporters respond that the two parties are not very far apart on the issues they care about, so even if the spoiler charge is sometimes true, it matters little.

E. Oklahoma 1994

The Democratic candidate was Jack Mildren, the lieutenant governor, and the Republican, and eventual winner, was Frank Keating, who was previously a member of the Oklahoma House and Senate, an assistant secretary of the Treasury under Reagan, and general counsel of the Department of Housing and Urban Development (HUD). The independent candidate was former Democratic House member Wes Watkins, who previously ran for governor as a Democrat in 1990 and lost the primary runoff by only 2 percent. In 1994, Watkins won 23 percent of the general election vote.

Like Fasi, Watkins had a varied relationship with the two major parties. In 1996, he ran as a Republican and won a House seat covering the same southeastern Oklahoma area. "I'm the same Wes Watkins," he claimed.[15] He later said that he never lost the third district, not as a Democratic House candidate, not as a Democratic gubernatorial candidate, not as an independent gubernatorial candidate, and not as a Republican House candidate.[16] Although the third district had a 4-1 Democrat advantage in voter registration, most voters did not seem to care what party label he chose to wear.

F. Pennsylvania 1994

The Pennsylvania governor's race of 1994 featured a third-party candidate different from those discussed above. Peg Luksik ran on the

Constitutional Party line and was widely perceived as the antiabortion candidate. Although she had never held a public office, she nearly upset Pennsylvania auditor general Barbara Hafer in the 1990 Republican gubernatorial primary, winning 46 percent of the vote. In 1994, Luksik won 13 percent of the vote, and Republican U.S. representative Tom Ridge beat Democratic lieutenant governor Mark Single by 5 percent.

Many third-party candidates find it difficult to attract media coverage and establish an image, and Luksik wanted to be known for more than her views on abortion. She said, "Nobody lives in a single issue world,"[17] but this was a perception that was hard to shake. For example, the *Lancaster New Era* described her as "a grassroots activist who branded Ridge [the Republican] an unacceptable liberal on abortion and other issues,"[18] and the *AAP 1996* (1126) referred to "the independent candidacy of antiabortion Peg Luksik." This issue might have attracted the most media attention because outgoing governor Bob Casey was well known as a pro-life Democrat, but both the Democratic and the Republican candidate were pro-choice.

G. Utah 1992 and 1988

Utah experienced two nonaligned campaigns by the same person in 1992 and 1988. The first effort came about because incumbent Republican governor Norman Bangerter supported a tax increase in 1987. When the Democratic candidate, Salt Lake City mayor Ted Wilson, did not criticize the increase, voters who disapproved of the tax were left with no electoral outlet to express their frustrations. This led to a challenge by "explosives manufacturer and antitax crusader" (*AAP* 1994, 1282) Merrill Cook. The final vote was Bangerter 40 percent, Wilson 38 percent, and Cook 12 percent.

In 1992, Cook ran again as an independent. This time he nearly tripled his votes, coming in second place with 34 percent. Democrat Stewart Hanson came in third with 23 percent, and the winner was Republican businessman Michael Leavitt with 42 percent. In 1996, Cook successfully ran for the U.S. House as a Republican.

H. New York 1990

In 1990, Mario Cuomo was finishing his second term as governor. His previous campaign gave him the all-time New York gubernatorial record (65 percent), and at the start of the 1990 election year the Republicans had difficulty finding a candidate. Their eventual nominee was Pierre Rinfret, an economic consultant. Rinfret was pro-choice and the Conservative Party nominee, Herbert London, was pro-life.

In addition, according to the *AAP*, "London was knowledgeable and competent while Rinfret came on like an ignorant blowhard, complete with insults for his Republican allies."[19] In the end, Rinfret finished just 1 percent better than London (21 vs. 20 percent), while Cuomo won with a surprisingly low 54 percent.

I. Oregon 1990

Like Pennsylvania in 1994, the 1990 Oregon gubernatorial election featured a nonaligned candidate known largely for a pro-life stance. Pro-lifers had demonstrated some political power in the 1986 Oregon Senate Republican primary election, where their candidate Joe Lutz gained 42 percent against pro-choice candidate Bob Packwood, a very large margin against a sitting senator (and this was before sexual harassment allegations were made against him).

The Democratic nominee in 1990 was Barbara Roberts, the two-term secretary of state. The Republican nominee was Oregon attorney general Dave Frohnmayer. If not for the pro-life independent candidacy of Al Mobley, Frohnmayer might have won in a year when Republicans took control of the Oregon state house. The final vote gave Roberts 43 percent, Frohnmayer 40 percent, and Mobley 13 percent. Although not all anti-abortion voters are Republicans, and not all Mobley voters would necessarily have turned out in his absence, in this case the independent might have played the spoiler.

J. Arizona 1986

Arizona in 1986 was the scene of an election in which one of the major-party candidates would later be an independent candidate in the 1992 Senate campaign. This candidate was Evan Mecham, former member of the Arizona state Senate and Republican nominee for the U.S. Senate in 1962 and for governor in 1978.

The 1986 election surprised many observers because almost nothing transpired as expected. First, Bill Schultz, the leading Democratic contender (who almost defeated Senator Barry Goldwater in the 1980 general election) withdrew before the primary. Second, the candidate endorsed by outgoing governor Bruce Babbitt was defeated in the Democratic primary by superintendent of public instruction

Carolyn Warner. Third, the state senate majority leader lost in the Republican primary to Evan Mecham.

Less than a week after the primary, Schultz reentered the race as an independent candidate, and the *AAP 1998* reported that "for a while it was a genuine three-way contest in the polls" (36). The election outcome was close, with Mecham winning 40 percent, Warner placing second with 36 percent, and Schultz receiving 26 percent. As mentioned earlier, independents are sometimes blamed by supporters of the losing candidate for the success of the winner. However, the *AAP 1988* suggested that Mecham might have won a one-on-one contest with Warner, although it is of course impossible to be certain.

K. Maine 1986

The 1986 Maine gubernatorial election is only the second instance in which two independent candidates in one election each won over 10 percent of the vote (the other was Connecticut in 1994, as discussed above). The winner was Republican John McKernan, a two-term House member and former assistant minority leader of the Maine legislature. His winning vote percentage was 40 percent, while Democratic attorney general James Tierney won 30 percent.

The *AAP 1988* described the third candidate, environmentalist Sherry Huber, as a nuclear power opponent. The fourth candidate was John Menario, a former Portland city manager who was described as a conservative with most of his support from the Portland area. Each candidate received 15 percent of the vote. Because the two independents were ideologically different and received the same vote percentage, it is unlikely that their presence changed the outcome.

L. Illinois 1986

One nonaligned candidate with a good chance of winning a governorship in 1986 was Adlai Stevenson III. At first, he challenged incumbent Republican Jim Thompson with no intention of running under any label but the Democratic one. As a Democrat he had come within five thousand votes (out of over three and one-half million cast) of defeating Thompson in 1982.

When a Lyndon LaRouche supporter unexpectedly won the Democratic primary for lieutenant governor, Stevenson resigned the

Democratic nomination, formed the Illinois Solidarity Party, and collected enough signatures to qualify it for the ballot.

It is difficult to tell how well Stevenson would have done had he run as a Democrat under normal circumstances. In the end, he received 40 percent of the vote, Thompson received 53 percent, and the Democratic line received 7 percent, even though there was no candidate.

This campaign points out that some nonaligned candidates are only reluctantly so. Stevenson originally wanted to run as a major-party candidate, and Schultz in Arizona and Fasi in Hawaii may also have preferred that option. That these candidates were among the best of the losing nonaligned candidates at the polls may be no coincidence.

M. Vermont 1986

The 1986 Vermont gubernatorial contest led to an outcome decided by the state legislature. Incumbent governor Madeleine Kunin won the previous race by only two percentage points and this time attracted two challengers: Republican Peter Smith, the lieutenant governor of the state, and independent Bernard Sanders. Sanders served as the mayor of Burlington from 1981 to 1989, winning his first victory by only ten votes. The *AAP 1990* (1989, 1238) described him as possessing "long curly hair and an effervescence that recalls the late 1960s on campus." He was certainly a political original, as demonstrated by his rare interest in discussing class issues on the campaign trail.

In the 1986 gubernatorial election, he won a respectable 14 percent of the vote, while Kunin won 47 percent and Smith 38 percent. Vermont state law required the legislature to decide the outcome when no candidate won 50 percent, but this vote went uneventfully to Kunin.

N. Hawaii 1982

The 1982 contest was between Frank Fasi and incumbent governor George Ariyoshi. This was their third gubernatorial match-up, although the first two had taken place in previous Democratic primary campaigns. This time, Fasi entered the general election as an independent after losing the mayoralty.

Fasi chose a good year to run, as Ariyoshi barely survived a primary challenge from his lieutenant governor. The incumbent nevertheless won the general election with 51 percent. Fasi came in second with 29 percent and Republican D. G. "Andy" Anderson (the state senate leader) won 26 percent.

O. Alaska 1982

The final election brings us back to where we began—Alaska. This was a unique election because it was the only example of a Libertarian Party candidate winning over 10 percent of the vote. The Libertarian candidate was Dick Randolph, a state legislator of that party. He was different from many of the other candidates discussed previously because he had held elected office under a third-party label and had not recently been involved with the other major parties. He won 15 percent, which was an improvement on the 12 percent of the vote the Libertarian presidential candidate won in Alaska in 1980.

As in the New Mexico and Arizona elections, some believed that without Randolph, the Republican candidate might have won. Democrat William Sheffield won with 46 percent, while Republican Thomas Fink came up short by nine points with 37 percent. But the *AAP 1984* pointed out that Sheffield's issue positions were generally in line with those of most Alaskans. In addition, even though Alaska votes Republican on the presidential level, the voters had previously demonstrated their willingness to elect Democratic governors.

Conclusions from Gubernatorial Nonaligned Campaigns

What conclusions can be drawn from these campaigns? First, there are relatively few candidates mounting credible nonaligned efforts. Only eighteen candidates—not including the four who won (and who are discussed in a later section)—ran credible campaigns, and it is still far from easy for nonaligned candidates to succeed. The 1994 elections in Alaska and Connecticut illustrate how difficult it can be to run, even while following on the heels of previous third-party success. Coghill and Groark might have hoped that victories by Hickel and Weicker would prove helpful, but their campaigns fell short of the previous mark.

Second, most of the eighteen relatively successful candidates ran either as independents or as members of parties formed by and for themselves. Only Mondragon of the Greens (NM) and Randolph of the Libertarians (AK) ran as the nominee of a party that sought to become a national force.

Third, did these candidates serve only to elect the major-party candidate farthest from their own ideological views? The campaign of Mondragon in New Mexico, for example, might have led to the victory of the Republican candidate. The problem is that this hypothesis is very difficult to prove and may not always be true. Exit polling can help to determine whether voters for the nonaligned candidate would have turned out without the candidate, and if so, whether they would have voted for someone else, but these questions are not always asked.

The possibility of playing the spoiler may discourage nonaligned candidates. They might be reluctant to risk helping defeat the candidate nearest to them in ideology and might worry that many potential supporters would have the same concern.

Fourth, did all the nonaligned candidates expect to win? It seems clear, at least in hindsight, that some candidates were largely promoting their particular issue position, their ideology, or themselves. Although any categorization is somewhat contaminated by actual results, it appears that of the eighteen respectable defeated candidates, perhaps six had a realistic chance of victory.

The idea that candidates who either do not expect to win or do not mind losing may run is not new; Jacobson and Kernell (1981) pointed out that some candidates run with goals in mind that have nothing to do with winning the race.[20] Much of this depends on the definition of "victory" or "defeat." Mondragon in New Mexico won only 10 percent of the vote, but this was enough to qualify the Greens as a major party. Was this a victory or a defeat? Does standing up for a strongly held belief mean more than the election outcome?

In addition, some of the more competitive candidates might have preferred a major-party label. Both Stevenson of Illinois and Schultz of Arizona began their campaigns as Democrats. Stevenson felt forced to leave the ticket because of his running mate. Schultz dropped out of the race because of his daughter's poor health, and when he decided to reenter after the primaries, the independent route was the only option. In fact, these two—in addition to Fasi and Watkins—had previously run unsuccessfully for either Senate or governor as a member of a major party, in either a primary or a general election. This suggests that the strongest nonaligned candidates for higher office may be those who have lost (although sometimes by very close margins) when using the traditional route.

Senate Races

The electoral experiences of the five independent or third-party Senate candidates who received 10 percent or more of the general election vote varied considerably. Twenty-twenty hindsight suggests that only one had a realistic hope of running a competitive campaign, and that candidate may not have preferred to run as an independent.

The motives of the others were mixed, and in several cases it is not clear whether the main goal of the candidate was to win the election.

A. Alaska 1996

Alaskan senator Ted Stevens, who first assumed office in 1968, was challenged in 1996 by Democrat Theresa Obermeyer and Green Party candidate Jed Whittaker. Obermeyer had previous political experience as a member of the Anchorage school board, but she reportedly charged that Stevens was responsible for her husband's repeated failing of the Alaska bar exam, and she sometimes appeared at the senator's public events wearing black-and-white prison stripes with a ball and chain around her leg.[21] Whittaker placed second with 13 percent of the vote, while Obermeyer won 10 percent. The Democratic governor, Tony Knowles, endorsed Stevens.

B. Virginia 1994

Marshall Coleman, who was previously a Republican, might have helped defeat the GOP nominee in 1994, Iran-Contra figure Oliver North. Coleman denied this motive and claimed that he wanted to win. Intentionally or not, Coleman's candidacy gave Republicans who did not want to vote for incumbent senator Chuck Robb an alternative to North; for instance, the *AAP 1998* reported that Virginia GOP senator John Warner voted for Coleman (1442). As discussed above, one must be careful when deciding whether a nonaligned candidate played the spoiler. The fact that Coleman received 11 percent of the vote while Robb defeated North by only 3 percent suggests that Coleman may have played the spoiler in this case. If true, this meant that Coleman's candidacy helped elect the person who defeated him in the 1981 Virginia gubernatorial election.

C. Arizona 1992

Evan Mecham was elected governor of Arizona in 1986, and his time in office was controversial. As noted by the *AAP*, he rescinded the proclamation of Governor Bruce Babbitt establishing a Martin Luther King, Jr. state holiday, was the subject of recall petitions, was impeached, and was removed from office in 1988 (*AAP* 1992, 38; *AAP* 1994, 36). After losing the Republican gubernatorial primary in 1990, Mecham entered the 1992 Senate race as an independent. His opponents were incumbent Republican John McCain and Democrat Claire Sargent. Mecham, claiming that McCain was "selling out his fellow POWs" (*AAP 1994*, 40), received 11 percent of the vote, while Sargent received 32 percent.

D. Hawaii 1992

Linda Martin ran as the candidate of the Green Party in the 1992 Hawaiian Senate race. She won 14 percent of the vote against Democratic incumbent Dan Inouye and Republican challenger Rick Reed. The Greens might have hoped that this relatively strong showing (and all for only $6,687 in total expenditures) would help generate momentum for their party. If so, it did not work in the short run. They failed to run a candidate in the 1994 Senate or gubernatorial elections,[22] and although there was a Senate and gubernatorial election in 1998, a Green Party candidate contested only the gubernatorial race.

E. New York 1980

Jacob Javits was one of the last prominent liberal Republicans, but by 1980, public support for big government was on the decline, particularly within the Republican Party. Alfonse D'Amato was a relatively unknown supervisor of Hempstead, New York (Long Island), but with "the strong support of Joseph Margiotta's Nassau machine, a conservative stand on issues, and an Italian name,"[23] he defeated Javits in the Republican primary.

Instead of retiring, Javits remained in the race as the candidate of the Liberal Party, one of the small parties within the previously discussed New York "fusion" system. Even the *New York Times*, which had long supported him, urged him to drop out of the race, but he did not and received 11 percent of the vote. Democrat Liz Holtzman lost by only 80,000 votes. According to the *AAP 1984*, "Javits's candidacy on the Liberal line helped D'Amato edge out Democratic nominee Holtzman" (783). Why did Javits stay in the race? Perhaps he felt that as the incumbent he had a reasonable chance of winning, regardless of party labels. He may have also thought that his presence on the ticket would draw away enough moderate or liberal Republican voters to defeat D'Amato.

Lessons from Nonaligned Senate Elections

The first point to note is the small number of candidates who were able to gain 10 percent or more of the vote. Not only are they fewer in number than in gubernatorial elections, but they also represent a smaller percentage. While there are fifty gubernatorial elections every four years, there are about sixty-six Senate elections in the same time period.

Second, while the previous section estimated that perhaps half a dozen gubernatorial nonaligned candidates had a reasonable shot at victory, perhaps only one of the five Senate candidates (Javits) was entitled to such a hope. The other four ran for a variety of reasons, but 20/20 hindsight suggests that the realistic expectation of victory was not one of them.

Campaign Expenditures

One important question in an age of expensive media campaigns is how the campaign expenditures of independent gubernatorial candidates compare with those of the major-party candidates. Do nonaligned candidates outspend the partisans, perhaps using personal resources, or do they run low-budget efforts because there is no established network of donors for them to tap? If they run relatively expensive campaigns, then their success might come as little surprise. Chapters 2 and 3 have already demonstrated that higher campaign expenditures lead to a greater percentage of the vote. If candidates run low-budget campaigns, then we would have to test other explanations for their relative success. Some candidate expenditure figures have been described previously, but this section will take a more comprehensive approach.

In order to compare expenditures accurately, a researcher should carefully weigh which actual candidates and campaigns to compare. It would be a mistake, for example, to compare expenditures by independent candidates in open seat elections with expenditures by major-party candidates challenging incumbents.

This section will therefore compare deflated (in 1996 dollars) per capita (voting age population) expenditures of the seven 1994 open seat nonaligned gubernatorial candidates with the overall average for all eighteen 1994 general election open seat gubernatorial candidates. This is because of the twelve nonaligned open seat candidacies that received over 10 percent of the vote, seven were in 1994, one each in 1992, 1990 and 1982, and two in 1986. In addition, expenditure data were not available for some of the third-party candidates from the 1980s. The per capita figure is important to use because a similar expenditure level will have a different meaning in different states.

The gubernatorial nonaligned candidates in 1994 spent on average 85¢ per voting age person. Frank Fasi of Hawaii spent the most, with $2.98 per person, followed by Angus King with $2.04, Wes Watkins with 45¢, Eunice Groark with 38¢, Peg Luksik with 4¢, Tom Scott with 2¢, and Jack Coghill with no expenditures. There is no clear pattern here, as two candidates had high expenditures, two were below average, and three spent very little. The one nonaligned candidate who won (Angus King) placed second in expenditures. The scattershot nature of the data is illustrated by a median (0.38) that is less than one-half the mean (0.85).

These figures do not compare well with the average per person expenditures of the major-party open seat candidates of 1994 was $1.47, and the latter spent, on average, $1.47, and the median was a relatively similar $1.59. Using the average figures, this small data set suggests that major-party candidates spent about 1.7 times more than nonaligned candidates. Whether this difference is large or surprisingly small depends upon the perspective of the reader. In general, it was surprising to find two nonaligned candidates spending substantially above the major-party average. Nonaligned candidates are, of course, usually considered underdogs with little financing. But while this may be largely true in Senate elections, it is less so in gubernatorial campaigns.

Another way to examine the role of money is to check the percentage of total spending by the nonaligned. The data show that the average nonaligned candidate was responsible for just under 16 percent of all expenditures. The figures in ascending order were 0 (Coghill), 0.7 (Scott), 1.7 (Luksik), 12.0 (Groark), 23.0 (Watkins), 26.3 (Fasi), and 47.1 (King) percent. In only one case did the candidate outspend the two major-party candidates and win. This was Angus King of Maine, the wealthy former businessman and public television commentator. The second-biggest relative spender was Frank Fasi of Hawaii, the former multiterm mayor of Honolulu.

How did these expenditures compare to votes received? Although the data are too limited to permit regression analysis, table 8.1 presents preliminary data on whether nonaligned expenditures paid off at the voting booth. These numbers suggest that better-funded candidates won a greater percentage of the vote. There is a pattern whereby the greater percentage of money expended, the greater the vote percentage gained.

When interpreting these data, the reader should keep in mind the well-known "endogeneity problem" in campaign finance research. As explained in Chapter 2, this suggests that the political causality does not always lead directly from expenditures to votes, but that

Table 8.1 Expenditures and vote percentages for 1994 independent and third-party candidates

Candidate	Expenditure Percent	Vote Percent
Angus King (ME)	47.1	35
Frank Fasi (HI)	26.3	31
Wes Watkins (OK)	23.0	24
Eunice Groark (CT)	12.0	19
Peg Luksik (PA)	1.7	13
Tom Scott (CT)	0.67	11
Jack Coghill (AK)	0	13

Source: Newspaper reports.

candidates who are expected to do better may receive more money. Indeed, King was well known and wealthy, and Fasi and Watkins were the most politically experienced candidates, so they might have been expected by political elites to do better than average for nonaligned candidates.

So, although limited by the low number of observations, these data suggest that the dynamics of third-party candidacies include the familiar combination of expenditures and expectations that the major-party candidates experience.

Time Trends for Gubernatorial and Senate Campaigns

One important question is whether nonaligned candidacies have gained more support over time. A large number of candidacies means little unless the candidates receive the support of voters. Therefore, to look at just the total number of nonaligned candidates would result in incomplete data.

Figure 8.1 therefore collapses the number of candidates and the support they received into one aggregate measure of the overall success of nonaligned candidates from 1980 to 1996. Each bar represents the total percentage vote received by third-party and independent candidates for the states that held gubernatorial elections in a given year. For example, if twenty states held a gubernatorial election in one particular year , and each such election had one nonaligned candidate running, and each such candidate received 10 percent of the vote, then the figure on the Y-axis (left hand side of the

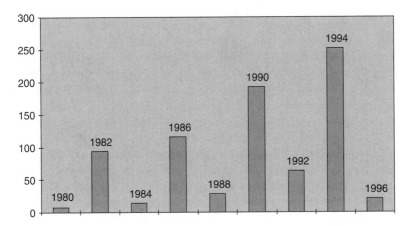

Figure 8.1 Total gubernatorial nonaligned percentage vote: 1980–1996

chart) would be 200 for that year.[24] Larger numbers over time could mean more minor nonaligned candidates or just a few more very successful ones, but in both cases it would represent declining support for the two major parties.

The graph therefore treats the state as the unit of observation. One alternative is to simply add up the number of individual votes for nonaligned candidates for each year, but this would be affected by the size of the states where such candidates ran. This method would suggest stronger popular support in a particular election cycle if a minor-party candidate ran poorly in California than if one ran strongly in Maine.

Elections held during midterm election years and presidential election years should not be compared with each other, because most states have moved their elections to the quieter midterm years. Not only does this give political actors and voters more time to focus on state elections, but it also helps prevent "contamination" of state elections by presidential campaigns and activists. One must therefore separately compare the 1980, 1984, 1988, 1992, and 1996 elections and then the 1982, 1986, 1990, and 1994 contests.

The results show that in both midterm and presidential election years there has been a steep increase in the total gubernatorial nonaligned vote percentage. The one exception is 1996, which registers a decline from 1992. Overall, the two major parties are slightly less secure each year in gubernatorial elections.

How does this compare with Senate elections? Perhaps this phenomenon is not unique to gubernatorial elections but is taking place

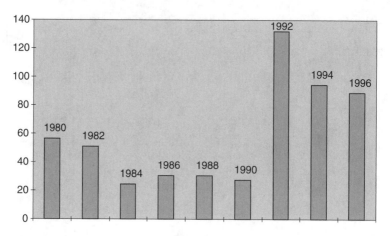

Figure 8.2   Total Senate nonaligned percentage vote: 1980–1996

across both major statewide elections. Figure 8.2 uses the same approach and covers the same time period as figure 8.1.[25]

Unlike figure 8.1, there is no meaningful pattern in these data. The nonaligned vote is not moving steadily upward in either midterm or incumbent elections, and while the vote is higher toward the end of the time frame than in the beginning, there is no clear explanation for the dip in the middle. This is not the first time in this book that important differences have been shown to exist between gubernatorial and Senate elections, and once again, we see the importance of examining these two statewide elections separately. Whether such patterns continue in subsequent election years is a question for future researchers to investigate.

Nonaligned Winners: Weicker, King, Ventura, and Hickel

This section will examine the four candidates who beat the odds to win a gubernatorial election. The discussion will be relatively brief, outlining their careers, the political context of the election, and their experiences with the two major parties and the other candidates.

A. Lowell Weicker

Weicker served as a four-term Republican senator from 1971 to 1989, and before that he was the first selectman of Greenwich, a member of the Connecticut legislature, and a U.S. Representative.

The *AAP 1988* (203) described him as "very much a maverick and a loner in Washington . . . [possessing] an aggressive, independent Republicanism, which gives him high marks from organized labor and Common Cause." Weicker even titled his autobiography "Maverick," defining the word on the front cover as "An independent individual who does not go along with a group or party."

In 1988, he was narrowly defeated by Democrat Joseph Lieberman, the attorney general of Connecticut. He blamed his loss on the right wing of the Republican Party (Weicker 1995, 176), as he did relatively well among Democrats and independents (169). In the 1990 gubernatorial elections, he skipped the GOP primary altogether and ran as the candidate of ACP. He said he had "toyed with third-party possibilities for years, ever since the Republicans started ostracizing me" (183), and now he had his chance.

He faced two House members: Republican John Rowland and Democrat Bruce Morrison. On election day, he won with 40 percent, while Rowland won 37 and Morrison trailed with 21 percent. Why did he win? One possible answer is that he remained popular with the public but lost in 1988 because "I ended up running a sloppy, lazy campaign . . . I didn't campaign physically. I disregarded the one-on-one style that had been so successful" (Weicker 1995, 176).

B. Angus King

Before 1994, Angus King had never run for political office. Although he worked as an aide to Democratic senator William Hathaway from 1972 to 1975 and considered a run for Congress in 1986 as a Democrat,[26] his political opinions were difficult to classify. In his book *Making a Difference* he wrote, "It's certainly true that my political philosophy has evolved over the years—from what would generally be called more liberal to more conservative—but I don't apologize for that, because the evolution was simply the result of experience."[27] He also said, "If I have to have a label, I guess it would [be] as a compassionate pragmatist."[28]

He used language common to candidates running "outsider" campaigns. For example, he said, "I'm not really interested in a political career. I just want the state to succeed."[29] He also said that his "secret weapon" for being a successful governor would be his disinterest in the job "as a career or to set myself up to run for anything else, which means I don't need the credit or the ego points."[30]

His support did not come from any particular sector of Maine society. An exit poll showed that "his support varied little by age, sex, ideology, education and income. He was backed by supporters of term limits and opponents . . . [and] received equal support from backers of all three major 1992 presidential candidates."[31]

Although he had never run for office, he was not without politically relevant resources. First, he was independently wealthy, having sold Northeast Energy Management Inc. for $8 million in 1994.[32] Second, he was well known in a nonpartisan way, having hosted a Maine Public Television show—*Maine Watch*—for eighteen years.

King's major opponent was Democrat Joseph Brennan, the governor from 1978 to 1986. The Republican nominee was Susan Collins, an aide to Senator William Cohen. An early September poll showed Brennan with 37 percent, King with 29 percent, and Collins with 18 percent,[33] but polls by early November showed Brennan and King nearly tied, with Collins a distant third.[34] In the end, King won by less than eight thousand votes (35 to 34 percent), while Collins received 23 percent and a Green Party candidate won 6 percent.[35]

Why did he win? King thought that his victory was part of the national dissatisfaction with partisan politics that had led to the defeat of incumbents almost everywhere. Former governor Brennan agreed that voters were "somewhat disillusioned with established political figures, and certainly I would come within that definition." King also thought that his pro-business and antibureaucrat platform had helped him.[36]

C. Walter Hickel

The 1990 Alaska gubernatorial race was one of two elections that year that put a third-party candidate into the highest state office. Walter Hickel was first elected governor as a Republican (1966–1967), was appointed to the cabinet by Richard Nixon, and ran unsuccessfully in GOP gubernatorial primaries in 1974, 1978, and 1986. In 1990, he entered the gubernatorial race in an unusual way. On the day of the filing deadline for the AIP gubernatorial ticket, John Lindauer and Jerry Ward resigned their spots on the ticket in favor of Hickel and Jack Coghill (who until that day was the running mate for the GOP candidate).

Hickel's Republican opponent was Arliss Sturgulewski, who had served in the Anchorage Assembly and subsequently won four terms in the state Senate.[41] She first ran for governor in 1986, losing by 4 percent to Steve Cowper. In the 1986 GOP primary, she beat Walter

Hickel. The Democratic candidate in 1990 was Tony Knowles, a former two-term mayor of Anchorage. This was Knowles' first run for statewide office.

Were Hickel and Coghill supportive of the stands of the AIP, and did they have much prior involvement with it? According to the *Seattle Times,*

> Hickel is running with the Alaskan Independence Party, a fringe group advocating that the 49th state declare itself a sovereign nation. But he's not a separatist; he's an opportunist: the Independence Party was the only 11th-hour ticket to the general election.[42]

Several reasons have been advanced for why Hickel won, ranging from voter populism, anti-incumbency, last-minute entry to avoid campaign negativity, and the effective use of polling and focus groups. One quantifiable factor is that he was able to raise a considerable amount of money in a relatively short period of time. Reports from the Alaska Public Offices Commission showed that Knowles raised $1,081,000, Sturgulewski raised $1,030,000, and Hickel raised $804,000.[43] When these figures are broken down by dollars per day of active campaigning, Hickel's short campaign allowed him to spend almost $17,000 a day, while his opponents each averaged less than $3,000 a day.[44] Of this money, Hickel himself contributed $615,000.

How did his lieutenant governor and the AIP fare in the next election? In that election, as described elsewhere in the chapter, the Democrat and Republican candidates nearly tied and Coghill won 13 percent. Hickel may have shaken up the political establishment in 1990, but by 1994, the major parties were again vigorously contesting gubernatorial elections.

D. Jesse Ventura

Unlike the other three governors discussed in this chapter, Jesse Ventura has attracted a great deal of national attention. Much has been written about him in the media, largely because of his colorful character and unusual background.

Ventura was the nominee of the Reform Party and a surprise general election winner. He beat two well-known candidates: the Republican was St. Paul mayor Norm Coleman, a former Democrat, and the Democrat (DFL) was Attorney General Hubert "Skip" Humphrey III, who possessed one of Minnesota's most famous political names. Ventura's campaign reportedly activated many voters with little previous electoral involvement and used relatively new campaign tactics such as soliciting campaign contributions through a website. Although he polled only 10 percent after the major-party nominating conventions, he eventually won with a 37 percent plurality; Coleman received 34 percent and Humphrey 28 percent.

Ventura joined the U.S. Navy after high school and became a SEAL, then gained a national following as professional wrestler Jesse "The Body" Ventura.[37] He subsequently appeared in the movies *Predator* and *The Running Man*, both starring Arnold Schwarzenegger. Ventura did gain some political experience from 1991 to 1995 as the mayor of Brooklyn Park, a sixty-thousand person middle-income Minneapolis suburb. He was also campaign chair of the Reform Party's candidate for U.S. Senate in 1996.

A parallel can even be made between Ventura's and Ronald Reagan's paths to the governorship. Both gained fame through the entertainment business. When Reagan left Hollywood, he spent years as a professional speaker. He toured the nation as a public relations personality for the GE corporation, which largely consisted of speaking before GE employees, thereby enabling him to hone his speaking and dramatic style. In a similar vein, Ventura retired from wrestling in the mid-1980s and concentrated on the speaking profession. He first became an announcer for professional wrestling and afterward hosted a radio talk show in Minneapolis. Unlike Reagan, Ventura would be coded in most quantitative political science research as a "quality candidate" because he held the prior elected office of mayor.

Few observers have a clear explanation of why he won, although many post hoc explanations have been advanced. These include his creative advertising, call for a tax cut, willingness to speak about controversial issues, an attentive media, the negative tone of the two major-party candidates, their lack of negativity toward Ventura, and the populist streak in Minnesota culture. From the political science perspective, however, Ventura might have been able to compete because he possessed high name recognition and politically relevant skills. As the state director of the Minnesota Democratic Party afterward said, "If you're up against a third-party candidate with name recognition and media skills, you'd better take them seriously, even if they're short of money" (Beiler 1999a, 121). According to Tom Kelley, communications director for the Democrats, "He had an asset that costs a lot of money: name ID and a personality."[38]

Although Ventura was outspent substantially, accounting for only 12.7 percent of expenditures, money did play a role in his victory. This is because Minnesota has a public financing system whereby candidates receive matching funds from the state if they promise to limit their overall expenditures. According to the *Star-Tribune* (MN), the public money

> helped even the odds at a critical time. After securing a loan that would be repaid by the subsidies, Ventura was able to compete on TV airwaves in the final days, and his imaginative TV spots undoubtedly helped put him over the top.[39]

Ventura therefore had some of the key characteristics common to traditional political candidates, a point often overlooked in the rush to treat him as sui generis. What was not relevant to his victory was financial support from the Reform Party. He raised almost no money from the party, and overall it was outspent 900 to 1 in Minnesota by the Republicans and Democrats. Ventura later claimed that the party had nothing to do with his victory: "They did nothing to help me to get elected, [and] they probably didn't support me in the first place anyway."[40]

Conclusions

This last section will draw lessons from the winners and the respectable losers. Then it will discuss the role of money in elections and the time trends for nonaligned candidacies. Comparisons with Senate elections are then made, followed by an overview of the future of independent and third-party efforts.

An important question is why so many nonaligned candidates choose gubernatorial elections. One potential answer is the executive nature of the office. If this were true, we would expect presidential elections to see similar efforts. In fact, a number of presidential elections in the 1990s have seen important third-party and independent efforts, which supports the theory that gubernatorial and presidential campaigns exhibit many of the same dynamics.

A. The Winners

First, most of the candidates who won or did relatively well had significant previous experience with one of the major parties. Both Lowell Weicker and Walter Hickel, for instance, had been elected to major statewide offices as Republicans. Hickel was first elected governor in 1966 as a Republican, and he subsequently served as Richard Nixon's secretary of the interior. Weicker served for twenty years in the House and Senate as a Republican.

For both candidates there were indicators that suggested a limit to party loyalty. In the words of the *Associated Press,* "Both Weicker and Hickel are maverick Republicans who, for years, were thorns in the side of a Republican establishment, Weicker as a liberal, Hickel as a conservative."[45]

One conclusion to draw from these experiences is that significant politically relevant resources are important to a nonaligned campaign. Whether this is prior electoral experience (Hickel and Weicker), an independent source of wealth (Hickel, Weicker, and King),[46] being a well-known persona outside of politics (Ventura and King), a state public financing system (Ventura), or best yet a combination of the above, there are no models of success without at least one of the four. Of course, this is barely different from the requirements for partisan office seekers, so perhaps what makes good party candidates also makes good nonparty candidates. Nonaligned candidates cannot merely hope that the public will arise and sweep them into office; they must run campaigns and convince voters just as the major-party candidates do.

Another explanation for the success of nonaligned candidates is that the cultures of Maine, Alaska, Minnesota, and, to a lesser extent, Connecticut, may be well suited for independent candidates. When trying to explain the victory of Angus King, the *Associated Press* reported that "Maine has frequently looked with favor on non-party candidates."[47] And in fact it has. Starting with the 1974 victory by independent James Longley, independent gubernatorial candidates have done well in all subsequent elections except in 1982. Herman Frankland won 17.8 percent in 1978; Huber and Menario, as discussed above, won a combined 30 percent in 1986; Andrew Adam won 9.3 percent in 1990; and of course, King won 35.4 in 1994 (along with Green Party candidate Jonathan Carter's 6.4 percent).

A similar political culture appeared to exist in Alaska during the same time period. The *Seattle Times* wrote that "Alaskans value political independence even more than four-wheel-drive vehicles or tickets to Hawaii in January,"[48] and nonaligned candidates have done well there. In 1974, AIP founder Joe Vogler won 5 percent of the vote; then Walter Hickel won 26.4 percent as a write-in candidate, and Tom Kelly received 12.3 percent as an independent in 1978; Libertarian Richard Randolph received 14.9 percent in 1982 (as discussed above); Joe Vogler received just over 5.6 percent in 1986; and then Hickel won the race in 1990 and Coghill received 13 percent in 1994.

The political culture of Minnesota is one of the main explanations analysts have used to explain Ventura's victory. "Ventura exploited the state's historical populism, which in the past has had both a right-wing and a left-wing character," reported one observer.[49] Although there is no long, nonaligned candidate history in Connecticut, *ABC News* called Connecticut "a stubbornly independent state that offers equally fertile ground for Republicans, Democrats, and third-party candidates . . . Connecticut has a habit of picking outsiders. The state went for Jerry Brown in the 1992 Democratic primary, and Gary Hart in 1984."[50]

It is difficult to define culture and understand how it affects politics. Voter records indicate that a large number of people in these states are willing to consider candidates without major-party affiliation. In 1990, 58 percent of Alaskan voters were registered with minor parties or were unaffiliated, along with 37 percent of Maine voters and 34 percent of Connecticut voters—percentages far higher than the average of 17 in the other states.[51] The Perot vote in 1992 also reveals support for nonaligned candidates. Alaska gave him 28 percent, Connecticut 22 percent, Maine 30 percent, and Minnesota 24 percent (an average of 26 percent for the four states), while the average for the other states was about 18 percent.

One problem with the cultural arguments is that they have a strong post hoc quality. Nobody predicted that Minnesota's populist history would help Ventura before his election, but many have turned to this explanation in the aftermath. The same is true for the other elections. Nonaligned candidates are often discounted for much of their campaigns, but after election day, reporters and commentators are forced to explain their victories. Rather than write a chapter such as this and compare and contrast candidacies, it is easier to argue that the unique culture of a state paved the way.

A third potential explanation for the four gubernatorial victories is based on the observation that the significance of a win depends partly on formal gubernatorial powers. Some governors are given less power by their state constitutions than are others, so perhaps voters and political and media elites are more willing to support nonaligned candidacies in states where their power is limited. If voters and elites are only gradually becoming comfortable with nonaligned elected officials in powerful positions, then they might be more willing to support them where they can do the least harm. This is reminiscent of Winger's (1997, 166) finding of the "tendency of voters to be more generous with their votes for minor party candidates for less important statewide office."

Beyle (1990) created a ranking of gubernatorial power based on features such as veto power, budget-making power, appointive power, and other factors. Alaska received an aggregate power score of 23, Connecticut 24, Maine 19, and Minnesota 25. The average score for all American states was 22. This comparison does not indicate that the governors of these four states are particularly weak, so the differential power thesis is not applicable here.[52]

B. The Respectable Losers

Of the respectable gubernatorial losers, all the candidates with the best chance of winning had strong previous partisan ties, and two might have preferred to run under a major-party label. Adlai Stevenson III in fact won the Democratic gubernatorial primary but felt compelled to resign the nomination. The candidate with the second-best chance of winning was probably Bill Schultz in Arizona, who ran for Senate in 1980 as a Democrat and came within one percentage point of defeating Barry Goldwater. Schultz dropped out of the Democratic primary in 1986 because of a family illness, and when he changed his mind and reentered the race, he could only run as an independent. Wes Watkins of Oklahoma previously served as a Democratic member of the House and ran in the Democratic primary for governor in 1990.

A further conclusion is that parties created as personal vehicles by well-known politicians do not often survive as meaningful political forces without the founder. Lowell Weicker set up ACP for his successful 1990 gubernatorial run, but his lieutenant governor was unable to use it successfully in 1994. It lost major-party status in 1994, and no candidate entered the 1998 contest on this line. Fasi of Hawaii, who created the BP for his 1994 campaign for governor, later ran unsuccessfully in the Republican gubernatorial primary in 1998. The BP merged with another party in 1997.

Returning to the issue of culture, four of the five respectable non-aligned Senate campaigns took place in states that had a successful or respectable gubernatorial nonaligned candidate. Alaska, Arizona, Hawaii, and New York all seem to be states relatively hospitable to a non-major-party effort. Of course, a number of states featured a non-aligned gubernatorial campaign without a Senate equivalent, so this point has its limitations.

Another problem with the culture argument is that the states where nonaligned candidates have done well do not appear to have much in common. Winger (1997) similarly found no obvious regional factor when he analyzed the eighteen states where minor parties had won some sort of election since 1945 (his analysis excluded independent candidacies). He did note that state ballot access laws "distinguish the eighteen states with minor party success from the other thirty-three states" (162). This could also apply to the states under consideration here. One might reasonably assume that states with lenient/strict third-party access laws have lenient/strict independent access laws. But a comparison of his state codings of strict/moderate/lenient to the states with strong nonaligned gubernatorial and Senate candidacies revealed no clear correlation.

It is also important to note that the candidates—winners and losers—did not appear to have any particular themes or issues in common. While they may all have taken advantage of voter dyspepsia over "career politicians" and "government as usual," their candidacies had largely different rationales. This has been noted previously by some observers. As University of Virginia historian Michael Holt said after the 1990 elections, "I don't think you're talking about a third party. When you have independent candidates it's precisely that: they're kind of lone rangers for one office."[53]

C. Time Trends

Even if there is no single underlying theme to their campaigns, there is a time trend from 1980 to 1996 favoring nonaligned gubernatorial candidates. The four winners ran in the 1990s, as did ten of the eighteen "moral victors." Of the six candidates in the 1980s, one was from 1988, three were from 1986, and two were from 1982. In other words, strong nonaligned campaigns were being run outside the two-party system with increasing frequency.

The data from figure 8.1 also corroborate the observation that the two major parties were finding less success over time in both presidential election and midterm election years, while figure 8.2 points out that this was not true in Senate elections. This shows once again how gubernatorial and Senate elections do not necessarily have the same electoral dynamics.

D. Campaign Expenditures

The perennial electoral topic of campaign finance was also investigated in gubernatorial elections. Table 8.1 shows that the rankings of spending percentage and vote percentage generally match. The limited number of observations, however, does not allow for definitive conclusions on the role of money in nonaligned campaigns.

Several of the successful candidates had significant personal funds. Walter Hickel was able to self-finance much of his campaign, as noted previously. Angus King of Maine became wealthy in January of 1994 through the sale of his energy conservation business. Lowell Weicker, whose grandfather started the Squibb pharmaceutical business, was frequently described as wealthy. Money was less of a concern for Jesse Ventura than for many other nonaligned candidates because of Minnesota's campaign finance system, whereby candidates receive public matching funds in exchange for an expenditure ceiling. Not only did this provide needed funds for Ventura during the critical final days of the campaign, it also limited his opponents to $2.1 million each. Taken together, this suggests that at this stage in the development of nonaligned politics, access to money, as well as the name recognition money is often used to buy, may be necessary for nonaligned success.

E. Comparisons with Senate Elections

Why did more nonaligned candidates either win or run respectable races in elections for governor than in elections to the Senate? The explanation cannot be state laws on party formation and ballot qualification: these laws govern Senate and gubernatorial candidates equally and therefore provide no advantage (or more accurately, no disadvantage) to either.[54]

A better explanation may lie in the nature of the two jobs; governors, like presidents, are the chief executives of their states, while senators are just one of a hundred colleagues (and one of 535 voting members of Congress). This point will be explored more fully below.

F. Governors and Presidents: The Executive Connection

As noted at the start of the chapter, the presence of nonaligned candidates in gubernatorial elections calls to mind their increasing involvement in presidential contests in the 1990s. In fact, Bill Clinton won both his elections with an Electoral College majority but only a popular plurality owing to Ross Perot's candidacy. Since 1980, only the 1984, 1988, and 2004 elections did not feature a credible nonaligned candidate. Although none of the post-1980 third-party presidential candidates won Electoral College votes, some observers believe that the outcome of the 1992 election was changed by Perot's candidacy (although most political scientists disagree), and it is likely that the 2000 outcome was influenced by the Green Party. In addition, the frequent presence of three choices for chief executive on the ballot may gradually increase voter willingness to consider nonaligned candidates at all levels of government. The nonaligned gubernatorial candidates of today often resemble their presidential colleagues. Rosenstone, Behr, and Lazarus (1996, 81) found that

> although the third parties of the 1800s closely resembled the major parties, the same cannot be said for those of the twentieth century. The most prominent movements of the 1900s . . . are all more accurately labeled independent campaigns than political parties. None had any real organization district from the candidate's own following, and for most of them the "party" would not have existed without the candidate.

This mirrors gubernatorial elections, where the modern nonaligned candidate runs not as the herald of an established third-party but as either an independent or the representative of his or her own personal party. Sometimes it is more convenient to run under a party label, but in no cases does a candidate build a mass party.

Successful nonaligned gubernatorial candidates do not run on single-issue platforms; the goods sold by the campaign are largely the candidates themselves. They may emphasize or dodge particular issues in their campaign, but this is no different from the behavior of major-party candidates.

Why do these people try for executive offices and only rarely for the Senate? One simple reason is that if successful, a nonaligned candidate can accomplish more as the single executive of a state than as one of a hundred senators in a complex legislative system.

The governor is the central political figure in a state. Just as the media spotlight in Washington focuses largely on the president, state media similarly pay close attention to the activities and opinions of the governor. The governor can also influence policy in a variety of arenas, from education reform to health care to taxation. These powers have significantly grown in the last few decades, as have the overall powers of state government. If state governments are indeed the "laboratories of democracy," then the governor is the chief scientist.

Aspiring nonaligned politicians may also believe that their odds of winning an executive office are higher than winning legislative office. Voters may have an intuitive understanding that an executive has the potential to change state or national political dynamics, or to "shake things up," while one senator will have a much less clear impact. This means that some voters may see a nonaligned executive vote as less likely to be "wasted" than a nonaligned legislative vote.[55]

G. The Future

What does the future hold for nonaligned candidates, particularly for prospective governors? One trend worth noting is that ballot access laws are gradually becoming less restrictive, either because the states have voluntarily lowered the bar or because they have been ordered to do so by the courts. Beck (1997) pointed out that recent Supreme Court decisions have overturned some state party regulations and simplified ballot access for independent and third-party candidates.[56] The court appears to find state regulation of electoral activities far less compelling than the value of an open electoral system, and Beck suggests that many current state laws might be overturned if challenged. This suggests that third-party and independent candidates are less hindered today than at any point in recent history, which perhaps helps to explain why successful and relatively successful nonaligned gubernatorial candidacies increased during the time period of this study (although it does not explain the lack of a trend in Senate elections).

Ultimately, the future is in the hands of the voters *and* in the perception of the voters by political elites. While some scholars have argued that voters increasingly find parties irrelevant (Wattenberg 1986), others have responded that the death of partisanship is greatly exaggerated (Keith et al. 1992). Not only does this have direct implications for elections, but there are indirect effects as well. The beliefs of candidates and other political actors (such as interest groups, consultants, and individual donors) about public support for the two major parties will likely have an effect on how well nonaligned candidates will do.

This parallels the theories of Jacobson and Kernell (1983), who pointed out the role of self-fulfilling prophecies in congressional elections. If strong potential candidates sense a bad electoral year for their party, they may choose not to run. With fewer quality candidates in the trenches, the party will lose more elections. While it may appear that the candidates were correct, the sum of their individual decisions may have contributed to the overall, national outcome.

In the gubernatorial context, if enough candidates with access to campaign resources (whether money or name recognition) decide that nonaligned candidacies are not only viable but under some circumstances advantageous, then more nonaligned candidates will win. If they decide that running outside of the two major parties sharply reduces the odds of victory, then strong nonaligned candidates will run less often and consequently win less often.

9

Conclusions

The introduction to this book suggests that the study of gubernatorial elections is important for several reasons. First, it helps us understand the dynamics that bring men and women into the increasingly powerful job of governor. Because governors are the most powerful political actors in their states; because the states have gained significant power vis-à-vis the national government; and because states have become more innovative in the policy arena, we care more about them now than at any other time in the postwar period.

The first section of this conclusion will therefore summarize the gubernatorial campaign dynamics discussed in the preceding chapters. It will cover the subjects of campaign expenditures, issue voting, candidate quality, voter turnout, political ambition, political competitiveness, and third-party and independent candidacies. As the individual chapters have pointed out, there has been relatively little research on these topics at the state level, and this section will discuss what the book has uncovered.

Second, the book points out that gubernatorial election dynamics differ from those of Senate elections, the other major statewide office. Relatively little comparative research on elections has been done across American political institutions, and the few existing studies largely compare Senate and House elections. Both offices are part of the legislative branch of government, which means that our quantitative knowledge about elections is largely intra-institutional. This book helps to address this imbalance by discussing to what degree and why these two statewide elections differ, and it does so in two ways. Three chapters directly collect and compare gubernatorial and Senate data, and several chapters compare their findings with parallel work in the Senate elections field. This constitutes the most comprehensive look at how dynamics for these two high-profile offices compare.

Third, this book argues that the executive nature of gubernatorial elections provides a theoretical explanation for the differences between gubernatorial and Senate elections, and the third section in this chapter therefore brings together the comparisons made between gubernatorial and presidential elections. As will be seen, the three most unique features of gubernatorial campaigns are best viewed through the lens of executive office. Little research has examined how the gubernatorial and presidential offices compare electorally, despite their similar placement in their respective political systems. Governors and presidents are both chief executives who must also work with a legislature, oversee a bureaucracy they only partially control, possess the best "bully pulpit" in their milieu,[1] and undergo significant media scrutiny. In other ways, they differ: the president of the United States works on an international stage, while governors seldom deal with any power more foreign than Washington, D.C. But the similarities between them well outweigh the differences and allow for meaningful comparisons.

The book therefore enables us to better understand which dynamics are unique to gubernatorial elections, which are common to statewide elections, and which are best explained by the executive nature of the office.

The Dynamics of Gubernatorial Campaigns

The first question addressed in this book is the long-standing debate over how candidate expenditures affect election outcomes. There has been much research conducted on whether the money spent by congressional incumbents affects outcomes, but there has been very little work on gubernatorial expenditures. As discussed in Chapter 2, early congressional research found no relationship between money spent and votes received.[2] The explanation was that incumbents have so many advantages over challengers, such as high name recognition and government-provided staffing and communication resources, that expenditures did not provide any extra electoral benefit.[3]

This theory was counterintuitive to many political professionals, but if proven true it would have had an impact on how campaigns are conducted. Such a finding would also have implications for campaign finance reform proposals at the state level. Proposals featuring incentives for incumbents to voluntarily lower their spending could be shelved, while plans providing additional resources to challengers would have more promise.

Recent congressional research has found that incumbent and challenger spending both matter (Gerber 1998; Ansolabehere and Snyder 1995), and Chapters 2 and 3 adopt their methodological approach. The conclusion is similarly that incumbents do not spend money fruitlessly; their expenditures have at least as much consequence as challenger spending. This not only adds to our knowledge of gubernatorial elections but also contributes to the development of a general understanding of the role of money in campaigns across political institutions.

The next question is whether a candidate's prior political experience affects electoral results. The regressions in Chapters 2 and 3 concluded that no particular political experience is associated with increased voter support. In addition, the Green and Krasno (1988) aggregate challenger measure was not associated with expenditures. This indicates that previous political experience does not play an important role in gubernatorial elections.

Another key electoral issue is how changes in economic and social conditions affect the vote. If governors are not held accountable for any declines in socioeconomic conditions, nor rewarded for improvements, then they will have less incentive to work for the best interests of their constituents. Of particular importance is the role of noneconomic changes, which have not been extensively investigated by the retrospective voting literature.

Chapter 3 was therefore unique among retrospective research because it examined such changes, specifically changes in the state crime rate and SAT scores. It found that incumbents were punished by the voters when the state crime rate increased, but not when any other factor changed. Tidmarch, Hyman, and Sorkin (1984) found that issues commonly thought to be more susceptible to state control, such as crime and education, were more likely to be discussed in gubernatorial election coverage. It therefore makes sense that voters would hold governors responsible for one of these state factors. While SAT scores were not a significant factor in this chapter, clear proxies for educational achievement are difficult to find.[4]

Open seat candidates, on the other hand, do not have to worry about state-level factors. Instead, they are affected by national-level political and economic conditions. Specifically, if open seat candidates are of the same party as the president, they should expect to receive fewer votes. In addition, open seat candidates of the same party as the president should expect to receive fewer votes when the national unemployment rate increases. In other words, open seat elections take on some of the characteristics of a national referendum on the president.[5]

Chapters 2 and 3 provide some additional insights into gubernatorial campaigns. First, incumbents who do poorly in primary elections are more likely, ceteris paribus, to receive fewer votes in the general election. This fits well with previous research on divided primaries, although the literature is split on whether this dynamic is at work in Senate elections as well. The regressions also show that challengers or open seat candidates who are famous or possess high name recognition do not receive a larger vote share than those who begin without this supposed advantage.

While scandals are often thought to hurt candidates, this does not apply to gubernatorial elections. Scandals involving incumbents do not appear to affect the vote, while there were not enough scandals in open seat elections to justify the inclusion of the variable. Perhaps incumbents are so well known and have such an established record on the issues that scandals either come as no surprise or are outweighed by other factors in the vote decision.

Another important electoral dynamic is voter turnout. Chapter 4 investigated the effect of social and economic changes on turnout and found that in incumbent campaigns an increase in the state tax rate is associated with higher turnout. In open seat races, increases in state unemployment and national per capita income increased turnout. We therefore see that bad news can spur turnout in both types of elections, and while incumbent races are affected by a state factor, open seat races are affected by a national factor (although in an unexpected direction).

Chapter 4 also showed that in incumbent elections, the ratio of money spent by the higher spender to money spent by the lower spender was negatively associated with turnout: the higher the ratio, the lower the turnout. This is the same variable used in Chapter 7 to measure electoral intensity, which suggests that less-intense elections draw fewer voters to the polls in addition to providing voters with less information about the challenger (Westlye 1991). Because low turnout often benefits incumbents, low-intensity campaigns can therefore hurt challengers in multiple ways.

In open seat elections, it is the total amount of money spent that increases turnout, not the ratio. Therefore, it is not the intensity that matters but the amount of political "noise" an election generates. This makes sense because open seat elections generally attract more attention than do incumbent contests. Open seat elections have a higher baseline of public awareness, so the intensity level may not lead to significantly greater public awareness or interest in the contest.

One of the unique features of gubernatorial elections is that independent and third-party candidates sometimes win or do well. While the media, the public, and scholars have shown much interest in "nonaligned" candidates in presidential elections , no comprehensive examination of this phenomenon in subpresidential contests has been attempted. Chapter 8 therefore studied the campaigns of candidates who won as well as of those who did relatively well (i.e., those who received 10 percent or more of the general election vote) in gubernatorial elections.

Three candidates without major-party affiliation won between 1980 and 1996, and there was an additional winner in 1998. While Angus King, Lowell Weicker, and Walter Hickel were not household names, Jesse Ventura's fame helped to increase the visibility of nonaligned candidates among voters (and perhaps nonvoters).

Chapter 8 noted some similarities among these nonaligned governors. Most importantly, they were all helped in their campaigns by prior politically relevant experiences. Hickel was a former governor, Weicker a former senator, and King was a wealthy and well-known public television host. While Ventura's background set him apart, he was not without resources. Although he first gained name recognition through professional wrestling as Jesse "The Body" Ventura, the source of his fame may have mattered less than the fact. He had also been the mayor of a Minneapolis suburb, the host of a radio show, and campaign chair for a 1996 Reform Party Senate candidate—experiences that are not often mentioned in popular accounts.

Political ambition is another key topic in electoral studies. It is important to know what factors lead to the emergence of quality candidates—particularly challengers to incumbents—and whether such candidates have any special effect on the outcome. Two chapters in this book directly examined these questions and several others touched on them. Chapters 5 and 6 examined the causes and consequences of quality challenger emergence in incumbent elections; Chapters 2 and 3 showed whether particular political backgrounds led to higher vote percentages in incumbent and open seat elections.

The data showed that the emergence of high-quality candidates in gubernatorial elections is not entirely random, as there are four factors associated with the decision to run (out of twenty tested). A higher national unemployment rate, a Republican incumbent, state political competition, and larger state size are associated with higher-quality challengers to incumbent governors. On the other hand, several seemingly important factors were not involved, such as the vulnerability of the incumbent, state party strength, whether it was a midterm year and the governor was of the same party as the president, and state economic and social change factors. In addition, the second part of Chapter 5 showed that the challenger quality variable was not associated with challenger expenditures. This once again suggests the limited role of candidate political experience in gubernatorial elections.

There is additional evidence supporting this general point. Chapters 2 and 3 showed that the previous political office of candidates in incumbent and open seat elections did not help these challengers do better on election day. Furthermore, Chapter 7 revealed that the aggregate challenger quality variable was not correlated with campaign intensity. This adds to the conclusion that candidate quality is not an important force in gubernatorial elections. As discussed below, Krasno (1994) and Abramowitz and Segal (1992) found that higher-quality challengers were more likely to run stronger campaigns against House and Senate incumbents.

Chapter 6 discussed the structural and personal factors that influence the decision of members of the U.S. House of Representatives to run for governor. House members were analyzed because they are the only politicians comprehensively studied in the political ambition literature, possibly the most important officeholders below governor and senator, and are found in every state. The data showed that only one variable was clearly associated with the decision to run for governor. The models also show that most of the factors determining ambition for the Senate do not apply in the gubernatorial context. This means that ambition for the two offices is structured differently.

There are several other conclusions that involve findings from different chapters. The first involves the role of state political competition. Chapter 4 found that turnout was positively associated with the level of recent state political competition. This is specified as the Holbrook and Van Dunk (1993) measure, which is based on state legislative election returns and confirms the argument that competitive environments affect turnout. Holbrook and Van Dunk (1993) pointed out two possible explanations behind the statistical association between competition and turnout: the first is that close elections increase interest in and information about elections, which reduces some of the costs associated with voting; and the second is that close elections prompt the parties and candidates to mobilize the electorate. In addition, Chapter 5 showed that state electoral competition was positively associated with the emergence of quality challengers to incumbents—although they do not seem to be politically advantaged in gubernatorial elections.

The findings of this book also have implications for partisanship and voting. First, the measures for the party strength of the candidates—the last four presidential election averages as well as the Erikson, Wright, and McIver (1993) specification—are insignificant in both incumbent and open seat election models. Gubernatorial candidates are therefore free to make their decision to run without considering whether the partisan leanings of the state will hurt or help them. In addition, only a small number of states exclusively elected governors of the same party from 1980 to 1996. States that are generally considered very conservative, such as Nebraska and Wyoming, sometimes elect Democratic governors; states that are thought very liberal, such as Massachusetts and Rhode Island, have elected Republicans.

Second, open seat candidates are punished when they share party affiliation with the president as well as when the national unemployment rate increases and they are from the same party as the president. There is no such presidential penalty in incumbent races. This shows that incumbents and their challengers do not have to worry about national forces, while open seat candidates begin with an advantage or disadvantage not of their making.

Third, in concurrent gubernatorial and Senate elections there is some evidence for similar partisan outcomes and levels of competition in open seat but not in incumbent races. This is the only evidence for any kind of "spillover" effect in simultaneous gubernatorial and Senate elections. Other evidence suggests that these elections are usually independent events, which is discussed in the next section.

Fourth, while Chapter 5 shows that Republican incumbents were more likely to attract higher-quality challengers than were Democratic incumbents, this book argues that challenger quality does not likely play any electoral role. More importantly, it argues that party is not associated with increased expenditures for quality challengers. On the other hand, the first-stage regressions in Chapters 2 and 3 showed that state party strength was positively associated with expenditures by open seat candidates, but not with expenditures by incumbents or their challengers. Taken together, this suggests that while partisanship itself does not matter, the strength of the party in a state can be indirectly helpful for some candidates.

Comparisons with Senate Elections

As mentioned previously, one goal of this book is to compare gubernatorial and Senate campaigns. This section will bring together the most important similarities and differences between campaigns for these two offices and show how the differences outnumber the similarities. One explanation for some of these differences is the executive nature of gubernatorial office. This is explored in more detail in the subsequent section, but will be briefly foreshadowed here along with a factual description of the differences.

A. Competition

One of the most important elements in an election is the level of political competition. What Price (1975, 35) wrote over thirty years ago is true today: "The possibility of opposition . . . remains a powerful factor in attuning the incumbent to the process of representation." If gubernatorial elections consistently produce minor levels of contestation, then governors may decide they have little reason to pay close attention to the wishes of their constituents.[6]

How do gubernatorial and Senate elections compare in terms of competition? Chapter 7 found that gubernatorial elections are highly competitive affairs. Governors are twice as likely to fail to win reelection as are senators and four times more likely than House members. Gubernatorial elections—both incumbent and open seat—are also much more likely to be "hard fought" (Westlye 1991) than are Senate elections.

What underlies these dynamics? Krasno (1994, 161) asked a similar question about Senate and House elections and found that an answer lay in the background of the opposition: "High-quality challengers are more partial to running for the Senate than the House." Abramowitz and Segal (1992, 228) similarly found that "the most important factor contributing to the level of competition in recent Senate elections has been the quality of Senate challengers." Squire (1989) discovered that not only did candidate quality directly affect Senate election outcomes, but it also affected how much money Senate candidates were able to raise.

This cannot be the answer for the gubernatorial/Senate competition differential. As discussed above, the effect of challenger quality in gubernatorial campaigns was examined in several chapters and found to be consistently minimal. Chapters 2 and 3 found very little evidence that any particular challenger background was associated with improved vote totals. Chapter 5 also showed that higher-quality challengers to governors did not spend more money than less-experienced challengers, and Chapter 7 found that an aggregate challenger quality variable was not statistically associated with campaign intensity.

Chapter 7 noted that governors and senators attracted different types of challengers, and in a way that was consistent with Schlesinger's (1966, 99) "manifest office" theory.[7] What the chapter did not find was a lack of experienced candidates running against governors vis-à-vis senators. Unfortunately for these experienced challengers, their prior experience did not affect election outcomes.

In addition, Chapter 6 examined whether House members' decision to run for governor was structured differently than the decision to run for Senate. The data showed that the gubernatorial decision was largely unstructured by political, institutional, or personal measures, while the senatorial decision was much more clearly structured by numerous factors. Because ambition theory assumes that a strategic, or "rational," candidate is one who follows a structured path based on the costs, benefits, and likelihood of winning, one might tentatively conclude that House members who run for governor are acting in a somewhat less-than-rational manner. It may be that their decisions are based on personal motivations that cannot be easily measured, but such decision making may reduce their odds of victory. This might help explain why House members, who are among the strongest candidates in Senate campaigns, do no better than anyone else in gubernatorial contests.

What might explain the differences in intensity and reelection rates? Chapter 7 posits several explanations, none of which are mutually exclusive. First, senators are members of a hundred-member body that is tied to an even larger House of Representatives, so they may be less accountable to the public. As one well-known political observer noted during the 1998 meeting of the Republican Governors Association,

> A senator is just one of 100 and therefore not personally accountable for what the Senate does or fails to do. The governor is judged by very different standards . . . Senators raise issues and make tough speeches; governors frequently have to raise taxes and make tough decisions."[8]

This theory has existed for some time; Chapter 7 noted Schlesinger's (1966) suggestion that as senators belong to a body of legislators, they are often shielded from public retribution, whereas solitary and visible governors cannot hide.

In fact, the level of incumbent security for governors, senators, and representatives is possibly related to this issue of accountability. House members are most numerous and most secure in any given election, senators place second in both categories, while governors, who have no peer in their states, are the most likely to be fired by the voters.

Second, the spending ratios listed in table 7.4 showed that governors were less likely to outspend their challengers than were senators. This was true for both per capita and total expenditures. Governors were therefore more likely to have more difficult and hard-fought campaigns than were senators, and, unsurprisingly, a greater proportion of defeats.

Third, governors are more likely to create controversy than are senators. As executives, governors must make decisions on controversial issues such as taxation and state spending, decisions for which they alone may be held responsible. Over time, each difficult decision may create opponents among previously neutral groups, or disappoint supporters who expected a more vigorous defense of their interests. We also know that governors receive far more media attention than do senators (Rosenthal 1990; Squire and Fastnow 1994). (These points will be discussed at length in the following section, which examines the electoral relevance of the executive nature of the office.)

There is no reason for these points to be mutually exclusive. In fact, the greater public accountability assumed by governors may help explain why they cannot outspend their challengers as can Senate incumbents. If by making difficult decisions they alienate people or groups who might have otherwise supported them, this may lead to lower incumbent revenues, increased funding for challengers, or both.

B. Candidate Quality

The second major difference between gubernatorial and Senate elections is that the effect of candidate political background is not the same. Scholars generally believe that candidates with political experience can raise significant amounts of money, start with an electoral base, enjoy credibility in political and media circles, and begin the race with more honed campaign skills. Krasno (1994) argued that whether or not quality challengers run for office is the major explanation for the low level of competition in House elections and the significant competition for Senate seats.

The previous section makes clear that candidate quality is not an important factor in campaigns for governor. Not only are the candidate experience measures not associated with election outcomes, but such candidates do not generally raise more money. Candidate background was discussed in several different ways in Chapters 2, 3, 5, 6, and 7, and none of the regression findings suggest it brings more to the political table.

Chapter 6 directly compared gubernatorial and Senate candidate data and examined the environmental and personal factors influencing whether House members run for governor or Senate, thereby building on the political ambition literature. For the office of governor, only the state size measure was clearly associated with the decision to run. Most of the variables associated with ambition for the

Senate—which included the length of House service, the age of the member at his or her first election, the distance of the district from Washington, D.C., and the political party of the member—did not apply in the gubernatorial context.

For purposes of comparison, a model was also tested in which the dependent variable was the decision to run for either governor or senator. This is the dependent variable usually tested by the literature. The regression results from this model closely resembled those found in the Senate model, thus showing that multiple factors previously thought to structure both gubernatorial and Senate ambition are only related to the latter.

These results suggest that House members have a well-structured decision-making process when it comes to senatorial ambition, but have a poorly structured process for gubernatorial ambition. This is important because the ambition literature theorizes that rational ambition takes into account the costs and benefits of running, but House members do not appear to do so when they run for governor. Perhaps they run for personal reasons that cannot be included in a regression model, but such motivations may not serve them well in their gubernatorial campaigns. These findings do not explain why other elected officials have no advantage in gubernatorial elections, but they show in another way that not only are gubernatorial elections unique, the role of candidate background in particular is different.

C. Independent and Third-Party Candidacies

Another difference between gubernatorial and Senate elections is the role of third-party and independent candidacies. Chapter 8 pointed out that while four nonaligned candidates became governor in the 1990s, no such Senate candidate approached victory. In addition, the gubernatorial nonaligned candidates who won 10 percent or more of the general election vote between 1980 and 1996 greatly outnumbered those in Senate elections. Eighteen gubernatorial hopefuls did at least this well while only five Senate candidates did, even though there were approximately 50 percent more Senate elections during this time period. Hindsight suggests that several of the losing nonaligned gubernatorial candidates had the potential to win, while none of the Senate candidates did.

When the percentage of the vote won by all nonaligned candidates in these two types of elections is aggregated for every election from 1980 to 1996, two different patterns emerge. In gubernatorial elections, increases over time are evident in both midterm and presidential election years. There is no similar temporal pattern in Senate elections. The percentages in the latter fluctuate randomly, so there is no indication that the lack of nonaligned Senate candidacies, or public support for those who do run, will change in the future.

D. Other

Three other differences between gubernatorial and Senate elections are brought to light in this book. The first concerns the effect of state party strength on election outcomes. Previous Senate research has found this factor significant; in particular, Gerber (1998) noted that the Wright, Erikson, and McIver (1985) measure of state partisanship was statistically significant in incumbent elections. Abramowitz and Segal (1992) found that voter partisan identification was significant in incumbent elections but not in open seat contests.

Chapters 2 and 3 tested two specifications of this concept: the Erikson, Wright, and McIver (1993) measure and the average two-party percentage vote for the presidential nominees of a candidate's party over the last four presidential elections. Although these two measures are quite different and do not closely correlate, neither is a significant explanation of incumbent or open seat gubernatorial voting outcomes.

The second concerns interactions between gubernatorial and Senate campaigns. As both types of elections sometimes take place in the same state at the same time, perhaps they affect each other in ways not well explored by the literature. Donors to Senate campaigns might decide, for example, to also give to the gubernatorial candidate of their party. On the other hand, a donor might decide to split his or her money between two campaigns instead of giving it all to one.

The book does not find any evidence of such financial "spillover" effects. There are several tests of this, the first involving campaign expenditures. Chapter 5 examined whether a concurrent Senate election affected the amount of money available to a gubernatorial challenger, and Chapter 7 tested whether a concurrent Senate election affected expenditures in open seat elections. The variable was statistically insignificant in both instances, which suggests that contributions to gubernatorial campaigns are unaffected by a concurrent Senate election.

Chapter 4 similarly examined whether gubernatorial turnout was influenced by the presence of a concurrent Senate or presidential election. The results showed a presidential election to be a significant influence, but a Senate election was not. Chapter 7 also compared partisan outcomes in gubernatorial and Senate open seat elections in the same year in the same state. In three-quarters of the cases, the winners were from the same party, and concurrent elections also tended to have similar levels of intensity. The low number of observations means that these findings are suggestive but tentative. There was no clear pattern in incumbent elections, despite the larger number of observations.

Perhaps there are spillover effects unrelated to finances, such as increased news media coverage of the two campaigns. This book does not collect data on media coverage of gubernatorial or Senate campaigns, but research by Kahn and Kenney (1999) has done so. They showed that a concurrent gubernatorial race leads to reduced media coverage of Senate campaigns, not increased coverage for both.

In addition, Chapter 6 tested whether the decision by House members to run for governor was encouraged or discouraged by a concurrent Senate election, and vice versa. The data show that neither dynamic took place; representatives were apparently interested in running for one office or the other and did not see them as interchangeable.

The final, and somewhat minor difference, concerns the role of scandals. Abramowitz and Segal (1992) and Gerber (1998) found that scandals hurt the general election vote of incumbents, which agrees with previous research on House campaigns (Peters and Welch 1980). Chapters 2 and 3 did not find any negative effect for incumbents. It is important to note that there were only a small number of such events,[9] but this only highlights the factor's lack of relevance in incumbent gubernatorial elections. In addition, the variable was not included in the open seat model because there was only one case. Why scandals are less commonly found in gubernatorial than Senate elections is not clear. Given the greater media scrutiny of governors than senators, perhaps candidates involved in scandals are less likely to run for governor.

E. Similarities

It is also important to note any electoral similarities between gubernatorial and Senate campaigns. The most important is one of the most contested issues in the elections literature: the association between expenditures and outcomes. Jacobson began this debate when he argued that expenditures helped House challengers win office but did not affect the chances of House incumbents.

Subsequent research tested this theory using a variety of methods in both House and Senate contests, and it generally concluded that challenger expenditures have several times the substantive effect of incumbent expenditures in Senate elections. Chapters 2 and 3 found that both incumbent and challenger expenditures mattered, and in approximately the same substantive range. This helps contribute to a more general understanding of the role of money in politics, as it confirms research on both Senate (Gerber 1998) and House (Ansolabehere and Snyder 1995) contests.

Gubernatorial Elections as Executive Elections

Presidents and governors occupy similar institutional landscapes. Both are single executives upon which much of the blame (or credit) for economic and social changes can fall. When problems arise, they cannot hide amid the legislative ranks or easily blame other institutions. They are both the subjects of intense media attention, and governors are the most well-known political personalities in their states, aside from the president.

The governor, like the president, is also the most important person in his or her political milieu. As Rosenthal (1990, 5) noted in his study of governors and legislatures, "Governors are believed to be the single most important figures in the process—truly the chief legislators in their state." King and Ragsdale (1988, 380) similarly wrote: "That the presidency is more important than any legislative seat (by any measure) and can be controlled for four years by winning only one election makes it a political prize almost unequaled in the democratic world." Although the formal powers of governors and the president vary, their institutional placement is the same in the state and federal political systems.

This similarity suggests that there may be parallel electoral dynamics, which this section will explore. One difficulty is that the study of presidential elections has been hindered by the "low n" problem and the resulting tendency to interpret each election in unique terms. The quantitative campaign expenditure studies done for House and Senate campaigns, for example, are not found in the presidential literature. Nevertheless, there is research on other aspects of presidential elections that can be examined for parallels with gubernatorial elections.

In particular, there are three dynamics uncovered in this book that require further analysis: the greater political competition for governor than for senator, the imbalance in the number of victorious and respectable third-party and independent campaigns for these offices, and the differential effect of challenger political experience. As will be discussed, these differences are not random; furthermore, they reveal parallels between gubernatorial and presidential elections that involve the executive nature of these two offices.

Governors are not, of course, the mirror images of presidents. Governors are not generally involved in foreign policy (although they do interact with other governors and states), their powers vary somewhat and do not always parallel those of the president, and the legislatures they deal with are not always as professionalized as the U.S. Congress. However, the similarities outweigh these differences: governors have more in common with presidents than with any other officeholder.

A. Competition

The first dynamic is the lower reelection rates of governors compared to senators and the concomitant greater degree of competition in gubernatorial campaigns. Chapter 7 considered and rejected the applicability of the major explanations for why senators are more electorally vulnerable than House members (which were reviewed earlier in this chapter). Fortunately, there is a significant body of research on presidential elections pertaining to this topic. This section therefore discusses the factors decreasing the electoral security of a president that are related to the institutional setting of the office. Few presidents seem able to escape them, and there are parallels in the political life of governors.

The first is the "coalition of minorities" dynamic first formulated by Mueller (1973). As discussed in Chapter 7, Mueller's work was built on the theories of Downs (1957), who argued that even if a president acted on each issue with majority public support, he would gradually alienate numerous people. These people could coalesce into a majority in the next election and defeat the incumbent or at least reduce the margin of victory. As Mueller (1973, 205) put it,

> This concept would predict that a president's popularity would show an overall downward trend as he is forced on a variety of issues to act and thus to create intense, unforgiving opponents of former supporters. It is quite easy to point to cases where this may have occurred.

Another explanation of this temporal pattern is that presidents are subject to a great deal of expectations, expectations that are likely to be slowly disappointed during the course of a term (Brace and Hinckley 1992). Not even schoolchildren are immune; Hinckley (1990) reports data showing that children assign to presidents the responsibility of not just giving money to the poor and protecting life but of helping ducks and assisting a lost puppy. She finds this functionally equivalent to how the general public views the president. Given such expectations, the public is bound to grow disappointed with any mortal who occupies the White House.

Regardless of the specific interpretation, the statistical evidence of this and other research suggests that presidential popularity declines as time in office progresses. Presidents generally lose popularity during their years in office, which can adversely affect their chances of reelection.[10]

That such a temporal dynamic might also apply to governors was suggested even earlier than Mueller. Schlesinger (1966, 69) noted that "the governor and the President are most vulnerable to the accumulated grievances of voters which produce the rejection of incumbents." His explanation was the singular nature of executive office, but it is similar in effect to the temporal arguments of the above research. More recently, Rosenthal (1990, 33) found that

> Not only do circumstances tend to eat into a governor's popularity, but the passage of time may be erosive as well. It may be part of the natural cycle of political life, as the office becomes diminished in the eyes of the public by their familiarity with the incumbent. Moreover, the governor may trade in some popularity in order to achieve objectives.

This is further evidence that while the two executives may work hard to maintain their popularity, they both find themselves opposed by forces exerting a downward pressure. This is reinforced by the media attention both offices receive. It is not surprising that media coverage of the president is overwhelming (Graber 1997). Congress is a large and complex body, while the president is a relatively solitary actor. Whether or not the president deserves such attention, the media need simple, thematic stories that are easy to understand as well as report. By their reporting, the media insinuate that executives embody the government: "The media amplify what we know to be a predisposition in the general public: namely, an impulse to understand public affairs mainly through a prominent political actor's behavior and not in terms of more complex, situational factors" (Heclo 1981, 8).

Regarding governors, Rosenthal (1990, 98) similarly found that "the governor commands the attention of the media" (198). While state legislators may seek media attention, they find it very difficult to compete with the focus on the governor. To illustrate this, Rosenthal (1990) quoted one Washington state legislator who said, "The cacophony of legislator voices can rarely compete with a governor who can capitalize on his singular visibility in the media" (25). Squire and Fastnow (1994) similarly reported that the governor received twice as much attention from state media during nonelection years than did both U.S. senators combined. The problem is that media attention is a double-edged sword; the focus on conflict and controversy means that over the length of a term, governors may long for more anonymity.

In addition, presidents and governors are rarely given power commensurate with public expectations. This is another reason they are more likely to disappoint voters than are other politicians. Neustadt (1990, ix) wrote that "presidential weakness was the underlying theme of *President Power*. This remains my theme . . . Weakness is still what I see: weakness in the sense of a great gap between what is expected of a man (or someday a woman) and assured capacity to carry through." Rosenthal (1990) similarly noted that the picture of gubernatorial power is sometimes exaggerated. Just as Congress has much to say about a presidential agenda, so does a state legislature about the plans of a governor. Like Neustadt's presidents, governors do not give orders to the legislature or bureaucracy: "They anticipate what leaders and members would like, they consult and negotiate, they compromise their positions, and they trim their proposals" (199). This does not mean that governors are not the center of state political life, but it does imply that it is easy for the public to misunderstand their role.

Executives may also be more convenient targets for voter anger over the direction of the state or nation, as "changing a legislative majority is both difficult and chancy" (Fiorina 1992, 69). A large number of seats are required to change partisan control, which is difficult to coordinate. It is also risky for a district to make such a change if few other districts follow suit. It will have replaced an experienced member of the majority with an inexperienced member of the minority, which may lead to fewer government benefits. Fiorina pointed out that in contrast, "neither consideration applies to executive office. Only one majority need be changed to shift control of the governorship. And the question of putting one's district at a disadvantage if control does not change simply does not arise" (70). This applies equally to the state and federal levels.

Some of the above factors may not apply to governors and presidents to the same degree. Media attention for the president will be greater than that for any particular governor, but the governor will still have the state political spotlight. The public may generally expect more from their president than from their governor, but the governor will bear more responsibility for state issues. "Institutional thickening," as Skowronek (1993) called the growing number of entrenched and independent interest and advocacy groups, will be greatest in Washington, D.C., but will still make life more difficult for governors.[11] The key point is not the absolute level of any dynamic for presidents and governors, but the relative effect.

All of this helps explain why executives in Washington, D.C., and the state capitals find maintaining public support a constant challenge. The combination of inflated public expectations, public overconfidence in executive power, executive decision making that can alienate supporters, and media attention that magnifies problems all make reelection more challenging. These dynamics have been most comprehensively researched in the presidential context, but their echo is heard in the gubernatorial literature.

B. Independent and Third-Party Candidacies

A second dynamic that needs explanation is the strong showings of gubernatorial candidates who are not Democrats or Republicans. Not only have four such candidates won office in the 1990s, but there were eighteen challengers and open seat contestants who received at least 10 percent of the vote during the same time period. Aggregate vote percentages for nonaligned gubernatorial candidates also increased from 1980 to 1996 in both presidential and midterm election years. Third-party and independent candidacies rarely experience much success in Senate elections, by contrast, and there was no upward trend in their public support over time.

In these ways, gubernatorial elections more closely resemble presidential contests than those for Senate. During the years of this study, three out of five elections saw a credible nonaligned candidate run for president. Although neither John Anderson nor Ross Perot won a single Electoral College vote, at various points their poll numbers were high. More recently, the Green Party candidacy of Ralph Nader may have affected the outcome of the 2000 presidential election.

It is also important to note that aside from Anderson and Perot, there has recently been a lot of activity by minor parties at the presidential level. As Herrnson and Green (1997, 10) found,

The 1990s were a period of intense minor party [presidential] activity . . . The candidates for the Reform and Libertarian parties appeared on the ballot in all fifty states and the District of Columbia, while candidates for the Natural Law, U.S. Taxpayers, and Green parties appeared on the ballots in forty-four, thirty-nine, and twenty-two states, respectively."

Whether this will eventually translate into increased electoral support for non-major-party candidates is unclear, but organizational activity is the first step toward future growth.

As in the states, presidential nonaligned candidates better resemble independent candidacies than third-party efforts, even when they officially run under the label of a party. John Anderson ran as an independent and under two party labels in 1980 in order to appear on as many state ballots as possible, but his "parties" did not survive long after his defeat. Ross Perot created the Reform Party for 1996 after an independent effort in 1992, but it declined in subsequent years without Perot.

As Chapter 8 detailed, nonaligned gubernatorial candidates largely run as independents or the candidate of their own party. While three of the four nonaligned governors ran officially as party candidates, closer inspection shows that this meant little. While Hickel ran as the candidate of the Alaskan Independence Party (AIP), it was a last-minute means to the ballot; few interpreted his victory as a call for the secession of Alaska from the United States. Ventura chose the Reform Party label in 1998, but later said that it was irrelevant to his victory. Few think that Lowell Weicker won because Connecticut voters wanted A Connecticut Party (ACP) to become an influential political force.

C. Candidate Quality

The third common electoral dynamic is the role of candidate political experience in both elections. This book finds that the prior elected office of challengers to governors and open seat candidates does not affect vote totals and is not related to campaign intensity, nor does overall challenger quality affect the amount of campaign expenditures. In Senate and House contests, by contrast, candidate political background strongly affects outcomes.

Consider how candidate prior political experience is discussed in the congressional elections literature by Jacobson, Green and Krasno, or other prominent scholars. The theory is that experienced candidates are especially good because they are better positioned to bring political resources to the table: money, an electoral base, credibility among political and media circles, and experience running for office.

Jacobson (1978, 474) argued that prior political experience measures "the effects of prior electoral success, and the exposure, experience, and contacts that come with holding elective office, on the ability to raise campaign funds." He later expanded on these points:

> Other things being equal, the strongest congressional candidates are those for whom politics is a career. They have the most powerful motive and the greatest opportunity to master the craft of electoral politics. They are most likely to have experience in running campaigns and holding elective office. They have the incentive and opportunity to build up contacts with other politically active and influential people and to put them under some obligation." (1987, 46)

The alternative is a race with an inexperienced candidate who overestimates his chances, spends little money and wastes much of it, receives little publicity, and ultimately loses.

Does candidate quality play the same role in presidential elections? Perhaps not, for three reasons. First, presidential campaigns always receive saturation media coverage, but media coverage is unrelated to candidate background. There are no contemporary examples where the media ignored a candidate because he or she was not thought to have the necessary political background. Whoever wins a major party primary is covered, for better or worse, and it is up to the nominee to make the most of it.

Second, campaign expenditures are not related to prior candidate political experience. Not since the Federal Election Campaign Acts (FECA) reforms of the early 1970s have general election candidates been able to directly raise money for their campaigns unless they also decline all public financing. The 1972 campaign was the last one fought under a largely unregulated financial environment.

Third, it is not clear whether skill at political campaigning is more common in candidates with particular electoral experiences and whether it has any impact on outcomes. Before being elected as president, the senior George Bush had won only a House seat and had lost his only Senate campaign. Michael Dukakis had contested multiple gubernatorial campaigns, which included one defeat followed four years later by a redemptive victory over his vanquisher. Few expected Bush to run the more skillful campaign.

Whether presidential candidates win or lose is often explained in terms of economics or personal variables; it is only rarely suggested that their prior electoral backgrounds directly affect vote totals. It is not easy to argue that Dukakis would have been more likely to win if he had served in the Senate.

In general, there does not seem to be any political background consistently favored in presidential elections for the reasons suggested in the congressional literature. Some time periods see more senators elected president, others more governors, but there is no clear explanation related to the nature of the offices. If candidate background affects presidential elections, it may only be as a symbol. Voters in the postwar era, when Washington was the epicenter of public policy, may have valued senators. As the glow of Washington diminished in subsequent decades, such thinking may have favored governors. The Watergate scandal may also have diminished public interest in presidential candidates with a Washington resume. From the mid-1970s to the present, successful candidates have largely been governors or former governors: Carter (1976), Reagan (1980, 1984), Clinton (1992, 1996), and Bush (2000, 2004). As is the case with presidential studies more generally, however, the relatively small number of observations makes patterns difficult to discern with any confidence.

This is not to say that presidential elections exactly parallel gubernatorial elections. Politically inexperienced people sometimes run for governor and raise relatively little money, receive little attention from the news media, and exhibit a damaging lack of political skills. Overall, however, there is a dynamic whereby executive elections are hard fought and difficult to predict regardless of the background of the candidates. This more closely resembles presidential rather than Senate elections.

Why might this be so? As discussed previously, much is at stake in an executive election that is not in a legislative election, even one for U.S. Senate. Except in unusual circumstances, political elites affiliated with a party work hard to support their presidential nominee. The presidency is too important to cede to the other party, even if the nominee is not the person they preferred. The same dynamic may be at work at the state level, where at stake is not just policy outcomes but jobs in the bureaucracy, state contracts, and sometimes judicial appointments. This may mean that gubernatorial candidates have more reliable access to campaign contributions, volunteers, get-out-the-vote efforts, party support, media coverage, and other politically important resources.

Further research on gubernatorial elections is needed to explore these possibilities. What is clear is that the role of candidate quality in congressional elections does not apply in either the presidential or gubernatorial context.

D. Final Thoughts

This book has highlighted the discordant and unifying features of executive and congressional elections in America today. The only feature that campaigns for different offices appear to share is the importance of money. Campaign expenditures by incumbents, challengers, and open seat candidates were significantly associated with gubernatorial election returns. This is in line with recent research on Senate and House elections. With the exception of this important common feature, there are more differences than similarities between gubernatorial and congressional contests.

It is unlikely that any convergence of electoral dynamics will take place. Several of the most important differences between gubernatorial and Senate elections involve the institutional placement of the offices. As long as this remains the same, there is bound to be significant variation in how those involved—voters, political elites, the media, and the candidates themselves—view elections to these two offices.

Balancing out the theme of gubernatorial/Senate differences are the similarities between gubernatorial and presidential elections. This book can only begin the development of an executive elections theory, however. Although Fiorina (1978, 442) noted over two decades ago that "to conclude a research report with a call for further study has become a platitude," hopefully, the study of elections across institutions will receive additional attention in the years to come.

Notes

Chapter 1   Introduction: Why Study How Governors Are Elected?

1. A relatively small but important and growing body of literature has examined gubernatorial elections. There have been edited volumes on gubernatorial elections, transitions, or experiences in a specific year or two (Beyle 1985, 1986, 1989, 1992); research on gubernatorial primary campaigns (Jewell 1984; Morehouse 1990; Morehouse 1998); work on gubernatorial campaign dynamics using polls and case studies (Carsey 2000); work on the role of issues, particularly abortion, in gubernatorial elections (Howell and Sims 1993; Cook, Jelen and Wilcox 1994; Berry and Winters 2001); and descriptive accounts of particular election campaigns (Sinclair 1935; Lubenow 1990, 1991, 1994; Whillock 1991; Morris 1992; Loevy 1996; Beiler 1999a, 1999b; Faucheux 1999; Wendel 1999). The previous electoral experience of governors and gubernatorial candidates has also received some attention (Schlesinger 1957, 1966; Squire 1992). None of these works has comprehensively examined the issues addressed in this book. Kingston (1989) and Squire and Fastnow (1994) are some of the few attempts to quantitatively examine multiple electoral factors in gubernatorial contests.

2. As the headline of a *New York Times* article read, "Forget Washington: Social Issues Shift to the States" (Berke 1997). It noted that although the Republican Party and Ronald Reagan in particular are often associated with devolution, even the Democratic Party platform now embraced shifting some power back to the states. The article cautioned that the federal government still takes the lead on some "big issues," especially those that are "a magnet for campaign donations."

3. Herzik and Brown (1991, x) noted that the New Federalism "expanded state policy responsibilities and forced governors to assume a greater policy leadership role."

4. Cox (1991, 59) found that gubernatorial staff is now much larger and more specialized than in previous times. He also pointed out that formal listings of staff often underestimate the level of personnel resources available to the governor, as employees from state agencies are often "loaned" to the governor's office and do not officially appear on the executive office roll (Beyle 1983).

5. Herzik (1991, 26) found that "the formal powers of governors have been upgraded across the states to the point where little variation exists between so-called strong and weak governor states (Dometrius 1988)."

6. The literature suggests that formal gubernatorial powers are necessary to affect policy change but not always sufficient. Herzik (1991, 27) wrote that "despite the intuitive idea that such formal powers should enhance gubernatorial influence, most research suggests they have little effect on policy (Dye 1969; Lester 1980) or the ability of governors to control state policy administration (Hebert, Brudney, and Wright 1983; Abney and Lauth 1983; Haas and Wright 1989)." He also cited the Sigelman and Dometrius (1988) study on how formal powers provide the opportunity to influence policy, but that these powers are most effective when combined with "informal political resources, most notably the electoral mandate enjoyed by the governor and the size of the same party representation in the state legislators" (27).

7. See Herzik (1991), preface (ix–x).

8. Kaplan and O'Brien (1991, 14) found that "institutionally and politically, the states' capacity to respond [to the New Federalism] was much greater in 1980 than it had been in earlier years. Beginning in the 1960s, states had modernized their governmental structures, including reforms of all branches of government. They had reduced the number of elected officials and strengthened the policy role of the governor. The skill and training of state administrative personnel had increased. Likewise, numerous reforms had been made affecting legislation and the courts."

9. The experience of governors in office has received more attention of late but is surprisingly small. Twenty-six years ago, Palmer (1972, I) optimistically claimed that "state government and politics are no longer dull topics in the study of American government," but few in political science seemed to receive the message. While there is a substantial literature on state politics from the 1960s and 1970s, much of that work included chapters on governors interspersed with chapters on local politics and other elements of state government (Munger 1966; Lockard 1969; Hofferbert and Sharkansky 1971; LeBlanc and Allensworth 1971; Adrian 1972; Dye 1973; Straayer 1973). As Jacob and Vines (1965, vi) noted early on, "most texts combine state politics with local politics."

This may be changing for the better. Morehouse (1998) examined the role of governor, and the early 1980s saw a renewed interest in the office (see works cited below). Former or current governors have written about their experiences in office (Williams 1961; Hodges 1962; Sanford 1967; Welsh 1981; Behn 1991; Hammond 1994; Thompson 1996), and scholars have discussed the experiences of particular administrations (Hamilton and Biggart 1984; Osborne 1988). Much of the best research on governors and state politics has examined elections as part of a larger look at the office (Key 1956; Beyle and Williams 1972; Morehouse 1981; Ransone 1982; Sabato 1983; Morehouse 1998).

10. They went on to add, "In education, 667 pages of regulations governing the 33 programs that were folded into the block grant were

replaced by 20 pages." Yet they also noted that the overall level of federal regulations for the states did not clearly decline during the New Federalism. Federal regulations through block grants were just the "tip of the iceberg" (7), and many other regulations remained in place.

11. Berke (1997). Beyle continued, "And it will continue that way until we have a major depression or other catastrophe," which suggests that this process is not irreversible.

12. He went on to explain that most governors "are too busy responding to their constituents to philosophize about the next political paradigm. But it is precisely their executive responsibility, their direct accountability for the health of their states, that has forced them to adapt their politics. And it is precisely this adaptation that distinguishes them from their counterparts in Washington. 'Washington has a way of dealing with yesterday's issues,' says Michigan Governor James Blanchard, who served in Congress for eight years. 'If you are a U.S. senator, you can give an ideological response to a serious problem and probably never be held accountable for it. Whereas the governors are dealing with the real world—they have to run things, to make them work'" (15).

13. For a recent account of state budgets, see "States' Coffers Swelling Again After Struggles." John Broder, *New York Times*, November 25, 2005.

14. The last time the states were such active policy participants was in the early part of the twentieth century. As Osborne (1988, 1) pointed out, "The groundwork for much of the New Deal social agenda was laid in the states during the Progressive Era." The "laboratories" analogy was made by Louis Brandeis, who was referring to the programs brought about by the Progressives (*New State Ice Co. v. Liebmann*, dissenting opinion). An important point on this subject was made by Walker (1969), who found that rarely do all fifty states conduct experiments in similar areas. Instead, innovations in one state are often subsequently adopted by other states without major adjustments.

15. This program does not directly give money to charter schools but first gives it to the states that then distribute the money. While Congress imposed stricter conditions in its 1998 legislation, states still had much discretion.

16. Leal (1999).

17. Such cynicism about gubernatorial motives may be misplaced. Bernick and Wiggins (1991, 82–83) argued that, "In the cynical world of today's politics, the media tend to stress the perspective that all gubernatorial actions stem from either political ambition or personal egos. Thus, few, if any, governors are considered to have strong and well-thought-out policy goals. This is neither a fair nor an accurate assessment of today's governor, however. Many are very desirous of shaping

the role of government within their own states (Sabato 1983). One should not underestimate a governor's desire to have a meaningful and constructive impact on the policy process as a determinant of one's decisions to enter the legislative arena. For some governors, good public policy is also good politics. Moreover, the marriage of political ambition and policy development makes for an even stronger and more active policymaker."

18. Berke (1997).
19. See Jacobson (1978, 1980, 1983, 1985).
20. Most notably Green and Krasno (1988).
21. Abramowitz (1988); Grier (1989).
22. Gerber (1998); Ansolabehere and Snyder (1995). As explained in Chapter 2, this means that while researchers want to know how money affects votes, expectations about the vote may influence how much money a candidate receives and therefore spends. In order to avoid this problem, the book uses instrumental variables—variables that directly affect the level of spending but do not directly influence the vote.
23. The term "retrospective voting" is used in this book to refer to how changes in economic and social conditions affect the vote. It is much simpler to write "retrospective voting," for example, than "how changes in economic and social conditions affect the vote."
24. Squire (1992).
25. Squire (1989); Lublin (1994); Adams and Squire (1997).
26. Bianco (1984); Green and Krasno (1988).
27. Squire (1989).
28. Where the dependent variable is coded 1 for a decision to run for either governor or Senate and coded 0 for the decision not to run for higher office.
29. Waterman (1990); Abramowitz and Segal (1992); Krasno (1994).
30. Although see Squire and Fastnow (1994).
31. As will be discussed, this is most likely caused by a political dynamic whereby contributors give large amounts of money to small-state Senate candidates because each Senate vote is equal. A contribution will have more impact in Vermont than in California, but no such dynamic exists in gubernatorial races.
32. In the first three chapters, some incumbent elections were deleted when a third-party candidate either won or gained over 10 percent of the vote because it was difficult to incorporate these candidates into the model. There were also several instances of incumbent governors losing in the primary, and these cases were not included. The unique single ballot of Louisiana is not comparable with the electoral arrangements of other states, so Louisiana elections were not included. Elections where one of the candidates either died before the general election or declined the nomination after the primary were also excluded.

Chapter 2 Election Outcomes: Campaign Expenditures and Candidate Quality

1. See also Alexander (1976) and Jewell and Olson (1978).
2. Even as far back as the 1979 elections, Beyle (1986, 20) noted that in several states "the most important expenditures as measured by money spent are for media advertising, political consultants, and public opinion polling." Beyle has also documented the increasing costs of gubernatorial elections over the years. See the articles by Beyle in the series *The Book of the States*, as well as Ransome (1982).
3. Jacobson (1980, 1983, 1984, 1985, 1990).
4. Jacobson (1978, 469). Italics in original.
5. Palda (1973, 1975); Welch (1974, 1977); Lott and Warner (1974); Dawson and Zinser (1976); Silberman (1976). However, some did show different marginal returns for challengers and incumbents, such as Glantz, Abramowitz, and Burkhardt (1976) and Silberman and Yochum (1978).
6. The initial Jacobson model used four explanatory variables to predict the challenger's percentage of the two-party vote: challenger campaign expenditures, incumbent campaign expenditures, challenger party, and strength of the challenger's party in the district. He also used two-stage least-squares (2SLS), but the results were essentially the same as those found using ordinary least-squares (OLS). The additional four variables used in the first stage of the 2SLS model included challenger political experience, whether the candidate faced a primary, whether the incumbent faced a primary, and the number of years the incumbent served in office.
7. See also Jacobson (1990, 341–342).
8. The approach of Abramowitz and Segal's (1992) book is almost exactly the same.
9. He presented only OLS results for these elections because 2SLS explained so little variance for one of the two years of the study.
10. Morehouse (1998, 10) is an extended discussion of "the relationship between the political efforts of party leaders and gubernatorial candidates to capture the nomination and their success when in office to put the program into effect." It is one of the few comprehensive studies of primary campaigns for any political institution. See also Jewell (1984) for other work on gubernatorial primaries.
11. Hinckley, Hofstetter, and Kessel (1974); Squire (1992); Squire and Fastnow (1994).
12. Lengle (1980); Southwell (1986); Stone (1986); Kenney and Rice (1987).
13. Hacker (1965) and Reiter (1979) found little evidence for this effect, but Bernstein (1977), Kenney and Rice (1984), and Westlye (1991) argued that it was a factor.
14. Sullivan (1977); Kenney and Rice (1987).

15. Buell (1986); Stone (1986).
16. Schlesinger (1965); Beyle (1983, 1990).
17. He noted, however, that this may be a statistical artifact of several unrelated factors.
18. The former is used in the models because the latter does not include data for Alaska and Hawaii.

Chapter 3   Election Outcomes: State and National Economic and Social Conditions

1. Fair (1978, 1988); Tufte (1978); Hibbs (1987); Erikson (1989).
2. Fiorina (1978); Kiewiet (1983); Markus (1988).
3. Kramer (1971); Tufte (1975, 1978); Jacobson and Kernell (1983); Hibbs (1982); Lewis-Beck and Rice (1984); Born (1986); Oppenheimer, Stimson, and Waterman (1986); although see Gough (1984); Campbell (1985); Alesina and Rosenthal (1989); Erikson (1990).
4. Fiorina (1978); Kiewiet (1983); Born (1986).
5. This is not to suggest that analysis at other levels of government is uncomplicated. As Fiorina (1978, 429) noted about the literature on congressional economic effects, "The specifics of the studies leave their authors wrangling about econometric techniques and their readers somewhat confused." The exchange between Fiorina (1978), Hibbing and Alford (1981), and Fiorina (1983) shows how different results can be obtained from similar or identical data studying similar questions depending on the methodology and approach.
6. Clarke (1986); Grady (1991).
7. Taxable resources and urban populations helped explain the variation. Politically, state legislative salary and percentage of Republicans in a legislature were positively associated.
8. Elkin (1984); Friedland, Piven, and Alford (1977); Mollenkopf (1983); Peterson (1981).
9. Levernier (1992); Peltzman (1987); Leyden and Borrelli (1995).
10. Svoboda (1995) analyzed 1982 and 1986 CBS/New York Times Exit Polls. Partin (1995) analyzed 1990 ANES surveys. Howell and Vanderleeuw (1990) analyzed a 1988 survey of Louisiana voters. Atkeson and Partin (1995) used 1986 and 1990 ANES data. Stein (1989) used 1982 CBS/New York Times Election Day Surveys.
11. In a reply, although Bennett and Wiseman (1993) took issue with some of the other arguments made by Chressanthis and Shaffer (1993), they acknowledged the points about the unemployment rate and inclusion of open seats.
12. Abramowitz (1980); Whitby and Bledsoe (1986); Abramowitz (1988).
13. Hinckley, Hofstetter, and Kessel (1974); Squire (1992); Squire and Fastnow (1994).

14. Iyengar and Kinder (1987).
15. Brody (1991) and Zaller (1992).
16. This is not the first study to suggest that the image of the president can have an impact on gubernatorial elections. King (2001, 585) used polling data to show that "voters with favorable images of the incumbent governor have a higher probability of voting for the candidate of the incumbent's party. The effect is greater when the incumbent seeks reelection, but it is present in open contests as well."
17. Peltzman (1987); Leyden and Borelli (1995).
18. Chubb (1988); Levernier (1992).
19. Adams and Kenney (1989); Leyden and Borelli (1995).

Chapter 4   Voter Turnout: Competition, Candidates, and Conditions

1. Ranney's (1976) index of interparty competition.
2. The 1980 CPS Election Study.
3. Using aggregate data, Kenney (1983b) found that both the presence of an incumbent in a primary and higher state income levels dampened turnout, while the closeness of the primary, the presence of a presidential primary, the traditional existence of contested primaries in the state, and the open primary rule all increased turnout. Jewell (1984) studied gubernatorial primary turnout in northern states using aggregate data. He used two dependent variables: turnout in Democratic and Republican primaries. He found that the smaller size of a winner's percent, the presence of open primaries, and the better the party had done in recent general elections, the greater was the primary turnout in both models. For Democrats, the presence of a Republican incumbent in the other primary served to decrease Democratic turnout, and concurrent presidential elections increased turnout. For Republicans, receiving the party endorsement decreased turnout. See also Jewell (1977).
4. Nagel and McNulty (1996).
5. It is not clear if their expenditure data were deflated.
6. It is also used by Westlye (1991) as a supplementary measure of intensity.
7. In incumbent elections, this is based on the premise that incumbent and challenger dollars have a roughly equal effect on the vote (see Chapters 2 and 3).
8. There is somewhat mixed evidence for whether differences in state voting procedures, such as registration laws, affect turnout. King (1995/96) used a time series design to show that the adoption of election-day voter registration was only marginally related to turnout, and King (1994, 127) used a recursive path model to suggest a prior cause: "Political cultures which value individual participation in the political

process have governments that adopt less restrictive legal requirements for registering voters and achieve higher rates of electoral participation."

9. Bruno (2000).
10. Although see the December 1999 issue of the *American Political Science Review* for additional research on this topic.
11. Gray (1987); Damasio (1994); LeDoux (1998).
12. He argued that several southern state outliers drove the relationship, but this is not the case here. When the southern observations are dropped and the regression rerun, per capita income is still significant and negative.

Chpter 5   Candidate Quality Revisited

1. Jacobson (1980); Jacobson and Kernell (1983); Green and Krasno (1988); Ansolabehere and Snyder (1995).
2. Abramowitz (1988); Stewart (1989); Abramowitz and Segal (1992); Squire (1992).
3. Krasno (1994, 154) explained that "senators lose more often because they are more likely to face formidable challengers who manage to wage intense campaigns. Based on their previous experiences, Senate challengers are usually better candidates—combining attractiveness and political skill—than the people who run against House incumbents."
4. Although the literature on shirking by members of Congress who have announced their retirement (Lott 1987; Van Beek 1991; Lott and Bronars 1993) supports the notion that they do not change their voting behavior, at least in terms of ideological index ratings. Whether or not continuity in these ratings accurately implies good representation, however, is unclear.
5. Squire (1992).
6. Squire and Smith (1996); Adams and Squire (1997); Squire (1989); Lublin (1994).
7. Bianco (1984) and Krasno and Green (1988).
8. Schlesinger (1966) and Black (1972).
9. Squire (1989) and Krasno (1994).
10. Which was found to be important in House elections by Krasno and Green (1988), Covington and Fleisher (1985), and Bianco (1984).
11. In House elections, Bianco (1984) similarly found that as per capita income declined, higher-quality candidates from the party out of power were encouraged to run.
12. As Jacobson (1987, 74) wrote, "The most important aspect of fundraising is convincing potential donors that their money will not be wasted. They must be persuaded that the candidate has a plausible chance of winning."
13. Such as *Congressional Quarterly Weekly Report* (*CQ Weekly*), CQ's *Guide to Elections*, and various editions of the *Almanac of American Politics* (*AAP*).

14. Westlye (1991, 13) discussed how there are multiple components to a quality challenger: "Challengers who have a background in politics, who have proven that they can win elections, and who are tied to the political infrastructure of a state are more likely to be able to put together the funding and organization needed for a highly visible statewide race. Potential contributors are more likely to risk their money, volunteers are more likely to give their time, and other politicians are more likely to offer their endorsements when the challenger has a proven political record. The more political experience a challenger has, the more likely he is to command the publicity and other resources necessary to conduct a hard-fought campaign and to achieve a high level of information dissemination. The news media have a special role in the dissemination of campaign information, and levels of information disbursement depend heavily on candidates' ability to attract free press coverage. The attraction of news coverage derives from candidates' ability to convince the press to take them seriously."

15. Bond, Covington, and Fleisher (1985); Green and Krasno (1988); Krasno and Green (1988); Squire (1989); Lublin (1994).

16. Bianco (1984); Abramowitz (1988); Krasno and Green (1988); Squire (1992); Lublin (1994).

17. Bond, Covington, and Fleisher (1985) and Jacobson (1989).

18. Squire (1989; 1992).

19. Ehrenhalt (1992); Jacobson and Kernell (1983); Fiorina (1994).

20. This is because gubernatorial candidates must meet the varying disclosure requirements of the states, unlike federal candidates, who must uniformly report to the Federal Election Commission (FEC).

21. It makes little difference if the dependent variable is specified as deflated challenger expenditures or deflated per capita expenditures.

22. Four states during this time period elected governors for two-year terms; only two did so by 1997.

23. Squire (1989) and Ansolabehere and Snyder (1995).

24. Jacobson (1980).

25. Chapter 3 has already demonstrated that open seat candidates who are of the same party as the president receive fewer votes.

26. Many interest groups are active donors to federal candidates, but few pay attention to state races. As Weicker (1995, 184) noted, "The nation's capital is not much of a place for gubernatorial fundraising under any circumstances; for an independent gubernatorial candidate, the thought of raising money in Washington is bizarre."

27. Although it was important to include them in this model to compare the results with those found in the literature discussed previously.

28. These variables include incumbent age, incumbent primary vote, challenger age, challenger primary vote, challenger party strength in the state, challenger wealth, and the five retrospective state and national economic change measures.

29. Ehrenhalt (1992) and Fiorina (1994).
30. An alternative to the presidential vote average is the Erikson, Wright, and McIver (1993) state partisanship measure. It is also insignificant, however, and slightly reduces the number of observations because data for Alaska and Hawaii were not available.
31. Bianco (1984), Bond, Covington, and Fleisher (1985), and Krasno and Green (1988) found that the previous margin of the incumbent was a powerful variable in House elections.

Chapter 6   Gubernatorial versus Senate Election Dynamics: Progressive Ambition

1. Kentucky, Louisiana, Mississippi, New Jersey, and Virginia.
2. Rohde (1979, 4) also excluded these cases and noted that "this eliminates from theoretical consideration the rare case of the representative who wants to leave the House and decides to run for higher office instead of retiring. This situation seems to occur so seldom that we can safely ignore it at this time."
3. These candidates include Bartlett of Texas, who left to become mayor of Dallas; Molinari of New York, who became borough president of Staten Island; and Lukens of Ohio, who took a position on the Cincinnati City Council. This follows the usual coding scheme in the literature (Loomis 1984; Kiewiet and Zeng 1993), according to which those who ran for lesser state office are considered to have retired.
4. This variable was obtained from various issues of *Congressional Quarterly Weekly Report* (*CQ*) and the *AAP*, along with the *Biographical Directory of the United States Congress: 1774–1989*.
5. One must be careful with this kind of coding, for victories sometimes have a way of looking inevitable when described years later. For example, were the many victories by the Watergate class against incumbents in 1974 inevitable, as they sometimes appear to be, or were they risky efforts by the challengers? The coding on such victories was not changed from "ambitious" to "unambitious."

   Another point is that a scandal sometimes had effects for two elections. When an incumbent was defeated because of serious scandal, the challenger was not coded as "ambitious." The challenger who challenged and defeated this new incumbent in the next election was also not considered "ambitious'" if the *AAP* described the freshman incumbent as highly vulnerable and likely to be defeated by whoever won the opposition party primary.
6. Such difficulties with the age variable may help explain the differing impact of age in the models of Kiewiet and Zeng (1993), who found that age strongly influences the decision to retire or to run for higher office but provides little information on whether a member will run for reelection.

7. Although Copeland (1989) found convergence in partisanship from 1980 to 1986.

8. Other researchers have noted that members with longer tenure travel home less often than those with less (Davidson 1969; Fenno 1978; Bond 1985). Hibbing (1991) argued that this is a political lifestyle effect, not a generational one. This should not affect the variable, because distance will affect all members regardless of their stage of career. A ten-term veteran from Oregon will be more bothered by travel than a ten-term veteran from Maryland.

9. The variable used in this study was obtained from the reference book *Direct-Line Distances: United States Edition*.

10. These figures were found in various issues of the *Book of the States* and the *AAP*.

11. These figures were taken from various issues of the *Book of the States*.

12. Brace (1984); Copeland (1989); although see Kiewiet and Zeng (1993).

13. Rohde (1979); Brace (1984); Kiewiet and Zeng (1993).

14. The regression was rerun excluding Alaska, but there were no differences. The subsequent regressions were also tested without Alaska and Hawaii. The only difference is that excluding both states changes the sign and significance of one variable in the gubernatorial ambition model. Distance from Washington, D.C., is now significant, but opposite the anticipated direction. This does not make much sense, and perhaps it is incorrect to consider Alaska an outlier. While Alaska is 500 miles farther from Washington, D.C., than is California, Hawaii is two thousand miles farther than Alaska.

15. The variables that helped channel progressive ambition in the Senate model and in the aggregate model include the age the member enters the House, the years served in the House, majority party status, the distance of the home state from Washington, D.C., and the number of House seats in the state. The significant variable in the final gubernatorial model was the number of House seats per state.

Chapter 7 Gubernatorial versus Senate Election Dynamics: Electoral Competition and Campaign Intensity

1. He showed that population size contributed to greater losses for senators only in the three largest states, and that even this minor effect varied across decades. Krasno also replicated contrary research by Hibbing and Brandes (1983), who used election results and not victory or loss as the dependent variable, and concluded that this phenomenon is limited to the very largest states. In addition, state size was not substantially related to attitudes toward the caseworker/ombudsman function of senators, assessments of voting records and ideology, or feeling thermometers and performance approval. Westlye (1991, ch. 7) similarly found that state size was not a generally important factor in election results.

2. This would affect senators more than House members not just because states are larger, but because state boundaries are set while House districts are often drawn by state legislatures to specifically suit a particular incumbent or type of candidate, as well as to comply with Supreme Court Voting Rights Act decisions on minority representation. Some previous research (Fiorina 1974; Bond 1983) tested this argument using the diversity measure developed by Sullivan (1973), but Krasno drew different conclusions from the same data. Krasno also used the pooled CBS/New York Times data assembled by Wright, Erikson, and McIver (1985) to test these hypotheses. Diversity was not related to election returns, ideological distance (between respondent's position and respondent's view of incumbent's position), agreement with voting records and general performance approval, or thermometer rankings. In sum, Krasno argued that "with regard to the impact of state population the conclusion is unambiguous: there is no evidence that the size matters" (70).

3. It was built around macrolevel electoral evidence (as is this book), whereas the Krasno (1994) study used public opinion data.

4. They examined the 1990 National Election Study (NES) Senate survey, several Heartland Polls, and a 1992 Political Media Research Poll.

5. While they found that senators were more likely to face the politically inexperienced than were governors, they might have noted that the inexperienced are not always less-formidable candidates than some office holders. Many of the politically inexperienced in these high-profile contests have significant accomplishments in the private sector.

6. Gubernatorial challengers also had higher name recognition than Senate challengers, yet surprisingly the former were only slightly better liked than the latter.

7. Hard-fought elections are not necessarily the same as close elections. A challenger may vigorously contest an election and the voters may receive excellent information about both candidates, but the incumbent could still overwhelmingly win. Krasno (1994) similarly found that "challenger quality and campaign intensity are closely related, but they are not identical. Furthermore, each concept has different implications for the study of Senate and House elections" (159). While some inexperienced candidates waged intense campaigns, other well-qualified candidates did poorly.

8. On the other hand, Erikson and Wright (1989) and Glazer and Grofman (1987) noted that the "survival rate" for House members and senators was about the same over a six-year period.

9. This does not include those incumbents who were prevented from running for reelection by state law. During the time period of this study, many states limited governors to two consecutive terms, while a smaller number did not allow reelection.

10. Thomas Judge of Montana and Dixy Lee Ray of Washington in 1980, Edward King of Massachusetts in 1982, William Sheffield of Alaska in

1986, and Walter Miller of South Dakota (who assumed office when Governor George Mickelson died in a plane crash in 1993), and Bruce Sundlun of Rhode Island in 1994.

11. Three were in 1980 and all three were Democrats: Donald Stewart in Alabama (although he was elected to serve the last two years of Senator James Allen's term, who died unexpectedly in 1978), Richard Stone in Florida, and Mike Gravel in Alaska. The fourth was Alan Dixon's loss to Carol Mosley-Braun in 1992.

12. Out of the 236 incumbent elections in the Senate data set.

13. Which is down from the 48 percent reported by Westlye.

14. Of these eight campaigns, it was the challenger who reported no expenditures in seven. The one incumbent who spent nothing was Senator William Proxmire of Wisconsin, who nevertheless won easily in 1982.

15. This contrasts with the 81 percent figure reported by Westlye (1991), but in either case gubernatorial contests were more likely to be hard-fought.

16. As opposed to comparing the average of all ratios from each election, as done in the above section. Although the ratios from both sections somewhat differ in number, the important point is that they both clearly demonstrate greater levels of contestation in gubernatorial than in Senate elections.

17. The voting age population is used instead of overall population because it more accurately reflects the audience politicians are trying to reach.

18. With the exception of state/local experience, which may lead to fewer votes in incumbent elections.

19. Squire's data covered elections from 1977 to 1989, while this table includes data from 1980–1996.

20. See the previous discussion of how Westlye defines these concepts. The number of elections in this table does not equal the number in some other tables. There are generally fewer observations in the former because it requires campaign finance data that are not available for every gubernatorial candidate.

21. CO, GA, HI, IL, IA, KY, MD, and SD.

22. One should be careful about joining the partisan-decline bandwagon. For an alternative perspective see Maisel (1994) and Keith et al. (1992).

23. According to which candidates of the party of the president are more likely to lose than in presidential election years.

24. A variety of studies in the 1980s also discussed the impact of challenger quality (Abramowitz 1980; Mann and Wolfinger 1980; Hinckley 1980, 1981; Kazee 1983) on incumbent reelection chances. Other research, however, has emphasized the advantages that come with incumbency (Mayhew 1974; Fiorina 1977; Cain, Ferejohn, and Fiorina 1987) as a way to understand incumbent success.

25. The sheer size of states, as compared with House districts, has been thought to make it more difficult for a senator to keep in touch with

even a substantial minority of his or her constituents. Others have noted that senators represent larger and less politically cohesive districts, whereas representatives often have districts tailored to meet their political preferences. On the other hand, "coherent media markets also encourage greater news coverage of Senate challengers and permit them to use campaign resources more effectively" (Jacobson and Wolfinger 1989, 511). Senate campaigns also receive more attention than House campaigns (Fenno 1982; Goldenberg and Traugott 1984), which may translate into problems for the incumbent.

26. Although members of the House may not enjoy the constant campaigning, it may be good for their careers. Previous researchers have thought that the six-year Senate election cycle "makes it easier to lose touch with constituents. New political trends and issues appear; old ones exploited successfully in the past fade. The two-year House term provides a good deal of campaign-to-campaign continuity" (Jacobson and Wolfinger 1989, 510). Fenno (1982, 16) also noted that "the key to trust may not be so much the sheer passage of time [in office] as it is the number of times a candidate encounters the electorate and wins an election. In a world calibrated by successive elections, the House member running after six years is in the same position as a senator running after eighteen years. Both are engaged in intensive or extensive contact with constituents for the fourth time." Jacobson and Wolfinger (1989, 510) concluded that "the six-year term may be a mixed blessing for incumbents, giving them relief from campaign pressures at a cost of weaker constituent ties."

27. Given their role as chief executives, governors should find both increased opportunity and danger in their disaster responses compared to representatives.

28. Edwards (1983); Lowi (1985); Neustadt (1990); Brace and Hinckley (1992); Nichols (1994).

29. Mark Shields, "Look to Montana," *New York Times*, November 28, 1993, A23.

30. Commenting upon the differences between being governor and senator, former senator and governor Chuck Robb of Virginia pointed out that [senatorial] "efforts tend to be more rhetorical." "Ex-Govs. Go From Top Spot to One in 100," *Roll Call*, December 3, 1998, p. 1.

31. He also calculated that "on average, the difference between a president's highest and lowest approval ratings is 42 percentage points" (166). King further noted that with the exceptions of Lyndon Johnson and Richard Nixon, "the correlations between time out of office and change in perceptions of the presidents are positive and extremely high, exceeding 80" (170).

32. Brody (1991) also found the "coalition of minorities" argument lacking (see also Kernell 1978) because while the effect itself may be descriptively true, it does not adequately explain why declines take

place. "The trend is evident but not self-explanatory. The meaning of 'time' as an explanatory factor is illusive: if we do not understand why a president loses support with each passing month, then time *per se* cannot offer much insight into the linkage between public policy and public opinions" (83). In his book, Brody argued that public opinion change is explained by media reports of presidential successes and failures as well as by unmediated policy outcomes.

Chapter 8   Gubernatorial versus Senate Election Dynamics: Third-Party and Independent Campaigns

1. *Almanac of American Politics* (*AAP*) 1996, 1358. One exception is Senator Bob Smith of New Hampshire, who switched from Republican to independent for just over a hundred days in 1999 to run as an independent or possibly third-party candidate for president. He switched back when the death of Senator John Chafee put him in line to chair the Senate Environment and Public Works Committee.
2. This can reflect the challenge presented by state law to ballot access. In some states, to qualify for the ballot as the candidate of a third party is more difficult than simply appearing on the ballot as an independent. In other states, the opposite is true.
3. In 1998, for example, U.S. Representative Charles Schumer (D-NY) also appeared on the Independence Party line in his race for Senate.
4. The campaign descriptions throughout this chapter are largely based on the accounts provided in various editions of the *AAP* as well as some editions of the CQ *Politics in America* series. Other sources are specifically cited.
5. He was not just given the nomination, however, but had to defeat three other aspiring AIP candidates in the primary.
6. "Name: Eunice Strong Groark," *Associated Press Political Service*, October 6, 1994.
7. In order to qualify for the ballot, Connecticut law stated that a potential party must gather the signatures of 1 percent of the total votes in the previous gubernatorial election. In this case, this requirement was at least 11,412 signatures of registered voters. Just to be safe, organizers turned in about 20,000 signatures. See "Income Tax Foe Files Petition for Governor," *Associated Press*, August 10, 1994.
8. "Gore, Stumping for Curry, Says Vote for Groark Will Give Rowland Election," *Associated Press Political Service*, November 3, 1994.
9. "Polls for the Picking as Gubernatorial Candidates Reach Final Stretch," *Associated Press Political Service*, November 4, 1994.
10. "Future of Weicker's Party on the Line," *Associated Press Political Service*, November 9, 1994.
11. Ibid.
12. *AAP 1996*, 389.

13. This means the Green Party primary is included on the ballot, and it puts their candidate's name at the top of the ticket with the Democrats and Republicans.
14. "Greens: Spoilers or Scapegoats?" *Chile Verde*, Fall 1996.
15. *AAP 1998*, 1165.
16. *AAP 1998*, 1165.
17. "Luksik Says She's More than a One-Issue Candidate," *Associated Press*, November 6, 1994.
18. *Lancaster New Era*, November 9, 1994.
19. *AAP 1992*, 829.
20. Jacobson and Kernell (1983, 89) wrote about some candidates who might be pursuing "various private goals that are not incompatible with losing."
21. *AAP 1998*, 80.
22. There were no statewide elections in 1996.
23. *AAP 1982*, 724.
24. Figures found in *Gubernatorial Elections: 1789–1997*.
25. It does not include special elections—only regularly scheduled elections.
26. "Angus King Not Looking for 'Ego Points,'" *Associated Press Political Service*, November 9, 1994.
27. "Maine Turns to Another Independent," *Associated Press Political Service*, November 9, 1994.
28. "Candidate Puts Platform in Book," *Associated Press Political Service*, February 15, 1994.
29. "King's Transition Council Meets for the First Time," *Associated Press Political Service*, November 22, 1994.
30. "Maine Turns to Another Independent," *Associated Press Political Service*, November 9, 1994.
31. "Poll: King Picks Up Voters of All Kinds," *Associated Press Political Service*, November 9, 1994.
32. "Governor-elect King: Lots of Work Ahead," Associate Press Political Service, November 14, 1994.
33. "New Poll Shows Brennan Leading, King in No. 2 Spot," *Associated Press Political Service*, September 8, 1994.
34. "Candidates Wind Up Campaigns, Wind Down Ads, on Election Eve," *Associated Press Political Service*, November 7, 1994.
35. Collins went on to win the 1996 Senate contest by defeating Brennan. This is reminiscent of how George Mitchell was one of the losing candidates to the last independent governor of Maine (Longley) but later won a Senate seat.
36. "King Vows to Work with Legislature to Solve Problems," *Associated Press Political Service*, November 9, 1994.
37. His legal name was James George Janos.
38. "Financial Reports Tally Size of Ventura's Win," *Star-Tribune* (MN), February 3, 1999.

39. Ibid.
40. "Meet the Press," NBC, October 3, 1999.
41. "Voters Get Variety in State's Gubernatorial Campaigns," *Associated Press*, October 22, 1990. Except where noted, the information for this section comes from stories in the *Anchorage Daily News*.
42. "Theater of the Bizarre: Alaska's Governor Race," *Seattle Times*, November 31, 1990.
43. "It Takes a Bundle to Run; Candidates Raise About $3 Million," *Anchorage Daily News*, November 4, 1990.
44. "Hickel Rode a Wave of Voter Discontent," *Anchorage Daily News*, November 7, 1990.
45. "Third-Party Governorships Reflect Dissatisfaction, Present Problems," *Associated Press Political Service*, November 7, 1990.
46. The *Associated Press* noted that "Weicker is frequently described as a 'Greenwich millionaire' and 'heir to the Squibb pharmaceutical fortune'" (*"Morrison Says Weicker Income May Reveal Conflicts," Associated Press Political Service*, August 21, 1990), but his campaign was not self-funded.
47. "Maine Turns to Another Independent," November 9, 1994.
48. "Theater of the Bizarre: Alaska's Governor Race," *Seattle Times*, November 31, 1990.
49. *AAP 2000*, 867.
50. ABC News, "Congress Watch: Connecticut," 1998, ABC News website.
51. *AAP 1992*. Only twenty-five states besides these three reported party registration figures. Minnesota was not one of them.
52. According to the series *The Book of the States*, Alaska and Connecticut in 1990 both provided full budget-making power, along with veto power requiring a two-thirds majority of legislators elected (as opposed to legislators present) for an override. In 1994, the governor of Maine had "full responsibility" for budget-making power but did not have veto power, while in 1998 the Minnesota governor had a two-thirds veto and full budget-making power.
53. "Third-Party Governorships Reflect Dissatisfaction, Present Problems," *Associated Press Political Service*, November 7, 1990.
54. Rosenstone, Behr, and Lazarus (1996, 19) found that "the Democrats and Republicans have constructed a maze of cumbersome regulations and procedures that make it difficult for minor parties and independent candidates to gain a spot on the general election ballot." These regulations vary from state to state. Beck (1997, 66) noted that "the laws range from those which specify party structure in detailed and full-blown provisions of more than 5,000 words to those of states that dispose of the parties in a few sentences or paragraphs." They found that a third party candidate for office in Tennessee must find only twenty-five signatures, while other states required signatures from 5 percent of the population.

Some states also have stringent signature verification procedures that in practice require candidates to collect many more signatures than the law requires.

55. There is evidence that presidential voters do worry about "wasted votes" (Abramson, Aldrich, Paolino, and Rohde 1995; Bibby and Maisel 1998), but there is no work on whether or how this might differ in executive and legislative elections.

56. See *Tashjian v. Republican Party of Connecticut*, 479 U.S. 1024 (1986) and *Eu v. San Francisco County Democratic Central Committee et al.*, 103 L. Ed. 2nd 271 (1989). See also *California Democratic Party v. Lungren*, no. C94-1703-WHO, Northern District.

Chapter 9 Conclusions

1. See Rosenthal (1990, 26–27) for some discussion of the gubernatorial "bully pulpit."

2. Although challenger and open seat expenditures were consequential.

3. It is reasonable to think that the office of governor provides some benefits similar to those enjoyed by legislators. Beyle (1986, xxvi), for example, referred to governors as having "the power of incumbency working for them" and found that "political money [challenger expenditures] cannot always overcome the other political powers that incumbents have" (xxviii). It is doubtful that incumbents would wish to rely exclusively on these resources.

4. Although this may be changing due to the student testing requirements of the No Child Left Behind (NCLB) legislation.

5. This recalls the finding from Chapter 7 that there are generally fewer victories for candidates of the president's party in open seat midterm elections. It is unclear whether potential candidates are aware of this effect or whether it influences decisions on whether to run in a given year. It is nevertheless important for political scientists and observers to be aware that some campaigns start with more obstacles to overcome than do others.

6. See also Schumpeter (1950).

7. Schlesinger found that there were "distinct career lines" (98) for each office. This means, for instance, that state legislators were much more likely to challenge governors than senators, but that House members were more likely to challenge senators than governors.

8. Mark Shields, "Look to Montana," *New York Times*, November 28, 1993, A23.

9. Abramowitz and Segal (1992) found five incumbent scandals over seven election cycles, while this study found two scandals over nine election cycles. This amounts to more Senate scandals, even when taking into account the larger number of Senate elections.

10. See also Stimson (1976), although see Brody (1992).

11. See Rosenthal (1993) for a discussion of lobbying in the state capitals.

Bibliography

Abney, Glenn, and Thomas Lauth. 1983. "The Governor as Chief Administrator." *Public Administration Review* 43:40–49.

Abramowitz, Alan I. 1980. "A Comparison of Voting for U.S. Senator and Representative in 1978." *American Political Science Review* 74:633–640.

———. 1988. "Explaining Senate Election Outcomes." *American Political Science Review* 82:385–403.

Abramowitz, Alan, and Jeffrey Segal. 1992. *Senate Elections.* Ann Arbor: University of Michigan Press.

Abramson, Paul, John Aldrich, and David Rohde. 1987. "Progressive Ambition Among United States Senators 1972–1988." *Journal of Politics* 49:3–35.

Abramson, Paul, John Aldrich, Phil Paolino, and David Rohde. 1995. "Third-Party and Independent Candidates: Wallace, Anderson, and Perot." *Political Science Quarterly* 110:349–368.

Adams, Greg, and Peverill Squire. 1997. "Incumbent Vulnerability and Challenger Emergence in Senate Elections." *Political Behavior* 19:97–111.

Adams, James D. 1986. "Equilibrium Taxation and Experience Rating in a Federal System of Unemployment Insurance." *Journal of Public Economics* 29:51–77.

Adams, James, and Lawrence Kenny. 1989. "The Retention of State Governors." *Public Choice* 62:1–13.

Adrian, Charles. 1972. *Governing Our Fifty States and their Communities.* New York: McGraw-Hill.

Alesina, Alberto, and Howard Rosenthal. 1989. "Partisan Cycles in Congressional Elections and the Macroeconomy." *American Political Science Review* 83:373–398.

Alexander, Herbert, ed. 1976. *Campaign Money.* New York: The Free Press.

Ansolabehere, Stephen, and Shanto Iyengar. 1995. *Going Negative: How Political Advertisements Shrink and Polarize the Electorate.* New York: Free Press.

Ansolabehere, Stephen, Shanto Iyengar, and Adam Simon. 1999. "Replicating Experiments Using Aggregate and Survey Data: The Case of Negative Advertising and Turnout." *American Political Science Review* 93:901–909.

Ansolabehere, Stephen, and James M. Snyder Jr. 1995. "Money, Elections and Candidate Quality." Paper presented at the Research Seminar in

Positive Political Economy, Harvard University and Massachusetts Institute of Technology, Cambridge, MA.

———. 1996. "The Inter–Election Dynamics of Campaign Finance: U.S. House Elections, 1980 to 1994." Paper presented at the annual meeting of the American Political Science Association, San Francisco, CA, August 30–September 3.

Arnold, R. Douglas. 1990. *The Logic of Congressional Action.* New Haven, CT: Yale University Press.

Atkeson, Lonna Rae, and Randall W. Partin. 1995. "Economic and Referendum Voting: A Comparison of Gubernatorial and Senatorial Elections." *American Political Science Review* 89:99–107.

———. 1998. "Economic and Referendum Voting and the Problem of Data Choice: A Reply." *American Journal of Political Science* 42:1003–1007.

Bailey Michael, Ronald Faucheux, Paul Herrnson, and Clyde Wilcox, eds. 1999. *Campaigns and Elections: Contemporary Case Studies.* Washington, DC: Congressional Quarterly Press.

Barone, Michael, and Grant Ujifusa. 1982–2000. *Almanac of American Politics.* Washington, DC: National Journal.

Beck, Paul Allen. 1997. *Party Politics in America.* New York: Longman.

Behn, Robert D., ed. 1991. *Governors on Governing.* Lanham, MD: University Press of America.

Beiler, David. 1999a. "The Body Politic Registers a Protest: Jesse Ventura's Stunning Victory for Governor of Minnesota in 1998." In Bailey et al. 1999.

———. 1999b. "Bama Bash: Endorsement Backlash Saves a Governor from Primary Defeat in Alabama in 1998." In Bailey et al. 1999.

Bennett, Randall, and Clark Wiseman. 1991. "Economic Performance and U.S. Senate Elections, 1958–1986." *Public Choice* 69:93–100.

———. 1993. "Economic Performance and U.S. Senate Elections: Reply." *Public Choice* 76:359–363.

Berke, Richard. 1997. "Forget Washington: Social Issues Shift to the States." *New York Times*, October 19, sec. 4, p. 5.

Bernick, E. Lee, and Charles Wiggins. 1991. "Executive–Legislative Relations: The Governor's Role as Chief Legislator." In Herzik and Brown 1991.

Bernstein, Robert. 1977. "Divisive Primaries Do Hurt: U.S. Senate Races, 1956–1972." *American Political Science Review* 71:540–545.

Berry, Matthew, and Richard F. Winters. 2001. "Abortion, Party, Candidate Positions, & Issue Salience in Explaining the Post–*Webster* Vote for Governor." Paper presented at the annual meeting of the Midwest Political Science Association, Chicago, IL, April 19–21.

Beyle, Thad L. 1983. "Governors." In *Politics in the American States*, edited by Virginia Gray, Harold Jacob, and Kenneth Vines. 4th ed. Boston: Little, Brown.

———. 1985. *Gubernatorial Transitions: The 1982 Elections.* Durham, NC: Duke University Press.

———. 1986. *Re-electing the Governor: The 1982 Elections*. Lanham, MD: University Press of America.

———. 1989. *Gubernatorial Transitions: The 1983 and 1984 Elections*. Durham, NC: Duke University Press.

———. 1990. "Governors." In *Politics in the American States*, edited by Virginia Gray, Harold Jacob, and Kenneth Vines, 5th ed. Boston: Little, Brown.

———, ed. 1992. *Governors and Hard Times*. Washington, DC: Congressional Quarterly Press.

———. 1997. "The State Elections of 1996." In *Toward the Millennium: The Elections of 1996*, edited by Larry J. Sabato. Boston: Allyn and Bacon.

Beyle, Thad, and Lynn Muchmore. 1983. *Being Governor: Views from the Office*. Durham, NC: Duke University Press.

Beyle, Thad, and Oliver Williams. 1972. *The American Governor in Behavioral Perspective*. New York: Harper and Row.

Bianco, William. 1984. "Strategic Decisions on Candidacy in U.S. Congressional Districts." *Legislative Studies Quarterly* 9:351–364.

Bibby, John F., and L. Sandy Maisel. 1998. *Two Parties – Or More? The American Party System*. Boulder, CO: Westview Press.

Black, Gordon. 1972. "A Theory of Political Ambition: Career Choices and the Role of Structural Incentives." *American Political Science Review* 66:144–159.

Bloom, Howard S., and H. Douglas Price. 1975. "Voters Response to Short-run Economic Conditions: The Asymmetric Effect of Prosperity and Recession." *American Political Science Review* 69:1240–1254.

Bond, Jon R. 1983. "The Influence of Constituency Diversity on Electoral Competition in Congress, 1974–1978." *Legislative Studies Quarterly* 8:201–211.

———. 1985. "Dimensions of District Attention Over Time." *American Journal of Political Science* 29:330–347.

Bond, John, Cary Covington, and Richard Fleisher. 1985. "Explaining Challenger Quality in Congressional Elections." *Journal of Politics* 41:510–529.

Borders, Rebecca, and C. C. Dockery. 1995. *Beyond the Hill: A Directory of Congress from 1984 to 1993*. Lanham, MD: University Press of America/Center for Public Integrity.

Born, Richard. 1986. "Strategic Politicians and Unresponsive Voters." *American Political Science Review* 80:599–612.

Box-Steffensmeier, Janet. 1996. "A Dynamic Analysis of the Role of War Chests in Campaign Strategy." *American Journal of Political Science* 40:352–371.

Boyd, Richard W. 1981. "Decline of U.S. Voter Turnout: Structural Explanations." *American Politics Quarterly* 9:133–160.

———. 1986. "Election Calendars and Voter Turnout." *American Politics Quarterly* 14:89–104.

———. 1989. "The Effects of Primaries and Statewide Races on Voter Turnout." *Journal of Politics* 51:730–739.

Brace, Paul. 1984. "Progressive Ambition in the House: A Probabilistic Approach." *Journal of Politics* 46:556–569.

———. 1985. "A Probabilistic Approach to Retirement from the U.S. Congress." *Legislative Studies Quarterly* 10:107–123.

———. 1989. "Isolating the Economies of States." *American Politics Quarterly* 17:256–276.

———. 1991. "The Changing Context of State Political Economy." *Journal of Politics* 53:297–317.

———. 1993. *State Government and Economic Performance.* Baltimore: Johns Hopkins University Press.

Brace, Paul, and Barbara Hinckley. 1992. *Follow the Leader: Opinion Polls and the Modern Presidents.* New York: Basic Books.

———. 1998. "Natural Disasters and Incumbency Advantage: Constituency Service Effects that Get Past the Endogeneity Problem." Manuscript, Department of Government, Harvard University.

Brody, Richard A. 1991. *Assessing the President: The Media, Elite Opinion, and Public Support.* Stanford: Stanford University Press.

Brody, Richard A., and Paul Sniderman. 1977. "From Life Space to Polling Place: The Relevance of Personal Concerns for Voting Behavior." *British Journal of Political Science* 7:337–360.

Bruno, Hal. 2000. "Campaign 2000: Do Polls Affect How People Vote?" CNN's TalkBack Live. Aired October 24.

Buell, Emmett Jr. 1986. "Divisive Primaries and Participation in Fall Presidential Campaigns: A Study of the 1984 New Hampshire Primary Activists." *American Politics Quarterly* 14:376–390.

Cain, Bruce, John Ferejohn, and Morris Fiorina. 1987. *The Personal Vote.* Cambridge, MA: Harvard University Press.

Caldeira, Gregory, Samuel Patterson, and Gregory Markko. 1985. "The Mobilization of Voters in Congressional Elections." *Journal of Politics* 47: 490–509.

Campbell, Angus. 1966. "Surge and Decline: A Study of Electoral Change." In *Elections and the Political Order*, edited by Angus Campbell, Philip Converse, Warren Miller, and Donald Stokes. New York: Wiley.

Campbell, James. 1985. "Explaining Presidential Losses in Midterm Congressional Elections." *Journal of Politics* 47:1140–1157.

Canon, David. 1990. *Actors, Athletes and Astronauts: Political Amateurs in the United States Congress.* Chicago: University of Chicago Press.

Carmines, Edward G., and James A. Stimson. 1989. *Issue Evolution: Race and the Transformation of American Politics.* Princeton, NJ: Princeton University Press.

Carsey, Thomas M. 2000. *Campaign Dynamics: The Race for Governor.* Ann Arbor: University of Michigan Press.

Carsey, Thomas M., and Gerald C. Wright. 1998. "State and National Factors in Gubernatorial and Senatorial Elections." *American Journal of Political Science* 42:994–1002.

———. 1998. "State and National Factors in Gubernatorial and Senatorial Elections: A Rejoinder." *American Journal of Political Science* 42:1008–1011.

Chressanthis, George, and Stephen Shaffer. 1993. "Economic Performance and U.S. Senate Elections: A Comment." *Public Choice* 75:263–277.

Chubb, John. 1988. "Institutions, the Economy, and the Dynamics of State Elections." *American Political Science Review* 82:133–154.

Clarke, M. K. 1986. *Revitalizing State Economics: A Review of State Economic Development Policies and Programs.* Washington, DC: National Governors Association Press.

Cohen, Jeffrey E. 1982. "Change in Election Calendars and Turnout Decline: A Test of Boyd's Hypothesis." *American Politics Quarterly* 10:246–254.

Congressional Quarterly. 1994. *Congressional Quarterly's Guide to United States Elections.* 3rd ed. Washington, DC: Congressional Quarterly Press.

———. 1998. *Gubernatorial Elections: 1787–1997.* Washington, DC: Congressional Quarterly Press.

Cook, Elizabeth, Ted Jelen, and Clyde Wilcox. 1994. "Issue Voting in Gubernatorial Elections: Abortion and Post-Webster Politics." *Journal of Politics* 56:187–189.

Copeland, Gary. 1989. "Choosing to Run: Why House Members Seek Election to the Senate." *Legislative Studies Quarterly* 14:549–565.

Council of Economic Advisors. 1996. *Economic Report of the President.* Washington, DC: United States Government Printing Office.

Council of State Governments. *The Book of the States.* Various editions. Lexington, KY.

Cox, Gary. 1988. "Closeness and Turnout: A Methodological Note." *Journal of Politics* 50:768–775.

Cox, Gary, and Michael Munger. 1989. "Closeness, Expenditure, and Turnout: The 1982 U.S. House Elections." *American Political Science Review* 83:217–232.

Cox, Raymond III. 1991. "The Management Role of the Governor." In Herzik and Brown 1991.

Damasio, Antonio R. 1994. *Descartes' Error: Emotion, Reason, and the Human Brain.* New York: G. P. Putnam.

Dantico, Marilyn, and Alvin Mushkatel. 1991. "Governors and Nuclear Waste: Showdown in the Rockies." In Herzik and Brown 1991.

Davidson, Roger H. 1969. *The Role of the Congressman.* New York: Pegasus.

Dawson, Paul A., and James E. Zinsser. 1976. "Political Finance and Participation in Congressional Elections." *Annals of the American Academy of Political and Social Sciences* 425:59–73.

Dometrius, Nelson. 1988. "Measuring Gubernatorial Power: The Measure vs. the Reality." *Western Political Quarterly* 40:319–334.

———. 1999. "Governors: Their Heritage and Future." In *American State and Local Politics: Directions for the 21st Century*, edited by Ronald Weber and Paul Brace. New York: Chatham House.

Downs, Anthony. 1957. *An Economic Theory of Democracy*. New York: Harper and Row.

Dye, Thomas. 1966. *Politics, Economics, and Public Policy in the American States*. Chicago: Rand McNally.

———. 1969. "Executive Power and Public Policy in the States." *Western Political Quarterly* 27:926–939.

———. 1973. *Politics in States and Communities*. Engelwood Cliffs, NJ: Prentice Hall.

Edelman, Murray. 1988. *Constructing the Political Spectacle*. Chicago: University of Chicago Press.

Edsall, Thomas B., and Mary B. Edsall. 1991. *Chain Reaction: The Impact of Race, Rights, and Taxes on American Politics*. New York: Norton.

Edwards, George C. III. 1983. *The Public Presidency: The Pursuit of Popular Support*. New York: St. Martin's Press.

Ehrenhalt, Alan. 1992. *The United States of Ambition: Politicians, Power, and the Pursuit of Office*. New York: Times Books.

Elkin, Stephen. 1984. "Twentieth Century Urban Regimes." *Journal of Urban Affairs* 8:11–28.

Epple, Dennis, and Allan Zelenitz. 1981. "The Implications of Competition Among Jurisdictions: Does Tiebout Need Politics?" *Journal of Political Economy* 89:1197–1218.

Erikson, Robert S. 1988. "The Puzzle of Midterm Loss." *Journal of Politics* 25:1011–1029.

———. 1989. "Economic Conditions and the Presidential Vote." *American Political Science Review* 83:567–576.

———. 1990. "Economic Conditions and the Congressional Vote: A Review of the Macrolevel Evidence." *American Journal of Political Science* 34:373–399.

Erikson, Robert S., and Gerald C. Wright. 1989. "Voters, Candidates, and Issues in Congressional Elections." In *Congress Reconsidered*, edited by Lawrence Dodd and Bruce Oppenheimer. Washington, DC: Congressional Quarterly Press.

Erikson, Robert S., Gerald C. Wright, and John P. McIver. 1993. *Statehouse Democracy: Public Opinion and Policy in the American States*. Cambridge: Cambridge University Press.

Fair, Roy. 1978. "The Effects of Economic Events on Votes for President." *Review of Economics and Statistics* 10:168–179.

———. 1988. "The Effect of Economic Events on Votes for President: A 1984 Update." *Political Behavior* 10:168–179.

Faucheux, Ronald. 1999. "Only in Louisiana: Populist Message Propels Republican to Governor's Mansion in Louisiana in 1995." In Bailey et al. 1999.

Fenno, Richard F. Jr. 1978. *Home Style.* Boston: Little, Brown.

———. 1982. *The United States Senate: A Bicameral Perspective.* Washington, DC: American Enterprise Institute.

———. 1989. *The Making of a Senator: Dan Quayle.* Washington, DC: Congressional Quarterly Press.

Ferejohn, John, and Morris Fiorina. 1974. "The Paradox of Not Voting: A Decision Theoretical Analysis." *American Political Science Review* 68:525–536.

———. 1975. "Closeness Counts Only in Horseshoes and Dancing." *American Political Science Review* 69:920–925.

Fiorina, Morris. 1974. *Representatives, Roll Calls, and Constituencies.* Lexington, MA: Lexington Books.

———. 1977. *Congress: Keystone of the Washington Establishment.* New Haven, CT: Yale University Press.

———. 1978. "Economic Retrospective Voting in American Elections." *American Political Science Review* 22:426–443.

———. 1981. *Retrospective Voting in American National Elections.* New Haven, CT: Yale University Press.

Fiorina, Morris P. 1983. "Who is Held Responsible? Further Evidence on the Hibbing-Alford Thesis." *American Journal of Political Science* 27:158–164.

———. 1992. *Divided Government.* New York: Macmillan.

———. 1994. "Divided Government in the American States: A Byproduct of Legislative Professionalism?" *American Political Science Review* 88:304–316.

Fitzpatrick, Gary L., and Marilyn J. Modlin. 1986. *Direct-line Distances: United States Edition.* Metuchen, NJ: Scarecrow Press.

Fowler, Linda L. 1979. "The Electoral Lottery: Decisions to Run for Congress." *Public Choice,* 34:399–418.

Fowler, Linda, and Robert McClure. 1987. *Political Ambition: Who Decides to Run for Congress.* New Haven, CT: Yale University Press.

Frantzich, Stephen. 1978. "Opting Out: Retirement from the House of Representatives." *American Political Science Review* 6:251–273.

Friedland, Roger, Frances Fox Piven, and Robert Alford. 1977. "Political Conflict, Urban Structure and the Fiscal Crisis." In *Campaigning for Public Policy,* edited by Douglas Ashford. Beverly Hills: Sage.

Gerber, Alan. 1998. "Estimating the Effect of Campaign Spending on Senate Election Outcomes Using Instrumental Variables." *American Political Science Review* 92:401–412.

Glantz, Stanton, Alan Abramowitz, and Michael Burkhart. 1976. "Election Outcomes: Whose Money Matters?" *Journal of Politics* 38:1033–1038.

Glazer, Amihai, and Bernand Grofman. 1987. "Two Plus Two Plus Two Equals Six: Tenure in Office of Senators and Representatives, 1953–1983." *Legislative Studies Quarterly* 12:555–563.

Goldenberg, Edie, and Michael Traugott. 1984. *Campaigning for Congress.* Washington, DC: Congressional Quarterly Press.

Goldenberg, Edie, Michael Traugott, and Frank Baumgartner. 1986. "Preemptive and Reactive Spending in U.S. House Races." *Political Behavior* 8:3–20.

Gough, Paul A. 1984. "Economic Conditions and Congressional Elections." *American Politics Quarterly* 12:71–88.

Graber, Doris. 1997. *The Mass Media and American Politics.* Washington, DC: Congressional Quarterly Press.

Grady, Dennis. 1989. "Governors and Economic Development Policy." *Policy Studies Journal* 17:879–894.

———. 1991. "Managing the State Economy: The Governor's Role in Policymaking." In Herzik and Brown 1991.

Gray, Jeffrey Alan. 1987. *The Psychology of Fear and Stress.* Cambridge: Cambridge University Press.

Gray, Virginia. 1976. "A Note on Competition and Turnout in the American States." *Journal of Politics* 38:153–158.

Green, Donald, and Jonathan Krasno. 1988. "Salvation for the Spendthrift Incumbent: Reestimating the Effects of Campaign Spending in House Elections." *American Journal of Political Science* 32:884–907.

Grier, Kevin B. 1989. "Campaign Spending and Senate Elections, 1978–1984." *Public Choice* 63:201–219.

Groseclose, Timothy, and Keith Krehbiel. 1994. "Golden Parachutes, Rubber Checks, and Strategic Retirements from the 102d House." *American Journal of Political Science* 38:75–99.

Gross, Donald A. 1989. "Governors and Policymaking: Theoretical Concerns and Analytic Approaches." *Policy Studies Journal* 17:764–781.

———. 1991. "The Policy Role of Governors." In Herzik and Brown 1991.

Haas, Peter, and Deil Wright. 1989. "Public Policy and Administrative Turnover in State Government: The Role of the Governor." *Policy Studies Journal* 17:788–803.

Hacker, Andrew. 1965. "Does a Divisive Primary Harm a Candidate's Election Chances?" *American Political Science Review* 59:105–110.

Hain, Paul. 1974. "Age, Ambition and Political Careers: The Middle-Age Crisis." *Western Political Quarterly* 27:265–274.

Hall, Robert, and Robert Van Houweling. 1995. "Avarice and Ambition in Congress: Representatives' Decision to Run or Retire from the U.S. House." *American Political Science Review* 89:121–136.

Hamilton, Gary, and Nicole Woolsey Biggart. 1984. *Governor Reagan, Governor Brown.* New York: Columbia University Press.

Hammond, Jay. 1994. *Tales of Alaska's Bush Rat Governor: The Extraordinary Biography of Jay Hammond, Wilderness Guide and Reluctant Politician.* Fairbanks: Epicenter Press.

Hansen, Mark, and Steven Rosenstone. 1984. "Context, Mobilization, and Political Participation." Yale University (typescript).

Hanson, Russell. 1998. "The Interaction of State and Local Governments." In *Governing Partners: State–Local Relations in the United States*, edited by Russell Hanson. Boulder, CO: Westview Press.

Hebert, F. Ted, Jeffrey Brudney, and Deil Wright. 1983. "Gubernatorial Influence and State Bureaucracy." *American Politics Quarterly* 11:243–264.

Heclo, Hugh. 1981. "Introduction: The Presidential Illusion." In *The Illusion of Presidential Governance*, edited by Hugh Heclo and Lester Salamon. Boulder, CO: Westview Press.

Hendrick, Rebecca M., and James C. Garand. 1991. "Variation in State Economic Growth." *Journal of Politics* 53:1093–1110.

Herrnson, Paul S., and John C. Green. 1997. "Making or Repeating History? American Party Politics at the Dawn of a New Century." In *Multiparty Politics in America*, edited by Paul S. Herrnson and John C. Green. Lanham, MD: Rowman and Littlefield.

Herzik, Eric B. 1991. "Policy Agendas and Gubernatorial Leadership." In Herzik and Brown 1991.

Herzik, Eric B., and Brent W. Brown, eds. 1991. *Gubernatorial Leadership and State Policy*. New York: Greenwood Press.

Hetherington, Marc. 1996. "The Media's Role in Forming Voters' National Economic Evaluations in 1992." *American Journal of Political Science* 40:372–395.

Hibbing, John. 1982. *Choosing to Leave: Voluntary Retirement from the U.S. House of Representatives*. Washington, DC: University Press of America.

———. 1991. *Congressional Careers: Contours of Life in the U.S. House of Representatives*. Chapel Hill: University of North Carolina Press.

Hibbing, John R., and John R. Alford. 1981. "The Electoral Impact of Economic Conditions: Who is Held Responsible?" *American Journal of Political Science* 25:423–439.

Hibbing, John, and John Alford. 1982. "Economic Conditions and the Forgotten Side of Congress: A Foray into U.S. Senate Elections." *British Journal of Political Science* 12:505–516.

Hibbing, John, and Sara Brandes. 1983. "State Population and the Electoral Success of U.S. Senators." *American Journal of Political Science* 27:808–819.

Hibbs, Douglas A. Jr. 1982. "President Reagan's Mandate from the 1980 Elections: A Shift to the Right?" *American Politics Quarterly* 10:387–420.

———. 1987. *The American Political Economy: Macroeconomics and Electoral Politics in the United States*. Cambridge, MA: Harvard University Press.

Hill, Kim Quaile, and Jan E. Leighley. 1993. "Party Ideology, Organization, and Competitiveness as Mobilizing Forces in Gubernatorial Elections." *American Journal of Political Science* 37:1158–1178.

Hinckley, Barbara. 1980. "House Reelections and Senate Defeats: The Role of the Challenger." *British Journal of Political Science* 10:441–460.

———. 1981. *Congressional Elections*. Washington, DC: Congressional Quarterly Press.

———. 1990. *The Symbolic Presidency: How Presidents Present Themselves*. New York: Routledge.

Hinckley, Barbara, Richard Hofstetter, and John Kessel. 1974. "Information and the Vote: A Comparative Election Study." *American Politics Quarterly* 2:131–158.

Hodges, Luther H. 1962. *Businessman in the Statehouse: Six Years as Governor of North Carolina*. Chapel Hill: University of North Carolina Press.

Holbrook, Thomas M. 1993. "Institutional Strength and Gubernatorial Elections: An Exploratory Analysis." *American Politics Quarterly* 21:261–271.

Holbrook, Thomas M., and Emily Van Dunk. 1993. "Electoral Competition in the American States." *American Political Science Review* 87:955–962.

Holbrook-Provow, Thomas. 1987. "National Factors in Gubernatorial Elections." *American Politics Quarterly* 15:471–483.

Howell, Susan E., and Robert Sims. 1993. "Abortion Attitudes and the Louisiana Governor's Election." *American Politics Quarterly* 21:54–63.

Howell, Susan E., and James M. Vanderleeuw. 1990. "Economic Effects of State Governors." *American Politics Quarterly* 18:158–168.

Iyengar, Shanto, and Donald Kinder. 1987. *News That Matters*. Chicago: University of Chicago Press.

Jacob, Herbert, and Kenneth N. Vines, eds. 1965. *Politics in the American States: A Comparative Analysis*. Boston: Little, Brown.

Jacobson, Gary C. 1978. "The Effects of Campaign Spending in Congressional Elections." *American Political Science Review* 72:469–491.

———. 1980. *Money in Congressional Elections*. New Haven, CT: Yale University Press.

———. 1983. *The Politics of Congressional Elections*. Boston: Little, Brown.

———. 1984. "Money in the 1980 and 1982 Congressional Elections." In *Money and Politics in the United States: Financing Elections in the 1980s*, edited by Michael J. Malbin. Chatham, NJ: Chatham House.

———. 1985. "Money and Votes Reconsidered: Congressional Elections, 1972–1982." *Public Choice* 47:7–62.

———. 1990. "The Effects of Campaign Spending in House Elections: New Evidence for Old Arguments." *American Journal of Political Science* 34:334–362.

Jacobson, Gary C., and Samuel Kernell. 1983. *Strategy and Choice in Congressional Elections*. 2nd ed. New Haven, CT: Yale University Press.

Jacobson, Gary, and Raymond Wolfinger. 1989. "Information and Voting in California Senate Elections." *Legislative Studies Quarterly* 14:509–529.

———. 1990. "National Forces in the 1986 House Elections." *Legislative Studies Quarterly* 15:65–87.

Jewell, Malcolm E. 1977. "Voting Turnout in State Gubernatorial Primaries." *Western Political Quarterly* 30:236–254.

———. 1984. *Parties and Primaries: Nominating State Governors*. New York: Praeger.

Jewell, Malcolm E. and David M. Olson. 1978. *American State Political Parties and Elections*. Homewood, IL: Dorsey.

Jones, Charles O. 1981. "The New, New Senate." In *A Tide of Discontent*, edited by Ellis Sandoz and Cecil V. Crabb. Washington, DC: Congressional Quarterly Press.

Kahn, Kim Fridkin. 1993. "The News Medium's Message: A Comparison of Press Coverage in Gubernatorial and Senate Elections." Paper presented at the annual meeting of the Midwest Political Science Association, Chicago, IL, April 15–17.

Kahn, Kim Fridkin, and Patrick J. Kenney. 1999. *The Spectacle of U.S. Senate Elections*. Princeton, NJ: Princeton University Press.

Kaplan, Marshall, and Due O'Brien. 1991. *The Governors and the New Federalism*. Boulder, CO: Westview Press.

Kazee, Thomas. 1983. "The Deterrent Effects of Incumbency on Recruiting Challengers in U.S. House Elections." *Legislative Studies Quarterly* 8:469–480.

Keith, Bruce, David Magleby, Candice Nelson, Elizabeth Orr, Mark Westlye, and Raymond Wolfinger. 1992. *The Myth of the Independent Voter*. Berkeley: University of California Press.

Kenney, Patrick J. 1983a. "The Effect of State Economic Conditions on the Vote for Governor." *Social Science Quarterly* 64:154–162.

———. 1983b. "Explaining Turnout in Gubernatorial Primaries." *American Politics Quarterly* 11:315–326.

———. 1988. "Sorting Out the Effects of Primary Divisiveness in Congressional and Senatorial Elections." *Western Political Quarterly* 41:765–777.

Kenney, Patrick, and Tom Rice. 1984. "The Effect of Primary Divisiveness in Gubernatorial and Senatorial Elections." *Journal of Politics* 46:904–915.

———. 1987. "The Relationship Between Divisive Primaries and General Election Outcomes." *American Journal of Political Science* 31:31–44.

Kernell, Sam. 1978. "Explaining Presidential Popularity." *American Political Science Review* 72:506–522.

Key, V. O. Jr. 1956. *American State Politics*. New York: Knopf.

———. 1966. *The Responsible Electorate*. New York: Vintage Books.

Kiewiet, D. Roderick. 1983. *Macroeconomics and Micropolitics*. Chicago: University of Chicago Press.

Kiewiet, D. Roderick, and Langche Zeng. 1993. "An Analysis of Congressional Career Decisions, 1947–1986." *American Political Science Review* 87:928–944.

Kinder, Donald. 1981. "Presidents, Prosperity, and Public Opinion." *Public Opinion Quarterly* 45:1–21.

Kinder, Donald, and D. Roderick Kiewiet. 1979. "Economic Discontent and Political Behavior: The Role of Personal Grievances and Collective

Economic Judgments in Congressional Voting." *American Journal of Political Science* 23:495–527.

———. 1981. "Sociotropic Politics: The American Case." *British Journal of Political Science* 11:129–161.

King, Gary, and Lyn Ragsdale. 1988. *The Elusive Presidency: Discovering Statistical Patterns in the Presidency.* Washington, DC: Congressional Quarterly Press.

King, James D. 1994. "Political Culture, Registration Laws, and Voter Turnout among the American States." *Publius* 24:115–127.

King, James D. 1999. "Looking Back at Chief Executives: Retrospective Presidential Approval." *Presidential Studies Quarterly* 29:166–174.

———. 2001. "Incumbent Popularity and Vote Choice in Gubernatorial Elections." *Journal of Politics* 63:585–597.

———. 1995/96. "Impact of Election Day Registration on Voter Turnout: A Quasi-experimental Analysis." *Policy Studies Review* 14:263–278.

Kingston, M. Jean. 1989. *Explaining Gubernatorial Election Outcomes: 1950–1985.* PhD diss., University of Georgia.

Kone, Susan F., and Richard F. Winters. 1993. "Taxes and Voting: Electoral Retribution in the American States." *Journal of Politics* 55:22–40.

Kostroski, Warren. 1978. "The Effect of Number of Terms on the Reelection of Senators, 1920–1970." *Journal of Politics* 40:488–497.

Kramer, Gerald. 1971. "Short-term Fluctuations in U.S. Voting Behavior, 1896–1964." *American Political Science Review* 65:131–143.

Krasno, Jonathan S. 1994. *Challengers, Competition, and Reelection.* New Haven, CT: Yale University Press.

Krasno, Jonathan, and Donald Green. 1988. "Preempting Quality Challengers in House Elections." *Journal of Politics* 50:920–936.

Leal, David L. 1999. "Congress and Charter Schools." In *School Choice in the Real World: Lessons from Arizona Charter Schools,* edited by Robert Maranto, Scott Milliman, Frederick Hess, and April Gresham. Boulder, CO: Westview Press.

———. 2002. "Home is Where the Heart is: Congressional Tenure, Retirement, and the Implications for Representation." *American Politics Research* 30:266–285.

LeBlanc, Hugh, and D. Trudeau Allensworth. 1971. *The Politics of States and Urban Communities.* New York: Harper and Row.

LeDoux, Joseph E. 1998. *The Emotional Brain: The Mysterious Underpinnings of Emotional Life.* New York: Simon and Schuster.

Lengle, James. 1980. "Divisive Presidential Primaries and Party Electoral Prospects, 1932–1976." *American Politics Quarterly* 8:261–277.

Lester, James. 1980. "Partisanship and Environmental Policy: The Mediating Influence of State Organizational Structures." *Environment and Behavior* 12:101–131.

Levernier, Willliam. 1992. "The Effect of Relative Economic Performance on the Outcome of Gubernatorial Elections." *Public Choice* 74:181–190.

Levine, Martin, and Mark Hyde. 1977. Incumbency and the Theory of Political Ambition: A Rational-Choice Model. *Journal of Politics* 39:959–983.

Lewis-Beck, Michael, and Tom Rice. 1984. "Forecasting U.S. House Elections." *Legislative Studies Quarterly* 9:475–486.

Leyden, Kevin, and Stephen Borrelli. 1995. "The Effect of State Economic Conditions on Gubernatorial Elections: Does Unified Government Make a Difference?" *Political Research Quarterly* 48:275–290.

Lockard, Duane, ed. 1969. *Governing the States and Localities.* Toronto: Macmillan.

Lockerbie, Brad. 1991. "The Temporal Pattern of Economic Evaluations and Vote Choice in Senate Elections." *Public Choice* 69:279–294.

Loevy, Robert. 1996. *The Flawed Path to the Governorship-1994: The Nationalization of a Colorado Statewide Election.* Lanham, MD: University Press of America.

Loomis, Burdett A. 1984. *The New American Politician.* New York: Basic Books.

Lott, John. 1987. "Political Cheating." *Public Choice* 52:169–187.

Lott, John, and Stephen Bronars. 1993. "Timer Series Evidence on Shirking in the U.S. House of Representatives." *Public Choice* 76:125–149.

Lott, William F., and P. D. Warner III. 1974. "The Relative Importance of Campaign Expenditures: An Application of the Production Theory." *Quality and Quantity* 8:99–105.

Lowi, Theodore. 1985. *The Personal President.* Ithaca, NY: Cornell University Press.

Lubenow, Gerald C., ed. 1990. *California Votes – The 1990 Governor's Race.* Berkeley, CA: Institute of Government Studies Press.

———. 1991. *The 1990 Governor's Race: An Inside Look at the Candidates and their Campaigns by the People Who Managed Them.* Berkeley, CA: Institute of Government Studies Press.

———. 1994. *California Votes – The 1994 Governor's Race.* Berkeley, CA: Institute of Government Studies Press.

Lublin, David. 1994. "Quality, Not Quantity: Strategic Politicians in U.S. Senate Elections, 1952–1990." *Journal of Politics* 56:228–241.

Luttbeg, Norman. 1983. "Television Viewing Audience and Congressional District Incongruity: A Handicap for the Challenger?" *Journal of Broadcasting* 27:411–417.

Magleby, David B. 1989. "More Ban for the Buck: Campaign Spending in Small-State U.S. Senate Elections." Paper presented at the annual meeting of the Western Political Science Association, Salt Lake City, UT, March 30–April 1.

Maisel, L. Sandy, 1994. *The Parties Respond: Changes in the American Party System.* 2nd ed. Boulder, CO: Westview.

Mann, Thomas E., and Raymond E. Wolfinger. 1980. "Candidates and Parties in Congressional Elections." *American Political Science Review* 74:617–632.

Markus, Gregory. 1988. "The Impact of Personal and National Economic Conditions on the Presidential Vote: A Pooled Cross-sectional Analysis." *American Journal of Political Science* 32:137–154.

Mayhew, David. 1974. *Congress: The Electoral Connection.* New Haven, CT: Yale University Press.

Milbrath, Lester. 1971. "Individuals and Government." In *Politics in the American States,* edited by Herbert Jacob and Kenneth Vines. 2nd ed. Boston: Little, Brown.

Mollenkopf, John. 1983. *The Contested City.* Princeton, NJ: Princeton University Press.

Moore, Michael K., and John R. Hibbing. 1992. "Is Serving in Congress Fun Again? Voluntary Retirements from the House since the 1970s." *American Journal of Political Science* 36:824–828.

Morehouse, Sarah McCally. 1976. "The Governor as Political Leader." In *Politics in the American States,* edited by Harold Jacob and Kenneth Vines. 3rd ed. Boston: Little, Brown.

———. 1980. "The Politics of Gubernatorial Nominations." *State Government* 53:125–128.

———. 1981. *State Politics, Parties and Policies.* New York: Holt, Rinehart and Winston.

———. 1990. "Money vs. Party Effort: Nominating for Governor." *American Journal of Political Science* 34:706–724.

———. 1998. *The Governor as Party Leader: Campaigning and Governing.* Ann Arbor: University of Michigan Press.

Morris, Celia. 1992. *Storming the Statehouse: Running for Governor with Ann Richards and Dianne Feinstein.* New York: Scribners.

Muchmore, Lynn R. 1983. "The Governor as Manager." In Beyle and Muchmore 1983.

Mueller, John E. 1973. *War, Presidents and Public Opinion.* New York: Wiley.

Munger, Frank, ed. 1966. *American State Politics.* New York: Thomas Y. Crowell.

Nagel, Jack, and John McNulty. 1996. "Partisan Effects of Voter Turnout in Senatorial and Gubernatorial Elections." *American Political Science Review* 90:780–793.

Neustadt, Richard. 1990. *Presidential Power and the Modern Presidents.* New York: The Free Press.

Nichols, David. 1994. *The Myth of the Modern Presidency.* University Park: Pennsylvania State University Press.

Niemi, Richard, Harold Stanley, and Ronald Vogel. 1995. "State Economies and State Taxes: Do Voters Hold Governors Accountable?" *American Journal of Political Science* 39:936–957.

Oppenheimer, Bruce, James Stimson, and Richard Waterman. 1986. "Interpreting U.S. House Elections: The Exposure Thesis." *Legislative Studies Quarterly* 11:227–247.

Ornstein, Norman, Thomas Mann, and Michael Malbin. 1996. *Vital Statistics on Congress 1995–1996*. Washington, DC: Congressional Quarterly Press.

———. 1998. *Vital Statistics on Congress 1997–1998*. Washington, DC: Congressional Quarterly Press.

Osborne, David. 1990. *Laboratories of Democracy*. Boston: Harvard Business School Press.

Palda, Kristian. 1973. "Does Advertising Influence Votes? An Analysis of the 1966 and 1970 Quebec Elections." *Canadian Journal of Political Science* 6:638–655.

———. 1975. "The Effect of Expenditures on Political Success." *Journal of Law and Economics* 18:745–771.

Palmer, Kenneth T. 1972. *State Politics in the United States*. New York: St. Martin's Press.

Parker, Glenn R. 1986. *Homeward Bound: Explaining Changes in Congressional Behavior*. Pittsburgh, PA: University of Pittsburgh Press.

Partin, Randall W. 1995. "Economic Conditions and Gubernatorial Elections: Is the State Executive Held Accountable?" *American Politics Quarterly* 23:81–95.

Patterson, Samuel C. 1982. "Campaign Spending in Contests for Governor." *Western Politics Quarterly* 35:457–477.

———. 1993. *Out of Order*. New York: Knopf.

Patterson, Samuel C., and Gregory Caldeira. 1983. "Getting Out the Vote: Participation in Gubernatorial Elections." *American Political Science Review* 77:675–689.

———. 1984. "The Etiology of Partisan Competition." *American Political Science Review* 78:691–707.

Peltzman, Sam. 1987. "Economic Conditions and Gubernatorial Elections." *American Economic Review* 7:293–297.

———. 1998. "How Efficient is the Voting Market?" *Center for the Study of the Economy and the State*, University of Chicago, Working Paper No. 53.

Peters, John G., and Susan Welch. 1980. "The Effects of Charges of Corruption on Voting Behavior in Congressional Elections." *American Political Science Review* 74:697–708.

Peterson, Paul. 1981. *City Limits*. Chicago: University of Chicago Press.

———. 1995. *The Price of Federalism*. Washington, DC: Brookings Institution/Twentieth-Century Fund.

Powell, G. Bingham Jr. 1986. "American Voter Turnout in Comparative Perspective." *American Political Science Review* 80:17–44.

Price, H. Douglas. 1971. "The Congressional Career: Then and Now." In *Congressional Behavior*, edited by Nelson Polsby. New York: Random House.

———. 1975. "Congress and the Evolution of Legislative Professionalism." In *Congress in Change*, edited by Norman J. Ornstein. New York: Praeger.

Ranney, Austin. 1976. "Parties in State Politics." In *Politics in the American States*, edited by Herbert Jacob and Kenneth Vines. 3rd ed. Boston: Little, Brown.

Ransome, Coleman B. Jr. 1982. *The American Governorship*. Westport, CT: Greenwood Press.

Reiter, Howard. 1979. "The Divisive Primary: A New Approach." Paper presented at the annual meeting of the American Political Science Association, Washington, DC, August 31-September 3.

Riker, William, and Peter Ordeshook. 1968. "A Theory of the Calculus of Voting." *American Political Science Review* 62:25–42.

Rohde, David. 1979. "Risk-Bearing and Progressive Ambition: The Case of Members of the United States House of Representatives." *American Journal of Political Science* 23:1–26.

———. 1988. "Studying Congressional Norms: Concepts and Evidence." *Congress and the Presidency* 15:139–146.

Rosenstone, Steven, Roy Behr, and Edward Lazarus. 1996. *Third Parties in America*. Princeton, NJ: Princeton University Press.

Rosenthal, Alan. 1990. *Governors and Legislatures: Contending Powers*. Washington, DC: Congressional Quarterly Press.

———. 1992. "Foreword." In *Governors and Hard Times*, edited by Thad L. Beyle. Washington, DC: Congressional Quarterly Press.

———. 1993. *The Third House: Lobbyists and Lobbying in the States*. Washington, DC: Congressional Quarterly Press.

Sabato, Larry. 1980. "Gubernatorial Politics and the New Campaign Technology." *State Government* 53:148–152.

———. 1983. *Goodbye to Good-time Charlie: The American Governorship Transformed*. Washington, DC: Congressional Quarterly Press.

Sanford, Terry. 1967. *Storm Over the States*. New York: McGraw-Hill.

Schlesinger, Joseph. A. 1957. *How They Became Governor: A Study of Comparative State Politics, 1870–1950*. East Lansing, MI: Governmental Research Bureau, Michigan State University.

———. 1965. "The Politics of the Executive." In *Politics in the American States*, edited by Herbert Jacob and Kenneth Vines. Boston: Little, Brown.

———. 1966. *Ambition and Politics: Political Careers in the United States*. Chicago: Rand McNally.

Schlozman, Kay Lehman, and Sidney Verba. 1979. *Injury to Insult: Unemployment, Class, and Political Response*. Cambridge, MA: Harvard University Press.

Schneider, Saundra. 1989. "Governors and Health Care Policy." *Policy Studies Journal* 17:809–826.

———. 1991. "Governors and Health Care Policymaking: The Case of Medicaid." In Herzik and Brown 1991.

Schumpeter, Joseph. 1950. *Capitalism, Socialism, and Democracy*. New York: Harper and Row.

Seroka, Jim. 1980. "Incumbency and Re-election: Governors v. U.S. Senators." *State Government* 53:161–165.

Shannon, John. 1987. "The Return of Fend-for-Yourself Federalism: The Reagan Mark." *Intergovernmental Perspectives* 13:34–37.

Sigelman, Lee, and Nelson Dometrius. 1988. "Governors as Chief Administrators." *American Politics Quarterly* 16:157–170.

Silberman, Jonathan. 1976. "A Comment on the Economics of Campaign Funds." *Public Choice* 25:69–73.

Silberman, Jonathan, and Gilbert Yochum. 1978. "The Role of Money in Determining Election Outcomes." *Social Science Quarterly* 58:671–682.

Sinclair, Upton. 1935. *I, Candidate for Governor: And How I Got Licked.* New York: Farrar and Rinehart.

Skowronek, Stephen. 1993. *The Politics Presidents Make: Leadership from John Adams to George Bush.* Cambridge, MA: Harvard University Press.

Southwell, Priscilla. 1986. "The Politics of Disgruntlement: Nonvoting and Defections from Supporters of Nomination Losers, 1968–1984." *Political Behavior* 8:81–95.

Squire, Peverill. 1989. "Challengers in U.S. Senate Elections." *Legislative Studies Quarterly* 14:531–547.

———. 1991. "Preemptive Fundraising and Challenger Profile in Senate Elections." *Journal of Politics* 53:1150–1164.

———. 1992. "Challenger Profile and Gubernatorial Elections." *Western Political Quarterly* 28:125–142.

Squire, Peverill, and Christina Fastnow. 1994. "Comparing Gubernatorial and Senatorial Research." *Political Research Quarterly* 47:705–720.

Stein, Robert M. 1989. "Economic Voting for Governor and U.S. Senator: The Electoral Consequences of Federalism." *Journal of Politics* 52:28–53.

Stewart, Charles. 1988. "On Vote Share and Turnout." Paper presented at the annual meeting of the Southern Political Science Association, Atlanta, GA, November 3–5.

———. 1989. "A Sequential Model of U.S. Senate Elections." *Legislative Studies Quarterly* 14:567–601.

Stimson, James. 1976. "Public Support for American Presidents: A Cyclical Model." *Public Opinion Quarterly* 40:1–21.

Stone, Walter. 1986. "The Carryover Effect in Presidential Elections." *American Political Science Review* 80:271–279.

Straayer, John. 1973. *American State and Local Government.* Columbus, OH: Charles E. Merrill.

Sullivan, David. 1977/78. "Party Unity: Appearance and Reality." *Political Science Quarterly* 92:635–645.

Sullivan, John L. 1973. "Political Correlates of Social, Economic, and Religious Diversity in the American States." *Journal of Politics* 35:70–84.

Svoboda, Craig J. 1995. "Retrospective Voting in Gubernatorial Elections: 1982 and 1986." *Political Research Quarterly* 48:135–150.

Thompson, Tommy G. 1996. *Power to the People: An American State at Work*. New York: HarperCollins.

Tidmarch, Charles, Lisa Hyman, and Jill Sorkin. 1984. "Press Issue Agendas in the 1982 Congressional and Gubernatorial Election Campaign." *Journal of Politics* 46:1226–1245.

Tuckel, Peter. 1983. "Length of Incumbency and the Reelection Chances of U.S. Senators." *Legislative Studies Quarterly* 8:283–288.

Tufte, Edward. 1975. "Determining the Outcomes of Midterm Congressional Elections." *American Political Science Review* 69:812–826.

———. 1978. *Political Control of the Economy*. Princeton, NJ: Princeton University Press.

Turett, J. Stephen. 1971. "The Vulnerability of American Governors: 1900–1969." *Midwest Journal of Political Science* 15:108–132.

Tushnet, David. 2005. *A Court Divided: The Rehnquist Court and the Future of Constitutional Law*. New York: W. W. Norton.

Uhlaner, Carole J., and Kay Lehman Schlozman. 1986. "Candidate Gender and Congressional Campaign Receipts." *Journal of Politics* 48:30–50.

Van Beek, James. 1991. "Does the Decision to Retire Increase the Amount of Political Shirking?" *Public Finance Quarterly* 19:444–456.

Walker, Jack. 1969. "Diffusion of Innovations Among the American States." *American Political Science Review* 63:880–899.

Ware, Alan. 1979. "Divisive Primaries: The Important Questions." *British Journal of Political Science* 9:381–384.

Waterman, Richard W. 1990. "Comparing Senate and House Electoral Outcomes: The Exposure Thesis." *Legislative Studies Quarterly* 15:99–114.

Wattenberg, Martin P. 1986. *The Decline of American Political Parties*. Cambridge, MA: Harvard University Press.

Weicker, Lowell. 1995. *Maverick: A Life in Politics*. With Barry Sussman. Boston: Little, Brown.

Welch, William. 1974. "The Economics of Campaign Funds." *Public Choice* 20:83–97.

———. 1977. "Money and Votes: A Simultaneous Equation Model." Paper presented to the Public Choice Society, New Orleans, Louisiana, March 11–13.

Welsh, Matthew. 1981. *View from the Statehouse: Recollections and Reflections*. Indianapolis: Indiana Historical Bureau.

Wendel, Peter. 1999. "The Squeaky Wheel(s) Make it Interesting: A GOP Star Barely Survives New Jersey Governor's Race in 1997." In Bailey et al. 1999.

Westlye, Mark. 1985. "The Effect of Primary Divisiveness on Incumbent Senators, 1968–1984." Paper presented at the annual meeting of the American Political Science Association, New Orleans, LA, August 29–September 1.

———. 1991. *Senate Elections and Campaign Intensity.* Baltimore: Johns Hopkins University Press.

Whillock, Rita Kirk. 1991. *Political Empiricism: Communication Strategies in State and Regional Elections.* New York: Praeger.

Whitby, Kenny, and Timothy Bledsoe. 1986. "The Impact of Policy Voting on the Electoral Fortunes of Senate Incumbents." *Western Political Quarterly* 39:690–700.

Wildavsky, Aaron. 1968. "The Empty-head Blues: Black Rebellion and White Reaction." *Public Interest* 3:16.

Williams, G. Mennen. 1961. *A Governor's Notes.* Ann Arbor: Institute of Public Administration.

Winger, Richard. 1997. "Institutional Obstacles to a Multiparty System." In *Multiparty Politics in America,* edited by Paul S. Herrnson and John C. Green. Lanham, MD: Rowman and Littlefield.

Wolfinger, Raymond, and Steven J. Rosenstone. 1980. *Who Votes?* New Haven, CT: Yale University Press.

Wright, Gerald C., Robert S. Erikson, and John P. McIver. 1985. "Measuring State Partisanship and Ideology with Survey Data." *Journal of Politics* 47:469–489.

Zaller, John. 1992. *The Nature and Origin of Mass Opinion.* New York: Cambridge University Press.